GW01316206

The Sacred Journey Islam Eman Islam

First Edition

Copyright © Ayman Abouzaid 2023/1445 AH. All Rights Reserved

ISBN: 9-798393-720797

In the Name of Allah, the Merciful, the Beneficent. Praise be to the Lord of all worlds. The First with no beginning and Last with no ending. Prayers and peace be upon our Prophet Muhammadﷺ, his blessed family, and companions.

"Focus on yourself and everything will fall in place"

Contents

PREFACE   1

INTRODUCTION   2

Chapter One: Understanding Islam   4

The meaning of Islam   5

The whole religion   6

What should be the priority?   8

Chapter Two: Allahﷻ   10

Your relationship with Allahﷻ   12

The Qur'an   13

The Names of Allahﷻ   16

Chapter Three: The Prophetﷺ   18

Your relationship with Prophet Muhammadﷺ   19

The need for prophets and messengers   22

The *sunnah* and *hadith*   23

The *seerah* and the *shamail*   24

Chapter Four: Mannerism in Islam (*akhlaq*)   26

Chapter Five: The Book of Islam - *fiqh* (jurisprudence)   28

What is *fiqh*?   29

What does the knowledge of *fiqh* cover?   29

Do you need to learn all areas of *fiqh*?   29

Legal/*fiqh* Schools – its history and development   30

The formation of Legal/fiqh Schools (*madhahib*)   31

Complying with *madhahib*   34

RITUAL PURIFICATION (*taharah*)   35

Types of water   36

Use of water/ruling on types of water   36

What is considered impure (*najas*/physical filth)   37

Levels of impurity and methods of removing   37

Toilet etiquette   38

Fitra actions   38

Use of containers (*aniyah*)   39

Ritual/purificatory bath (*ghsul*) - major ritual purification   39

Ritual/purificatory wash (ablution/*wudu*) - minor ritual purification   42

The use of toothstick (*miswak*)   44

Wiping over the footgear (*khuff*)   44

Dry ablution (*tayammum*)   45

For women (vaginal bleeding)   48

PRAYER (*salah*)   49

Introduction   49

The obligatory/fard prayers   50

Sunnah/recommended prayers – *rawatib*   51

Sunnah/recommended prayers – *nawafil*   51

Conditions for a Muslim to pray   53

Conditions prior to performing prayer (prerequisites)   53

Prayer fundamentals (*arkan*)   54

Greater recommended actions   54

Lesser recommended actions (*hay'at*)   55

Differences between men and women in the prayer   56

What causes the prayer to be invalidated   56

Inability to pray   57

Times when it is not permissible to pray   57

Performing the prayer, *step-by-step*   58

Friday prayer (*jummah*)   61

Congregational/group prayer (*jama'ah*)   61

Shortening and combining prayers (*jam' and qasr*)   62

THE DECEASED   63

Obligations towards a deceased Muslim   64

FASTING (*sawm*)   64

Conditions for a Muslim to fast   65

Obligatory actions of fasting   65

What invalidates the fasting and what does not   65

Sunnah/recommended actions of fasting   66

Days fasting is not permissible   66

Making up for fasting and expiations   66

Spiritual Retreat (*itikaf*)   67

Conditions for *itikaf*   67

ALMS (*zakat*)   68

Zakat of fast-breaking (*zakat al-fitr*)   68

Conditions for a Muslim paying *zakat al-fitr*   68

Zakat on wealth (*zakat al-mal*)   69

Conditions for a Muslim paying *zakat al-mal*   69

Distribution of the *zakat*: types of people (the beneficiaries)   69

HAJJ AND *UMRAH*   69

Objectives and benefits of *hajj*   70

Conditions for a Muslim to perform *hajj* and *umrah*   71

Umrah fundamentals (*arkan*)   71

Impermissible things while in the state of *Ihram*   71

Performing *umrah, step-by-step*   72

Hajj fundamentals (*arkan*)   72

Hajj obligatory (*fard*) actions   72

Hajj recommended (*sunnah*) actions   73

Types of *hajj*   73

Performing *hajj,* step-by-step   73

What are educational ojectives?   76

Examples of educational objectives of *hajj*   76

Chapter Six: The Book of Eman - *Aqidah* (principles of faith/belief)   77

KNOWLEDGE, OUR LIMITATIONS AND ALLAH ALMIGHTY   78

How we comprehend things   78

Limitation of senses   79

Imagination   79

Limitations of the human mind   80

Conclusion   80

What is *aqidah*?   81

What does the knowledge of *aqidah* cover?   81

BELIEF IN ALLAH   82

How do we believe in Allah (in general)?   82

How do we believe in Allah (in detail)?   82

    His essence (*dhat*)   82

    His attributes (*sifat*)   82

    The Necessary   83

    The Impossible   86

    The Possible   88

What is the meaning of *shirk* (polytheism)?   88

    Levels of *shirk*   88

    Major shirk (*al-shirk al-akbar*)   88

    Attributing ability and actions independently from Allah 88

    Hidden Shirk (*al-shirk al-khafi*)   88

The meaning of 'There is no Lord but Allah: La Ilaha Ila Allah'   89

Misinterpretations and misconceptions   89

BELIEF IN PROPHETS AND MESSENGERS 95

Introduction 95

The difference between a prophet (*nabi*) and messenger (*rasul*) 96

Miracles 96

The difference between a miracle and other events or actions 97

How do we believe in prophets and messengers (in general)? 97

How do we believe in prophets and messengers (in detail)? 97

The Necessary 98

The Impossible 100

The Possible 100

Misinterpretations and misconceptions 101

The duties of prophets and messengers 112

Following Prophet Muhammad 114

THE DIVINE BOOKS 115

The Qur'an (*al-qur'an*) 115

The Torah (*al-taurat*) 118

The Gospel (*al-injeel*) 118

The Psalms (*al-zabour*) 120

BELIEF IN THE UNSEEN (*ghayb*) 120

Belief in the Last Day 120

Questioning in the grave, the bliss and punishment (or torment) of the grave 120

Resurrection (*al-ba'th*) 121

The Gathering (*al-hashr*) 121

Questioning, Judgement, Reward and Punishment 121

The Scale (*al-mizan*) 122

The Bridge (*al-sirat*) 122

Basin of the Prophet (*al-hawd*) 122

Paradise and Hellfire 123

Seeing Allah in Paradise 127

Intercession (*shafa'ah*) 127

Signs of the Last Day 128

Jinn 130

Angels (*malaikah*) 130

BELIEF IN *QADAR* (*fate*) 133

Qada' - pre-knowledge 134

Qadar – the pre-known becoming reality 134

The relationship and agreement between the will of a person and the Will of Allah 135

The Will of Allah and the actions of a person 136

Chapter Seven: The Book of Ihsan – *Tazkiyah* (Spiritual Purification)   138

What is *ihsan*?   139

What does the knowledge of *ihsan* cover?   139

Importance of ihsan   141

The elements and process for purification   145

The Practicalities   146

    One: who are your friends and companions?   146

    Two: what are you looking for in your spiritual guide?   148

    Three: the pledge of faithfulness and commitment   150

    Four: purification without knowledge is controversial & knowledge without purification is negligence   151

    Five: are you willing to put in the effort?   152

    Six: do you expect a journey to Allah☀ to be without remembering Allah☀?   154

    Seven: understanding your journey and experiences   159

Inner (heart) traits   161

    One: clear the heart, to pave the way – repentance (*tawba*)   161

    Two: awaken to take accountability and be accountable to remain awakened   162

    Three: fear (*khouf*)   163

    Four: hope (*rajaa*)   164

    Five: truthfulness (*sidq*)   165

    Six: sincerity and pure intentions (*ikhlas*)   165

    Seven: patience (*sabr*)   167

    Eight: scrupulousness (*wara*)   169

    Nine: asceticism (*zuhd*)   170

    Ten: satisfaction (*rida*)   172

    Eleven: reliance on Allah☀ (*tawakul*)   173

    Twelve: gratitude (*shukr*)   174

The fruits and outcomes of purification   175

Realities and Certainty   179

CONCLUSION   181

PREFACE

Since the early days of Islam, the preserving and spreading of Islamic knowledge has been an ongoing activity, revealing the truth, serving the seekers, opening the eyes of humanity to realities, and accommodating changes. What then is the purpose of writing a single book about the teachings of Islam when we have a rich library in both scope and quantity? The need for this would be highly regarded when one appreciates that manifestation, development, and change through the religion and in line with the purpose of the Qur'an, "**guidance**"[1] is not just about content but about also context, dealing with barriers, core values, intellectual discipline, self-control and a conviction that the source of knowledge must be correct just as the methods are, for the outcome to be sound and acceptable. If there is inconsistencies in the source, methodology, and priorities, there will be disconnection and flaws in the outcome.

A key milestone in teaching and preaching the religion over many years in mosques, centres, lectures, courses, 1-2-1s, and sermons in different parts of the world was interacting with my respected brothers in a UK prison establishment. There were those who had almost everything they needed. Above all, repentance, the desire to learn, free time, a chaplaincy department (an imam on site) and access to resources and Islamic material. But there was still a gap. Working with them closely re-triggered my attention to much needed work in presenting core Islamic teachings in a simple and methodical way while deepening insight on how to change with this knowledge. An approach that works to nourish minds and organise thoughts with structure and clarity. A person may possess authentic knowledge but lacks the ability to develop deep understanding and connect information. Along with practical solutions.

It quickly became obvious they are no different. Their knowledge, guidance and refinement needs mirrored that of the masses. Coming across many beautiful hearts, the interaction showed they share the same concerns, thoughts, inner and outer issues, much of which they are unable to grasp the root causes of or resolve. And they too have rights upon us, to show empathy, sincerity, and mercy, "**Every son of Adam commits sin, and the best of those who sin are those who repent**".[2] We are all in this together as we all need refining. We too can be prisoners, to our egoistic desires. Hence there is no separation and the 'target audience' is one. Everyone is serving time in this life, will stand for questioning and judgement in the Next, and will be greeted by the guards on the Gates of Paradise or Hellfire.

How we relate to, embrace, and implement the practices of a fundamental *hadith* serves as a key indicator as to where we are and to what extent we understand [authentic] Sacred Knowledge, in a well-guided and thorough way that brings about change, development, and righteousness. However, change cannot proceed knowledge, "*knowledge comes before speech and actions*".[3] Therefore, this book is offered to beginners just as it serves everyone seeking assurance their *Islamic knowledge* and practices are genuine and encompassing of all elements, "**O Believers! Enter Islam completely**"[4] i.e., embrace it wholly and wholeheartedly with a serious commitment to change through it.[5]

---

[1] Qur'an 2:2.

[2] Al-Tirmidhi (2667), Ahmad (13049), Ibn Majah (4251).

[3] The words of Imam al-Bukhari in his Sahih (Book of Knowledge).

[4] Qur'an, 2:208.

[5] Tafsir al-Tabari, tafsir Ibn Kathir, tafsir al-Baydawi, tafsir al-Jalalin.

INTRODUCTION

Our worldly life is only a milestone which carries the characteristics of a journey, is a means to the Next life and a temporary stop. It is limited, perishable, short-lived, and above all, "**a test**".[6] In it are many bounties, pleasures, and joys, but they remain "**nothing but an amusement and distraction**"[7] whereas "**the true life is in the Hereafter**"[8] and is "**far better and more lasting**".[9] When Allah﷾ tells us "**do not neglect your rightful share in this world**"[10] and warns "**do not let the present life deceive you**".[11]

The Prophetﷺ guides us to a fitting conclusion and mindset, "**be in this world as if you are a stranger or a traveller passing-by**".[12] A traveller is conscious and focused on where to get to (the aim) and at the same time does not neglect the present responsibilities and duties (the means).

As with every travel, there needs to be direction and clarity. *From here we start* being that direction; sound and authentic knowledge to embark on a '*Sacred Journey*' on board "**the Straight Path**".[13] A 'straight path' is the shortest route to reaching from one point to another. A believer, a true seeker, should aim to be guided through the shortest [authentic] route.[14] Anything other than that is heedless and longwinded.

The *Sacred Journey* is teachings of the religion aimed to be manifested in actions, thoughts, and condition, while elevating through the ranks of piety and noble character. This first starts with acquiring *Sacred Knowledge*. Those who do not acquire this knowledge do not compare to those who do, who are chosen for goodness and Paradise, more conscious of their Lord, raised, and in the sight of Allah﷾ superior.[15] There is no option, you cannot fulfil or progress in something you do not know about, hence "**Seeking knowledge is an obligation upon every Muslim**".[16]

"**We have revealed to you the Book [O Muhammad], as an explanation of all things, and as guidance**".[17] This is a core verse that paves the way to success and salvation for mankind, in this life and in the Next. Revelation sent to Prophet Muhammadﷺ to convey to people clarity and purpose of life. A path and guidance that guards every individual from shackles of confusion and distortion.

Islam is a broad religion that serves the needs and assures the wellbeing of not only the individual but families, communities, societies, economies, plants, animals, the environment … and everything. It provides wide scope and comprehensive guidance and solutions to assist in fulfilling our duties and purpose in life in the most efficient way. Many

---

[6] Qur'an, 67:2.

[7] Qur'an, 6:32. See also Qur'an, 10:7-8, 14:3, 16:107, 87:16-7.

[8] Qur'an, 29:64.

[9] Qur'an, 87:17.

[10] Qur'an, 28:77.

[11] Qur'an, 35:5.

[12] Al-Bukhari (6416), Ahmad (4764).

[13] Qur'an, 1:6.

[14] Tafsir al-Sha'rawi (Qur'an, 1:6).

[15] Qur'an, 39:9, 35:28, 58:11. Al-Bukhari (71), Muslim (2392), al-Tirmidhi (2682), Ibn Majah (223), Abi Dawud (3641), Ahmad (16931).

[16] Ibn Majah (224).

[17] Qur'an, 16:89.

rulings tell us specifically what to do while other types of rulings guide to adopting ethical and principled ways of going about our day-to-day affairs.[18] One still, however, needs to be conscious of the challenges they may face in implementing. Modernity, traditions, social conditioning, ideologies etc do impact and do create veils which must be addressed and dealt with, "***Those who <u>strive</u> hard for Our cause, We shall be sure to <u>guide</u> to Our way***".[19]

The general aim and method of this book is to bring the reader in line with a pure state of heart, mind, and actions, harmonious with the purity of this religion. Then, not only becomes far from darkness and close to light but shall increase "***Light upon light***".[20] However, one cannot increase in something that is not founded in the first place. The first layer or '*foundational light*' needs to be established to be able to supplement, and develop: "***Allah <u>increases</u> in guidance those who acccept guidance***" and "***those who <u>are</u> <u>guided</u> – He <u>increases</u> in guidance***".[21] Those who have willingness to be guided and refined, acquire the necessary knowledge, follow the path, and deal with the challenges shall increase in guidance, wisdom, and success.[22] The verse concludes, "***and blesses them with righteousness***".[23]

It is important you approach the religion slowly and focus on how to better yourself in worship, character, and conduct. This allows you to absorb well the knowledge acquired and deal with obstacles wisely. Whilst our worship is to adhere to the command of Allah﷾ and please Him, we are the ones in need. Focus on quality and excellence and be not driven by quantity and speed. Know that "***Successful indeed are those who purify themselves***".[24]

Reading through this book, there may be things you did not know or understand well enough, especially if you are new to practising the religion. As you continue to develop and grow in Islam, your knowledge, understanding, and faith shall also increase, and you will appreciate more and more its beauty and refinement methods. The true fruits are increased love for Allah﷾ your Creator and the Prophetﷺ your guide, mentor and purifier, develop in noble character, and establish a well-founded, ignorance-free attachment to Islam. Take this opportunity to learn and change. There are people who have not reached this point. Many days, weeks, months, and a whole lifespan goes by but have not allowed themselves to reflect or have chosen to not face their character flaws and knowledge gaps. You have this great opportunity. Do not lose it. *The only barrier would be you!*

---

[18] Qur'an, 6:36. Tafsir al-Qurtubi, tafsir al-Razi, tafsir zad al-masir and Qur'an, 5:3. Al-Zuhaili. W. *Johoud taqneen al-fiqh al-Islami*, pp.14-5.

[19] Qur'an, 29:69.

[20] Qur'an, 24:35.

[21] Qur'an, 47:17.

[22] Tafsir al-Tabari, tafsir Ibn Kathir, tafsir al-Qurtubi, tafsir al-Baydawi, tafsir al-Baghawi, tafsir Abu al-Saud.

[23] Qur'an, 47:17.

[24] Qur'an, 87:14.

CHAPTER ONE
Understanding Islam

The meaning of Islam

Let us start with the most basic yet important question: what does the word 'Islam' mean?

'Islam' is an Arabic word that derives from the three-letter root S-L-M which carries the meaning of 'submission, sincerity, purity, and peace'.[25] Islamically, is 'to submit'. This means:

If you **SUBMIT** fully to Allah ﷻ alone and worship Him **PURELY**, you will achieve **PEACE** in this life and in the Hereafter[26]

The previous Abrahamic religions may have difference names of Christianity and Judaism but the actual religion - in its original form - has always been one. Simply because the Sender (Allah ﷻ), the message (belief system), the transmitters (prophets and messengers) and the recipients (jinn and humans) are the same, all along.[27]

The Final Message:

Allah ﷻ sent numerous prophets throughout history and chose to send a final one with the continued message. This final prophet and messenger would be for all of mankind from his time until the End of Time,[28] so had to be different from the previous ones in some ways. It is the Prophet Muhammad ﷺ who fits all these criteria:

- Since no one comes later to correct any mistakes or distortions, the revelation he receives must remain preserved in its original form, "***It is certainly We Who have sent down the revelation, and We will surely preserve it***".[29] As it is divinely preserved and free from any outside influence, the Qur'an continues to have an amazing effect on many minds, as it presents a particular attraction for mankind. It accommodates the true manner of thinking and feeling, answers people's requirements of belief and action, and brings an exact solution to the great problems which disturb them. In summary, it gives complete satisfaction to their need for truth, goodness, and beauty, through a work that is at the same time religious, moral, and literary.[30]

- The miracle would be different as well. This is because the 'sign' would have to affect not only the people of his time but all later generations: "***this is the book [i.e., the Qur'an]***" described as "***guidance for those mindful of God***".[31] One of the Qur'an's [miraculous] methods, for example, is inviting non-believers to the truth through communication where inferences and conclusions are 'commonly accepted'[32] using logical arguments, reasoning, rhetorical questions, and by stimulating reflection and encouraging self-correction.[33]

---

[25] Lisan al-arab, al-mujam al-wasit.

[26] Qur'an, 2:112. Tafsir Abu al-Saud.

[27] One sender (Qur'an, 2:21), same message (Qur'an, 21:25) and al-Muwata' (511), same transmitters (Qur'an, 15:10) same receipents (Qur'an, 51:56).

[28] Qur'an, 33:40.

[29] Qur'an, 15:9.

[30] Draz, M.A., Introduction to the Qur'an, p.39.

[31] Qur'an 2:2.

[32] Such as the 'whole' of something is greater than the 'part,' the number 1 is less than 2. These are commonly accepted as a sound, logical conclusion, and inference. Likewise, the arguments the Qur'an makes with regards to God, prophets and messengers, and matters of belief are done in a way that any sound mind would accept, providing the person is not clouded by desire or arrogance.

[33] See Qur'an 2:171, 23:71, 26:70-82, 21:22, 7:191-5, 10:34-5, 4:82, 11:13-4, 17:56-7.

- The final prophet would put an end to those being sent to certain communities, as is sent for the entire global community. All of humanity, "***And We have not sent you, [O Muhammad], except as a mercy to the whole of mankind***".[34] In this beautiful *hadith*, a description of how he is a completion and seal of all prophets, ***My similitude in comparison with the other prophets before me, is that of a man who has built a house nicely and beautifully, except for a place of one brick in a corner. The people go about it and wonder at its beauty, but say: 'Would that this brick be put in its place!' So I am that brick, and I am the last of the Prophets***".[35]

- The teachings and rulings of this message had to be fixed in matters that need to be fixed and at the same time flexible in matters to accommodate changing times, needs and circumstances.[36]

The whole religion

If a person is to fulfil their religion and practice fully, it is important to understand exactly what it comprises of. You may have already heard of different Islamic knowledges/sciences and may be asking where this all fits in, which ones do you have to learn and what are the priority ones. The Prophet in a *hadith* presents the three aspects of Islam. We shall see also what knowledges these relate to. Three keywords and a conclusive statement provide the answer to what is expected of us. One of his close companions named `Umar mentioned that Angel Jibril[37] came to ask certain questions. The idea was to teach the companions who were present by Angel Jibril asking and the Prophet responding. This way they would hear the answers and learn. Our focus is on the words in **BOLD**:

On the authority of `Umar who said:
"While we were one day sitting with the Messenger of Allah there appeared before us a man dressed in extremely white clothes and with very black hair. No traces of journeying were visible on him, and none of us knew him. He sat down close by the Prophet resting his knees against the knees of the Prophet and placed his palms over his thighs and said: "O Muhammad! Inform me about **ISLAM** "The Messenger of Allah replied: "Islam is to testify that there is no deity worthy of worship except Allah and that Muhammad is His Messenger, that you should perform salah (ritual of prayer), pay the zakah (alms), fast during Ramadan, and perform Hajj (pilgrimage) to the House (the Ka`bah at Makkah), if you can find the means for making the journey". He said: "You have spoken the truth". We were astonished at his thus questioning him and then telling him that he was right, but he went on to say, "Inform me about **EMAN** (faith)". He (the Prophet) answered, "to believe in Allah and His angels and His Books and His Messengers and in the Last Day, and in fate (qadar), both in its good and in its evil aspects". He said, "You have spoken the truth". Then he (the man) said, "Inform me about **IHSAN** "He (the Prophet) answered, "to observe and worship Allah as though you could see Him, for though you cannot see Him yet He sees you". He said, "Inform me about the Hour".[38] He (the Prophet) said, "About that the one questioned knows no more than the questioner". So he said, "inform me about its signs" He said, "They are that the slave-girl will give birth to her mistress and that you will see the barefooted ones, the naked, the destitute, the herdsmen of the sheep (competing with each other) in raising lofty buildings" Thereupon the man went off. I waited a while, and then he (the Prophet) said, "O `Umar, do you know who that questioner was?" I replied, "Allah and His Messenger know better." He said, **"THAT WAS JIBRIL. HE CAME TO TEACH YOU YOUR RELIGION".**
Muslim (97) another narration exists: Al-Bukhari (50)

---

[34] Qur'an, 21:107.

[35] Al-Bukhari (3535), Muslim (5961), Ahmad (9167).

[36] This is in the rich and extensive work of scholars is in the methodology of *usul al-fiqh* (principles of jurisprudence) with *fiqh* (jurisprudence) being it's the end product. Kamali, M. *Principles of Islamic Jurisprudence*, p.1.

[37] The angel assigned to communicate revelation from Allah to His prophets and messengers.

[38] This is not a separate category. It falls under the category of Eman.

At the end of the *hadith* – after explaining the three categories - we see the conclusion being, "**That was Jibril. He came to teach you your religion**". Not parts of the religion but the **whole** religion.[39]

Therefore:

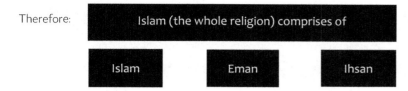

What do each of these mean, so we know what to study and how to practice?

- The response to **Islam** was practical actions; the knowledge of *fiqh* (jurisprudence).
- The response to **Eman** was matters of the mind; the knowledge of *aqidah* (principles of faith/belief).
- The response to **Ihsan** was matters of the heart; the knowledge of *tazkiyah* (spiritual purification).

The source for all these knowledges is the Qur'an and Sunnah meaning they originate from verses of the Qur'an and teachings of the Prophet.

Each of these also develops a part of the human structure. The body, mind, and heart. While fulfilling the commands of the religion the person also becomes a well-developed human through pure actions (the body), pure perception and mindset (the mind) and a pure inner self (the heart). Leaving out any of these leads to, on one hand, religious disobedience, and on the other hand gaps and flaws in their character. Islam develops the Muslim physically, intellectually, and spiritually to fulfil the purpose they are created for, be worthy to establish civilization, and spread prosperity in the world.

Aspect/category	Knowledge of	Works on	Develops & Disciplines	Objective - ensures you
Islam	*Fiqh* (jurisprudence)	The Body	Actions	Carry out your actions correctly
Eman	*Aqidah* (principles of faith/belief)	The Mind	Thinking	Develop correct mindset and perceptions
Ihsan	*Tazkiyah* (spiritual purification)	The Heart	Feelings	Refine and purify your inner self

All other Islamic sciences are 'tools' or 'means' to knowing how to read and understand the Qur'an and Sunnah text, derive rulings, and be equipped to provide fatwas ("explanation" or "clarification") on matters of the religion.[40] These three elements (*fiqh, aqidah* and *tazkiyah*) are '*Intended Knowledge*' or known also as '*Objective Knowledge*' where every person's primary focus should be on fulfilling and perfecting.

---

[39] Collectively these are also called *Shariah* i.e., the complete laws and commands; the way of life prescribed by Allah to mankind.

[40] For example, many branches of Arabic language, *tafsir* (explanation of the Qur'an), *usul al-fiqh* (principles of jurisprudence), Science of Qur'an, Science of Hadith, *Tajwid* etc.

An overview of each category/knowledge:

Islam	*Fiqh* (jurisprudence)	The Body	Actions	Carry out your actions correctly
Performing rituals, acts of worship and day-to-day matters in a correct and complete way: purifying physically, prayer, fasting, pilgrimage, alms, charitable giving, marriage, having children and their upbringing, relationships (family, friends, neighbours, Muslims and non-Muslims, society etc), financial transactions, economy, judiciary, politics and more. All practical affairs, at every level.				

Eman	*Aqidah* (principles of faith/belief)	The Mind	Thinking	Develop correct mindset and perceptions
Its end result is affirmation in the heart but starts with the mind. If one has an incorrect understanding of something, affirming it in the heart can corrupt their belief. *Aqidah* helps understand correctly matters relating to (a) Allah☬ (b) prophets and messengers (c) the unseen (ghayb). Then from the [correct] understanding and mindset, knowledge penetrates to becoming heart-affirmed.				

Ihsan	*Tazkiyah* (spiritual purification)	The Heart	Feelings	Refine and purify your inner self
Works on removing negative traits, replacing with good character and positive traits, and dealing with the barriers that prevent or hinder this process to continue in a thorough and productive way. This is achieved through various means of purifying the heart.				

What should be the priority?

One important thing to always remember about your worship and obedience is that you take it with you everywhere. Wherever you are now or in the coming months and years is only a change in circumstances. It does not and should not change the reality and responsibility of worshiping fully, sincerely and continue to be a better person.

Your **heart** is the centre of the relationship with your Lord and the starting point for your actions. As your heart accompanies you everywhere, no one can stop, delay, or interrupt that connection and no one can take control of its intentions. What you do need is will, perseverance, and real determination. It starts with you and remains with you!

The simple answer is to prioritise what Allah☬ and His Messenger☬ have prioritised. Allah Almighty commands and the Prophet☬ is the guide to fulfilling those commands. Focus should not just be on we are taught in terms of content but also on the priorities set out for us. The religion is no burden, but a person can make it burdensome for himself by restricting and constraining. You **must** be focused on knowing the priorities and following them, to avoid going around in a vicious circle, causing yourself confusion and frustration. The Prophet☬ says clearly, "***Verily, in the body is a flesh which, if sound, the entire body becomes sound, and if corrupt, the entire body is corrupt. Verily, it is the heart***".[41]

---

[41] Al-Bukhari (52), Muslim (4094), Ahmad (18374).

8

In Islam the heart is viewed as the essence of the individual and focuses greatly on its condition. This is since it occupies a core position in spiritual development and actions. Nothing shall benefit a person on the Day of Judgement "***Except the one who returns to Allah with a pure sound heart***".[42] The 'heart' referred to is the Spiritual Heart. This is when it becomes free from spiritual illnesses and character defects.

Here are some of the immense benefits of a sound and pure heart:

- The heart is where intentions are:[43]

If the intention is sound the deed will be met with acceptance.[44] If corrupt, the act will be rejected. A small act can become enormous by an intention and likewise a great action can be rejected by an intention.

- The heart is where Allah﷾'s focus is turned to:

Indeed, God does not look at your forms or your appearances, but He looks at your hearts".[45] And in another *hadith* "...***does not look at your appearances or your wealth, but He looks at your hearts and action***".[46]

- The heart is where the Qur'an is understood:

True understanding and realisation come from the heart which contains deeper intelligence and wisdom. To be enlightened with the truth means there is real understanding, so if there is not, it can be concluded this is due to the heart being corrupt or impure. If a person is ignorant of purifying himself, he shall be left ignorant of true Sacred Understanding. The link between the heart and understanding is clear throughout the Qur'an, for example, "***will they not reflect on the Qur'an, or do they have locks on their hearts***".[47]

- The heart is where piety and God-consciousness (*taqwa*) is:

"***And be mindful of God. Surely God knows best what is in the heart***".[48] In a *hadith*, the Prophetﷺ explains, "***Taqwa is here***" *pointing to his heart three times*"[49] and when asked by a companion, "***who is the best of people?***" He explained, "***Those with a pure heart and a truthful tongue***". Heﷺ was then asked to clarify, "We understand what a truthful tongue is, but what is a pure heart?" He replied, "***It is one that is pious and pure, with no sin, injustice, rancor[50] or envy in it***".[51]

---

[42] Qur'an 26:88-9. Tafsir al-Qurtubi.

[43] Al-Bukhari (54), Muslim (4927), Ahmad (168).

[44] Providing the action itself is also acceptable. Qur'an, 67:2. Al-Bukhari (2697), Muslim (4492), Ahmad (26033).

[45] Muslim (6542).

[46] Muslim (6543), Ahmad (10960).

[47] Qur'an, 47:24. Tafsir al-Tabari. Qur'an, 2:118, 4:63, 6:25, 7:100, 9:127, 18:57, 22:54, 63:3.

[48] Qur'an, 5:7.

[49] Muslim (6541).

[50] Bitterness or resentfulness.

[51] Ibn Majah (4216), al-Bayhaqi, *Shu'aib al-eman* (4462).

CHAPTER TWO
Allah ﷻ

Allah﷾ is our aim. Whom our life is centred round. We yearn His forgiveness, plead his mercy, and beg His acceptance. f a person has Allah﷾ in his life he has everything and if a person does not, he has nothing.

This relationship, however, depends on how much you know Him. If we aim to build a strong and deep relationship, we must know Him well. The more the knowledge increases the more appreciation and devotion increases.[52] Here are other important indicators/signs that tell us how we are developing on the scale of love and submission:

True love involves sacrifice	When you act from a loving heart you show commitment and willingness to overcome any barrier or distraction to please the one you love. Even if it is against what you like, you are more willing to sacrifice everything knowing He is worthy and that His blessings and bounties upon you deserve every sacrifice to show gratitude and appreciation. As this develops, there becomes only one thing you love. To love what He chooses. With Him, to choose not to choose.[53]
Pay attention to the actions Allah﷾ loves and does not like	Whenever you hear a Qur'anic verse or *hadith* that says "**Allah loves**" you are attentive, enthusiastic, and eager. Devoted to practice with sincerity and consistently what pleases Him, reject and move far from what "**Allah does not like**."
Following the commands of the Prophetﷺ and voluntary actions	Following the Prophetﷺ is a sign of loving Allah﷾ as he was sent and praised by Him, "**Say [O Muhammad], "If you [sincerely] love God, then follow me; God will love you and forgive your sins**"[54] and practicing his teachings, "**My servant continues to draw near to Me with supererogatory works (nawafil) so that I shall love him**".[55]
Seek the company of those who love Allah﷾ and the Prophetﷺ	This is your opportunity to see an example of true love and obedience in their silence speech, and actions. It is also a motivation for you to progress in your journey to please and devote to the one you love.
Continuously remembering Him	If one loves someone they will keep mentioning and remembering them. Remembrance (*dhikr*) is an indicator of evolving love and ongoing consciousness of the Beloved.
The commitment to purify yourself	If someone truly loves, they will want to be in their presence in the most presentable and honourable manner and image; clean and pure internally and externally.

---

[52] Qur'an, 35:28. Tafsir al-Tabari, tafsir al-Razi.

[53] Qur'an, 4:65.

[54] Qur'an, 3:31.

[55] Al-Bukhari (6502).

Let no moment of your life be without reflection. What you are doing and where you are going. What is good be grateful to your Lordﷻ and what is not (a) admit you are the reason and nothing else (b) regret (c) insist on not returning to it again (d) if this involves the rights of anyone, return those rights.

Spend time regularly with Allahﷻ just you and Him, alone with the Alone, yearning His forgiveness and acceptance. Talk to Him, express your concerns and worries. Share your happiness and ambitions towards Him. Remove the barriers. He should be your first point of contact. He is not far, "*I am Near. I respond to those who call Me*".[56]

If you do this - along with other means of purification and practicing the religion wholly (Islam, Eman and Ihsan) - you shall see your life transform and He will embrace you with His generosity. Such humility will lead to honour, darkness replaced with light and the veils hindering you bettering yourself reduce. His light is never extinguished, we are the ones who allow the veils to thicken. The more effort you put in the more veils are removed and replaced with guidance, just as reflection is a sign of an awakened heart.

This does not mean we will not fall into mistakes. But 'falling into' is different to insisting or being heedless in your ways. Even then, the door to Allahﷻ is always open, "*Indeed, [it is] We who created mankind and [fully] know what their souls whispers to them: and We are closer to them than their jugular vein*".[57] Heﷻ is aware of our nature. Of course knows we are not infallible, and we will not be without mistakes.

However, effort and strive is essential, "*Those who strive hard for Our cause, We will surely guide to Our way*".[58] In this verse there are two parts. The first is your duty and the second is an outcome:
"*Those who strive hard for Our cause*" - Your duty: strive and preserve to please Him and deal with the egoistic self.
"*We will surely guide to Our way*" - The outcome: be rightly guided with discipline, and in His presence.
Even then, not only guided but once guided, shall increase in guidance, "*And those who are guided – He increases them in guidance and blesses them with righteousness*".[59] Guided in the heart, mind and body serving both the inner and outer condition.

---

[56] Qur'an, 2:186.
[57] Qur'an, 50:16.
[58] Qur'an, 29:69.
[59] Qur'an, 47:17.

The Qur'an is the word of Allah﷾ revealed to Prophet Muhammadﷺ. It is the starting point and primary source for all three areas (Islam, Eman and Ihsan), for every person's faith, practice, means to developing in good character and attain success in this life and the Next. It is in every way a book of guidance for "**those who are mindful of God**".[60]

It was revealed over 23 years bit-by-bit and in the Arabic language. Therefore, the Arabic text is what refers to the direct word of God and used in rituals and acts of worship. Translations are considered only the meaning of the Qur'an and not the word of God itself.[61] It consists of 30 parts (*juz*) and 114 chapters (*surah*). The order of both and the verses is not according to when they were revealed, just as the Qur'an is not a book of law that treats each subject in a separate chapter. It may deal with matters of belief, morals, rituals, and legislation all in the same chapter giving its teachings more power and persuasion. This approach shows how the Qur'an is a living doctrine that serves as a practical solution to human intellectual, spiritual, and ethical needs. Quantitatively, matters of *aqidah* (belief) take up the largest part. Morals, manners, and good character come next, followed by rituals, and lastly the legal provisions.[62] The *aqidah* being first as a 'framework' or structure to the religion.[63] Then comes manifestations of good character, submission through rituals and worship, and religiously-sound actions and dealings.

When connecting and living with the Qur'an you will see how each passage, chapter, and verse is presented in a way that brings guidance in the best way possible. Deep pondering and contemplation (and of course the purified state of the heart) when reading the Quran is the way to understand its signs, wisdom, and benefit from its methods of instilling discipline and refinement. It is talking to you. It relates to you and serves you. Every verse. All of it.

Do not focus on parts and less on others. For example, the verses addressing believers are talking to you and so are the verses describing and talking to the non-believers or hypocrites. As a book of guidance, practicality is a distinctive feature. Practical matters are mentioned frequently and explicitly as a necessary condition for final salvation and eternal happiness.[64] Knowing the characteristics of a believer helps you be and remain steadfast as one. Likewise, knowing the traits of non-believers and hypocrites helps understand and avoid declining into their traits. The Qur'an is not helping work only on specific traits but guides the reader to change as a person holistically and completely. It gives the core solution to problems and core reasons for nobleness and righteousness. The divine miracle of the Qur'an is that it speaks to you, and you will find your own life story in it.

Its beauty is appreciated when you read verses and passages in their context and not take a verse-by-verse approach,[65] and to understand the chapter theme (or overview) through its own coherence. Each chapter has its unique coherent character.

---

[60] Qur'an, 2:2.

[61] Abdel Haleem, M. *Understanding the Qur'an*, p.8.

[62] *Ibid*, p.6.

[63] Hence the five pillars of Islam start with the 'Testimony of Faith'. Al-Bukhari (8), Muslim (114), Ahmad (6301).

[64] Draz, M.A., Introduction to the Qur'an, p.62.

[65] The approach of literalism, atomism, and disregard for context.

This is defined by a main subject or a theme of interrelated topics which together form the body of the chapter's subject matter. Once the core theme or subject matter is identified the jigsaw pieces come together revealing how the rest of the chapter falls in line with or can be related to that theme.[66] You will see also how it accurately relates to little-known events of the past, true prediction of future events, and the unique relationship between words and meaning (the *nazm*[67]).[68] It is rightly described as "*a well-composed and well-knit discourse*",[69] which goes beyond any linguistic study, owing to the images it portrays and fine expressions in conveying the intended meaning.[70]

Its guidance encourages the reader to seize every opportunity for direction and helps remove every possible obstacle to reach salvation and happiness.

Memorising the whole Qur'an is not obligatory, but you do need some verses to pray with. Start with chapter one (*al-fatiha* – The Opener) as this must be read in your daily prayers (*salah*) and read correctly. If you want to memorise larger parts of it, the best way is to follow the steps of the companions of the Prophetﷺ and that is to read, understand, and memorising 10 verses at a time while implementing.[71] This way you understand what you are memorising and practice what you are understanding. Then another 10 verses and so on.

Understanding its meaning comes from the commentary and interpretation of the scholars of Islam. These books are called *tafsir*[72] or 'commentary of the Qur'an'. This is different to translations of the Qur'an which are only translating the words from its original Arabic text.[73]

The important thing is to not neglect the Qur'an. Do not be amongst those the Prophetﷺ will complain about, "**And the Messenger will say, "My Lord, my people have abandoned this Quran**"[74] i.e., to be disconnected with it by not Reading/listening, pondering (*tadabor*), understand what is expected of you, and implement its teachings.[75] The following is an overview of its main themes and objectives:

The necessity[76] of God and his unity[77] - the Qur'an aims to address people's heart about firm and deep-rooted belief in God through belief in and awareness of the unseen. It proves there is God Who created this world, and its ongoing existence and sustenance cannot be without a god.

---

[66] Al-Ghazali, M. A thematic commentary on the Qur'an, p.viii.

[67] Al-Baqillani, A. *I'jaz al-qur'an*, p.279.

[68] *Ibid*, pp.48-51.

[69] Tafsir al-Kashaf (1/3).

[70] Draz, M.A., *An Eternal Challenge*, Translated by Adil Salahi, p.91.

[71] Tafsir al-Tabari (1/42), al-Hakim in *al-Mustadrak* (2070).

[72] The works of scholars who interpret and explain the context, text, and provide sound commentary for understanding what is intended.

[73] E.g., *The Qur'an. A new translation* by M.A.S Abdel Haleem, *The clear Qur'an* by Dr. Mustafa Khattab, *The Qur'an* by The Qur'an Project. These are also used for this book.

[74] Qur'an, 25:30.

[75] Tafsir Ibn Kathir, tafsir al-Baghawi, tafsir Abu al-Saud, tafsir al-tahrir wa al-tanwir, tafsi al-Sha'rawi.

[76] Necessity meaning a person cannot imagine this world without a god. His existence is therefore Necessary.

[77] Meaning it cannot be imagined there can be more than one unique god.

Prophethood and Revelation – explaining how Islam is the complete and preserved religion. Whilst all prophets and messengers spread the same core message, the sending of Prophet Muhammadﷺ is the final of the process of religious teachings and revelation. Prophethood is an essential part of human history as Allahﷻ chose them to reveal his truth just as they are the channel through which revelation became known to humanity. Revelation and prophethood are therefore interrelated and their miracles serve as a way of affirming their legitimacy.

The universe and creations – proving existence of the Creator and the demonstration of His ultimate Wisdom and Power by observing and pondering on the universe, oneself, and all created things. His sound judgement is evident in everything around us for those those who ponder with objectivity and hearts are unclouded with desire and minds with stubbornness.

Humankind as Individuals - granted free choice, everyone is created in a neutral state with no inherited sins and a readiness to submit to the Will of God or otherwise. The Qur'an guides man to make the choice of worship, righousness and obedience over submitting to the of evil of Satan (*shaytan*), negative traits, and one's egoistic self. To become enriched with a sound mind, honourable character, pure heart and correct acts of worship and deeds. There is immense focus in the Qur'an on purification, refining of character, and being good-hearted.

Society – it aims to help people and societies achieve success and prosperity and oppose all forms of corruption and injustices. The development or decline of a healthy society lies on the individual. The forms of injustices that should be condemned relate to all aspects of life. This includes - but not limited to - mental, physical, economical, political, distribution of wealth, family unity and parenthood. The Qur'an is filled with principles and guidance on people and society. The Qur'anic approach to the wellbeing of mankind and civilization is about developing individuals and developing society through the individual, "***Indeed, Allah does not change the condition of a nation until they change the condition of themselves***".[78]

Death, resurrection, and reward/punishment in the Hereafter – there will come a day when the realities are known, every person faced with the truth about themselves, and will be handed their book. In it is a record of everything they did. Every deed and every act will testify for or against the person, and their fate will depend on this and on the mercy of Allahﷻ. The Qur'an places strong emphasis on the fear of Judgment Day in the mind and hearts of people so that the effect of this is manifested in a way that makes them obedient and good-natured.

Satan and evil - Satan is a creation called *jinn*.[79] Like humans, there are good and evil *jinns* and Satan is the most evil of them. He is opposed to man and seeks to corrupt, destruct, and deceive into disobeying God. The Qur'an speaks of his ways and tactics, danger of following, and importance of being God-conscious to overcome his whispers and defeat his attempts to instil hopelessness and misery.

---

[78] Qur'an, 13:11.

[79] A creation from fire and can manifest into different forms.

Belief and trust in the unseen (*ghayb*) – not everything that exists is only what we can see and touch. Man is faced with danger when he relies fully on material and physical things. It corrupts his perceptions and impacts his actions and feelings. For example, a person with little financial income may feel hopeless in resolving an overwhelming debt problem leading to a self-declared 'dead end' with no solution in sight. This causing him to live in despair, anxiety, and could lead to mental pressures and/or emotional imbalance. In the chapter 2, the first characteristic of a believer mentioned is "**those who believe in the unseen**". Conscious that Allah is all-knowing of his needs, listens to his prayers, is the all-Provider and can relieve from debt. This solidifies reliance on Allah and instils hope, inner-peace, and contentment. The Qur'an teaches in many ways the importance of the unseen and its impact.

The names of Allah

Every teaching in Islam is interrelated. Being the Qur'an, *hadith*, what relates to the Prophet and even the names and attributes of Allah. This is not information for just mental satisfaction or intellectual stimulation but a way of life. As well as knowing His words and commands - through the Qur'an - it is important to know His names. Knowing Him better removes doubts and uncertainties from the heart and replaces with clarity, faith, and determination. Taking from His names develops and deepens the relationship, helping become a righteous slave and noble being.

How can we take from these names when He is the Creator with such attributes and we are creations, limited?

You are only taking the word. As for the essence of the word there is a difference. The names and attributes of Allah is one thing and the attributes of human beings is another. For example, He has mercy and people can also have mercy. What is in common is only the word 'mercy'. However, He is **all**-merciful and always had this attribute: "*just as He was eternally characterised by His attributes, He will likewise continue to be characterised by them neverendingly*"[80] whereas the mercy in mankind is limited and has been created by Him. There is no comparison.

The names and attributes of Allah influence the universe and all creations. It is important to understand how to deal with these to benefit far beyond knowing just the definition or basic meaning. The perfection and happiness of man comes from complying to His perfections in His names and attributes and to regard them with love, respect, and honour.[81] There must be a process. Starting from understanding the name progressing onto changing with the name, *from defining to refining*. This requires you:

- Read the linguistic definition of the name carefully with much focus, thought, and attentiveness
- Ponder on what the name means in relation to Allah, through the works of scholars
- Take your time, allowing meaning to deepen in the mind and heart. Spend time with the thought of the name
- Then read what the name means in relation to us, reflecting much on what is intended from it

---

[80] The Creed of imam al-Tahawi (line 15).

[81] Qur'an, 7:180. Tafsir al-Tabari, tafsir al-Qurtubi, tafsir Ibn Kathir, tafsir al-Razi, tafsir al-tahrir wa al-tanwir, tafsir al-muharar al-wajiz.

- Reflect on how you will start to implement and how the name will become part of you. As a manifested characteristic not just isolated actions
- Allow yourself time before moving on to a new name. If the above is done correctly you will see the effect and change from the first name. Focus on quality not quantity.

How many names of Allah﷾ are there?

There is a common *hadith* that lists 99 names[82] which many people think are the only ones. There are many more which are either:[83]

- Mentioned in the Qur'an
- Taught to His creations (prophets, messengers, etc)
- Allah﷾ has kept to Himself and not exposed

Are there names which have exact same meaning?

No. There are no two names that will be exactly the same. Each will have detailed meaning(s) that is not in the other, such as:[84]

'Al-Ghafir' the Forgiver - refers to the origin/principle of forgiveness

'Al-Ghafur', the all-Forgiving - forgives a lot, multiple sins

'Al-Ghaffar', full of forgiveness - repeatedly forgives, ongoingly

How does the name 'Allah' differ to the other names?

Allah is the name used to refer to His Being. It is therefore the name that encompasses all the other names and attributes and can only be for Him.

Allah is considered the greatest of His names and the mostly used in the Qur'an.

Allah is the mostly used name amongst Muslims regardless of their background and language.

---

[82] Al-Bukhari (2736), Muslim (6809).

[83] Ahmad (3712), Ibn Hibban (972).

[84] Al-Qurtibi, Al-asna fe sharh asmaa Allah al-husna wa sifatihi, p.46.

CHAPTER THREE
The Prophet ﷺ

Allah♦ created us for an honourable purpose: to worship Him alone and maintain a life in line with His noble teachings. His mercy was such that He did not leave us without close guidance or in confusion. He sent us humans just like us. They can relate to us, communicate, and demonstrate how His message is to be implemented. These are prophets and messengers. The likes of *Adam, Nuh, Ibrahim, Musa* and *'Isa*, and *Muhammad* - peace and blessings be upon them. A detailed account of their life is unnecessary as the Qur'an is focused on guidance and practicality. The mention of only 25 in the Qur'an guides to understanding the message and implementing its teachings.

Think of the Prophet Muhammad♦ as a means to your Lord. Allah♦ commands and the Prophet♦ guides us to fulfilling those commands. Born in the year 570 CE in Makkah (Saudi Arabia today), his father died before he was born, and he was raised first by his grandfather then his uncle. His mother died at the age of six. He belonged to a respectable family and a pure linage. He lived 63 years. Of that was 23 years as prophet and messenger when at the age 40 he began to receive revelation that became the basis for the Qur'an. His teachings were in line with and mirrored the Qur'an, "**Nor does he speak out of [his own] desire. It is not but a revelation revealed**".[85] All prophets and messengers have Necessary qualities and characteristics. To be discussed later in the *aqidah*/principles of belief section.

Your relationship with Prophet Muhammad♦

Sent to reveal the truth and open people's eyes to their purpose in life, he was a unique example of uprightness and objectivity. He used to prevent the companions from worshiping excessively and overburdening themselves[86] and at the same time taught them strength and perseverance.[87] He represents balance and perfection in every way.

We are ordered to love and devote to the Prophet♦. This is not limited to an emotional feeling or merely to honour his prophethood. Nor should his teachings be seen as just a list of dos and don'ts. The relationship should never be stern and stiff but is about a real connection, increasing appreciation and love, a commitment to follow his footsteps to progress in good character and righteousness, and to take him as a perfect example. There are many Quranic verses that help us understand how to relate to the Prophet♦.[88] One important one is:

"***Those who <u>believe</u> in him, <u>honour</u> him, <u>support</u> him, and <u>follow the light which is sent down with him</u>; they are the successful***".[89]

We see from this verse that following his teachings is only part of the relationship not all of it. Many people follow his teachings robotically but the spirit of love, wholehearted attachment and bond is casual or almost non-existent. Do remember all four: ***believe - honour - support – follow the light which is sent down with him***.

---

[85] Qur'an, 53:3-4.
[86] Al-Bukhari (5063), Muslim (6966).
[87] Muslim (6774).
[88] Qur'an, 4:136, 4:80, 3:81, 48:10, 3:31, 108:1, 17:1, 53:8-9, 2:144, 93:3-5, 17:79, 52:48, 68:4, 33:21, 3:164, 2:151, 33:45-6, 53:3-4, 5:15, 21:107, 33:40, 24:63, 33:56.
[89] Qur'an, 7:157.

(1) Believe

Anyone can claim to have love for the Prophetﷺ. This can only be true if the real conditions for love are there. First and foremost is to believe him and believe in him. Believing he is a true Prophet as part of one's faith is one level, but to have real loyalty and commitment is a level far beyond even reading his *hadiths* and practicing them.

There can be a basic acceptance or there can be a deep conviction. This is when the belief becomes not only deep rooted but comes with eagerness and submission. To love to know about him, eager to learn from him, and yearn to connect with and relate to him. Where love and trust are firmly embodied in the heart. The confidence that his personality and mission is divinely guided and only through him we attain righteousness, divine connection, and enlightened guidance. Believing in him as a perfect teacher, mentor, and purifier. Accepting, without a doubt, his way is what we need going forward in our individual lives, for our societies to prosper and for the welfare and wellbeing of our *ummah*[90] and the whole of humanity.

(2) Honour

Not honour in the basic common understanding but an intense feeling of fondness, admiration, and attachment, "**No one of you will become a [true] believer until he will love me [i.e., the Prophet] more than his parents, children and all other people**".[91] In another hadith, the great companion 'Umar was once with the Prophetﷺ and said to him "**O Messenger of Allah! You are dearer to me than everything except my own self." The Prophet said, "No, by Him in Whose Hand my soul is, [you will not have complete faith] till I am dearer to you than your own self." Then `Umar said to him, "it is, now, by Allah, you are dearer to me than my own self." The Prophet said, "Now, O `Umar, (now you are a believer)**".[92]

(3) Support him

To support his mission. As the companions were around the Prophetﷺ assisting him in spreading the message and guiding people, we too have a duty to preach and teach. Like he strived and worked restlessly to save every possible soul from the trauma of Hellfire, we should also share this heart-felt desperation and devote to what he devoted to.

We should equip ourselves with knowledge and be in tuned with modern methods of communication and objective reasoning to prove the truthfulness of Islam. A Muslim should work to be characterised with strong principles, moral conduct, a high level of social order, a balance with materialism, and a deep-rooted spiritual state. Through our spiritual condition and mannerism (i.e., inner and outer perfections) we spread the religion and draw hearts to it. And should not through bad manners and spiritual emptiness move people away from the religion, "**Our Lord, make us not [objects of] torment for the disbelievers**".[93] i.e., do not allow our condition to be a reason for them to transgress and deviate.[94]

---

[90] Meaning the global Muslim population/community

[91] Al-Bukhari (15).

[92] Al-Bukhari (6632).

[93] Qur'an, 60:5.

[94] Al-tafsir al-wasit lilquran al-kareem.

(4) Follow the light which is sent down with him

The light is the Qur'an, so to follow him, along with the Qur'an.[95] Once the above is achieved (to believe, honour and support), a desire to follow will naturally unfolding and enhance. Following him is not just the limbs in action. Rather, the heart, mind, and limbs (Islam, Eman and Ihsan) all harmoniously abiding to his path, following his way and seeking to take from his perfections, "***It is not for any believer, man or woman, when Allah and His Messenger have decided a matter, to have liberty of choice in their decision***"[96] simply because the term 'believer' comes with established traits, "***None of you [truly] believes until his desires are subservient to what I have brought***".[97]

How can this all be achieved?

- The first important thing is to believe this can be achieved. One cannot be reading about change and righteousness through the Prophet⌖, be motivated and ambitious, yet sceptical or in doubt
- Secondly, it is a process and is ongoing. It is not a list of tasks or a box ticking activity
- Thirdly, both the inner and outer need to be worked on together

Whilst there is more detail to this, which will follow (under spiritual purification), it is necessary to:

- Read and contemplate his *shamail* and *seerah*. Start **first** with the *shamail*[98]
- Study his *hadiths*. Ponder deeply and look for what is intended from each one, the change and refinement
- Do lots of *salawat*.[99] The Qur'an explains the Prophet⌖ has been sent not just as a teacher but also a **purifier**.[100] Through *salawat* you gain immense benefits, is a means for purifying yourself,[101] and a spiritual connection with the Prophet⌖ develops
- To love all those whom he loved. His companions (*sahaba*), his family (*ahl al-bayt*), his *ummah*, and all people regardless of colour, race, and status. And to hate what he hated. He hated the actions of the wrongdoers not the individuals themselves
- Embark on a journey of purification with a spiritual guide who can take your hand and mentor you. This is the Prophet⌖'s method of guiding his *ummah* spiritually. He mentored the companions who became righteous and were qualified to take those of the next generation on a spiritual purification journey and this method continues to our time today

One of the beautiful things about prophet Muhammad⌖'s perfection is that for you it constantly raises the limits for perfection and development potential. You will never reach his perfection, but you will always have more perfections you can advance in and work towards, progressing in ranks of uprightness, purity, and piety. If his perfection stopped at a certain point we can reach, we would not be able to progress any further.

---

[95] Tafsir Abu al-Saud.

[96] Qur'an, 33:36.

[97] Al-Nawawi's Forty Hadiths (41).

[98] Both explained in the next section.

[99] *Salawat* is an Arabic word, meaning prayer or salutations upon the Prophet⌖ who himself, responding to a companion named Ubayy, assured him that if all his *dhikr* (Remembrance) was devoted to *salawat*, "**your needs will be sufficed, and your sins will be forgiven**". Al-Tirmidhi, (2625), Ahmad (21241). Prayers refers to Remembrance (*dhikr*).

[100] Qur'an, 2:151. 3:164.

[101] Qur'an, 33:43. Muslim (912). This shall be discussed in detail under the *ihsan* section later.

The need for Prophets and Messengers

Never has a person of even great abilities, skills, intellect, or experience been able to initiate or add to previous attempts to create a complete way of life. One that serves the interest and wellbeing of humanity and encompasses every aspect of both this life and the Hereafter and in context of Allah﷾'s governing ways (the systems He has placed, unchanging laws of our universe). Even if there were attempts, this would be done by those with their own flaws and are not infallible. The sending of prophets and messengers is a mercy that protects us from dilemma and difficulties, instead focusing our efforts on implementing divine commands and succeeding. They had certain qualities and characteristics the average person lacks. These include:

- Directly linked to the [divine] source of all-knowledge for information which is real, credible, and authentic.
- They knew the very detailed nature of human beings; physically, psychologically, emotionally, spiritually, mentally etc. Afterall, it is this [human] being they would be teaching and guiding. It is only through revelation they could know this, as only Allah﷾ knows every detail of His creations.[102]
- They were familiar with details of past nations and the history of humanity. This can only come from revelation as no person can know or comprehend this fully. They knew how to understand and relate to historical events and Universal Laws that govern the universe we and all creations operate within. Simply because they were connected to The Fashioner of all things,[103] *"[This is] the established way of God also occurred in the past. And never will you find in the way of Allah any change "*[104] and in another verse, *"And never will you find in the way of Allah any substitute"*.[105]
- They can carry a message which is clear and objective, that relates to and serves every person in any setting. People of all different nations, backgrounds, languages, and times.
- They were free from desire, personal agenda and characterised with total purity, sincerity, trustworthiness, flawlessness and free from sinning, *"We sent Our messengers with clear signs, the Scripture and the balance that the people may uphold [their affairs] in justice"*.[106] Balance meaning justice. In every sense. infallibility.

Mankind is lost and left in darkness without proper guidance. With prophethood and divine direction comes light and success. The conclusion is that real guidance and a sound way of life can only come from one source: Allah﷾. Once prophets and messengers are sent to humanity and the message is clear, there remains no excuse and everyone is accountable, bearing in mind *"And never would We punish [people] until We sent a messenger [to warn them]"*[107] nor will He leave those who know and choose to deny without accountability when the truth is not just clear to them but are constantly being reminded, *"Which, then, of your Lord's blessings and signs can you deny?"*[108] An awakening verse that comes after a list of many blessings and bounties He has bestowed upon every individual.

---

[102] Qur'an, 67:14.

[103] The Fashioner is a translation of His name *Al-Musawir*, meaning He fashioned everything He created i.e., determined its image, shape, colour, attributes etc.

[104] Qur'an, 48:23. Known as *sunnan of Allah* (the ways of Allah﷾, His Universal Laws, and measures in place).

[105] Qur'an, 35:43.

[106] Qur'an, 57:25.

[107] Qur'an: 17:15.

[108] This verse is repeated 31 times in the same chapter of the Qur'an to highlight how hearts should be awakened and ignorant minds unlocked through pondering and observation. Chapter 55, verses 13, 16, 18, 21, 23, 25, 28, 30, 32, 34, 36, 38, 40, 42, 45, 47, 49, 51, 53, 55, 57, 59, 61, 63, 65, 67, 69, 71, 73, 75, 77.

We mentioned before the Qur'an is the primary source for teachings of the religion. Likewise, the Sunnah. These two primary sources form the basis of Islam and its sciences/knowledge.

'*Sunnah*' means the 'path' and 'practices' of Prophet Muhammad.[109] His way of doing things which the companions who were around him observed and which formed a model and perfect example for them to follow. They were the ones who passed these on to the following generations through transmission, leading to the documenting of *hadiths*.

'*Hadith*' means 'news' or 'story'[110] and is a record relating to the Prophet. A transmitted record of what he said, did, approved, and disapproved of, explicitly or implicitly.[111] It extends to his attributes, features, and characteristics.[112] Each report is a piece of information that when collected paints a larger picture of his teachings which formed the *Sunnah*. There are two types of hadith:

Hadith Nabawi (Prophetic *hadith*)	The words and actions of the Prophet
Hadith Qudsi (Holy *hadith*/divine saying)	The meaning is from Allah but words of the Prophet [113]

There are several books of *hadith*, some compiling hundreds and others in the thousands, including the works of great scholars such as *al-Bukhari, Muslim, al-Nasa'i, Abu Dawud, al-Tirmidhi, ibn Majah, and Malik*. Other books are compiled with a lot less, focusing on theme topics or to serve a specific purpose.[114]

Each *hadith* is intended to present a core message(s) to guide to righteousness. It is up to the reader to build a bond with every *hadith* to know what is intended of it and its manifestations. A deep reflective approach is important. One cannot claim to have understood a *hadith* until the core message and '*educational objective(s)*'[115] is grasped. Once analysed and its core intent understood (through the works of scholars and those of sound understanding), only then can a person develop and change through it.

Start by studying a book called *The 40 Nawawi hadiths* (by Imam al-Nawawi) which is a collection of fundamental *hadiths* highly regarded for centuries in the Muslim world. Each one consists of an important underlining principle(s) of the religion, helping develop sound Muslim intellect and carve a godly character.

---

[109] Al-Jurjani. *Al-ta'rifat.*

[110] Al-Kofwi. *Al-koliyat mu'jam fi Al-mustalahat wa Al-forouq Al-loghawiyah,* p.370.
Hadiths have different levels of strength according to transmission and other reasons which are outlined in the Science of Hadith. This is different to the hadith itself. It is a scholarly study of the wording and transmitters, placing the *hadiths* into different categories. See *Al-manthouma al-bayquniyah, matn nokhbit al-fikr.*

[111] Siraj Al-Din, A. *Sharh al-manthouma al-bayquniyah,* p.21.

[112] Al-Minshawi, M. *Qamous mustalahat al-hadith al-sharif.*
The same term is used for the words of companions and ta'bieen (the successors, i.e., generation after the companions). Siraj Al-Din, A. *Sharh al-manthouma al-bayquniyah,* p.21.

[113] Al-Jurjani. *Al-ta'rifat,* Al-Minshawi, M. *Qamous mustalahat al-hadith al-sharif.* Or both the meaning and wording is from Allah but said by the Prophet.

[114] A great collection of *hadiths* of the Prophet on good traits, manners, and noble character is *Riyadh al-saliheen* by the renowned scholar and jurist, Imam Al-Nawawi.

[115] An explanation of 'educational objectives' will following in the *hajj* and *umrah* section (under *What is an educational objective? And Examples of educational objectives in hajj*).

The *seerah* is a timeline of the Prophet's life and biography. Generally speaking, it does not go into details of his character but focuses more on the pre-prophethood period and his broad role as a prophet and leader, his linage, birth, upbringing, in his community, prophethood, with his companions, how he dealt with enemies and fought battles, his travels and efforts to spread the message, how he developed society, and developed his companions spiritually, with knowledge and wisdom, his migrating from Makkah to Madinah, sermons, final days and death, *peace and blessings be upon him.*

The Qur'an says, "**We alternate these days amongst people**",[116] teaching us that history repeats itself. People and times change but the broad lines remain the same.[117] When we read and understand the journey of the Prophet over 1440 years ago we are also getting to know our own journey and being guided on how he dealt with matters in his time and for all times. When one acknowledges that the Universal Laws of God that governs this world is consistent, the message and nature of mankind are the same, we then understand how the essence of human life and broad lines of history are also the same.

The *seerah* is important as it helps:

- Observe the ways of Allah in governing His universe and the manifestation of His laws and names
- Understand and appreciate what he went through for the sake of the truth
- Increases love towards Him
- Understand how to approach matters in a balanced way
- Educates us about the meaning of the Qur'an
- Raises hope and uplifts our spirit in times of hardship, turbulence, and affliction
- Lays out a precise methodology on how to revive the *ummah*
- Understand how he mentored and developed his companions

The *shamail* is more specific knowledge that relates to his physical and character perfections. While there is no picture or portraits of his exact image, the *shamail* is a collection of *hadiths* that portrays such perfections.[118] Focus is on detailed characteristics, physical appearance, and his features such as height and build, hair, and clothing. How he sat, ate, his speech and sense of humour. How he slept, what he liked and disliked of food, his manners, humility, modesty, and more.

Knowing his beautiful appearance, character, and lifestyle paves the way for developing deep and holistic appreciation of him as a messenger and as a human being. Islam has put emphasis on collecting the qualities of the final messenger so that people may get glimpses of real perfection and be devoted to taking from it.

---

[116] Qur'an, 3:140.

[117] Tafsir Abu al-Saud, tafsir al-tahrir wa al-tanwir.

[118] This collection of *hadiths* was first made by Imam al-Tirmidhi who collected 415 in his book *Al-shamail al-muhammadiyah.* Many such books exist today. All intending to celebrate his beauty of character and perfect being.

Knowing his *shamail* has proven to be a means for instilling love towards him and a deep convince of his perfect state, inwardly and outwardly. It also provides context to understanding Islam. Without properly understanding his *shamail* and *seerah* one can be left to understand Islam and the Prophetﷺ through their own opinion and tendencies where desire can lead, and people go astray by tweaking the Qur'an and *hadith* to what they think it means or what they want it to mean. This is very dangerous and sinful. Reading the *shamail*, you shall see that even the most basic piece of information about him will be an eyeopener to understand divine teachings and his perfect character.

The *shamail* is important as it helps:

- Develop love through his beautiful character
- Devote to perfection and excellence
- Relate to him, creating a strong bond
- Understand he is human so one can imitate and follow his footsteps and guidance

Read the *shamail* before the *seerah*. This way you know the *character* before the *journey*. Both, along with other aspects of purification shall help adorn the soul with good qualities and perfect traits. Reading, however, is not to scan through or just memorise dates, events, and features. It is to reflect and confirm your understanding and developing thoughts. This religion focuses strongly on the importance of contemplating[119] and rejects following blindly,[120] which comes with consequences.[121] We are here to gain sound understanding. And for information to penetrate, the heart must be present with the mind. Bringing both together develops positive and progressive impact.

[119] Qur'an, 4:82, 10:3, 12:111, 23:68, 38:29, 47:24.
[120] Qur'an, 2:170, 5:104, 7:179, 8:22, 21:53, 26:74, 43:23.
[121] Qur'an, 11:109, 67:10.

CHAPTER FOUR
Mannerism in Islam
(*akhlaq*)

Islam provides a body of knowledge on manners and etiquette that covers every aspect of life for Muslims to adopt and the whole of mankind to benefit from. It clarifies the nature of an ethical life, offering a scale by which we be guided by and assess our mannerism against. It is knowledge that enlightens the path for what it is supposed to be.[122] Once adhered to and manifested in a Muslim, it becomes through them that Islam is introduced to others and brings about harmony amongst people.

Enhancing inner and outer qualities causes hearts and minds of others to be drawn close, "**The best amongst you are the best in character and manners**".[123] It can be concluded through studying the life of the Prophetﷺ, non-believers of his time turned to Islam not by counting the different forms of worship he practiced or the number of rituals he performed. They observed his conduct and distinguished character.

Mannerism in Islam is key to a healthy individual, society and human family. It spells out exactly what everyone is required to do and what can be expected of one another, creating common understanding and appreciation. Morals and high principles are outlined in a clear and precise way leaving no room for ambiguity. Huge emphasis is placed on enhancing mental objectivity, purifying the conscience, habituating the self (*nafs*), and training individuals to adopt righteous behaviour towards everyone and everything.[124]

Mannerism requires regular attention not a surface level 'brushing activity', a 'superficial polish', or limited to certain occasions or calibre of people. It is about moulding a deep inner condition where actions arise naturally without the need for thought or effort. A natural moral-value-tendency. However, any moral concept worthy of the name is based on the idea of obligation. This is its most fundamental basis and core foundation around which the whole ethical system revolves, which if absence, would destroy the essence of practical wisdom. For without obligation there is no responsibility and without responsibility there can be no return of just behaviour or treatment which leads to chaos, disorder, and lawlessness according to the moral principle itself.[125]

"Verily, the most beloved and nearest to my gathering on the Day of Resurrection are those of you with the best character".[126]

"There is nothing is weightier on the Scale of Deeds than one's good manners".[127]

---

[122] Zakzouk, M. Introduction to the knowledge of mannerism, pp.18-9.

[123] Al-Bukhari (3559), Muslim (6033).

[124] Many verses and *hadiths* speak of a wide range of manners, ethics and opens many doors for spreading peace, mercy, empathy, social harmony and goodness. Some of these in the Qur'an: 22:30, 49:12, 28:76, 49:11, 17:26, 22:36, 5:89, 9:4, 3:134, 24:15-6, 24:12, 33:58, 17:23, 23:3, 49:11, 25:63, 41:34, 6:108, 6:152, 5:101, 25:67, 53:32, 76:9, 58:11, 8:61, 4:86, 2:264, 49:9, 31:19, 6:108, 2:273, 4:135, 20:44, 9:79, 24:63, 4:128, 49:4, 2:217, 16:125, 24:4, 33:6, 49:2, 4:94, 24:59, 4:29, 31:18, 24:22, 24:62, 58:9, 2:44, 17:28, 3:159, 49:6, 33:53, 24:27-8, 2:231, 16:126, 49:13, 4:19.

[125] Draz. M. A., The moral world of the Qur'an, p.13.

[126] Al-Tirmidhi (2137).

[127] Al-Tirmidhi (2121), Abi Dawud (4799).

CHAPTER FIVE

The Book of Islam
(Fiqh/Jurisprudence)

What is *fiqh*?

Linguistically, *fiqh* means 'to understand'.[128]

Islamically, is 'to understand detailed rulings that relate to a Muslim's practical rituals and acts of worship'. Referred to as Islamic jurisprudence, is a scholarly understanding of divine Islamic law of the Qur'an and the Sunnah.[129]

What does the knowledge of *fiqh* cover?

It explains what is expected and the 'know how' of outward physical actions. Some examples:

Rituals - physical purity (*taharah*), ablution (*wudu*), prayer (*salah*), pilgrimage (*hajj*), alms (*zakat*).

Family - marriage, upbringing of children, relations with parents, spouses, and wider family ties, inheritance, divorce.

Other - social legislation, charity, business & finance, politics, war and peace-making, inheritance, food and drink, clothing, and appearance.

This is just a glimps. Matters of *fiqh* are very broad and detailed (in the thousands) as it covers all practical matters.

By studying *fiqh* a person ensures:

- Fulfilling their duty of servanthood and rights towards their Lord
- Rituals and acts of worship are free from error and deficiency
- Actions and conduct become religiously-sound and acceptable
- Fulfilling rights and responsibilities towards one's self and others, including non-human creations

In return, this:

- Develops peace, tranquillity, justice, stability and consistency towards oneself and others
- Attains happiness and success in this life and the Hereafter

Do you need to learn all areas of *fiqh*?

No. But you may be asking why not. Is this all not part of the religion and should be practised?

These are physical actions. In other words, practical responsibilities. Say if a person is not physically (or financially) able to perform *hajj*, then they are not [yet] obliged to practice this ritual until they are able to do so. Therefore, are not required to know the rules of it. Or if a person does not own or manage a business, they are not expected to study the [relevant] *fiqh* of financial transactions and trade dealings. But say a person intends to marry, they would need to know the conditions of marriage, how it is conducted, and each person's role and responsibilities in the marriage. Islam is a practical religion and does not burden the average person to seek knowledge for the sake of knowledge. It urges Muslims to be focused and purposeful.

---

[128] Al-mu'jam Al-wasit.

[129] Al-Zurqa. M. Al-madkhal al-fiqhi al'am., p.65.

There are, however, parts of *fiqh* everyone must know. Such as whoever meets the conditions and is required to pray must know about purifying physically and how to perform the prayer. It is their duty to study the *fiqh* relating to this. You do not need to study every detail. Only the essentials. Whenever you have questions beyond this or need clarification, revert to those with knowledge or scholars who are expected to study the entire knowledge of *fiqh*.[130]

Legal/*fiqh* Schools – its history and development

The knowledge of *fiqh* and its preservation throughout the history of Islam went through three phases:

- The time of Prophet Muhammad☷
- The period of The Companions (*sahabah*)
- The generation of The Successors (*tabi'in*)

The time of Prophet Muhammad☷

In many verses of the Qur'an and reasons for revelation (*asbab al-nuzoul*) we see questions being presented to the Prophet☷ on a wide range of matters. Revelation would then come down to give answers, or intended to highlight something important, "**They ask you [O Prophet]**" is repeated numerous times. This and similar statements formed part of the initial examples of *fiqh* i.e., the first mention of rulings to practical matters. They asked, for example, about the crescent/phases of the moon, charitable giving, fighting in the Sacred Month, intoxicants, gambling, [the property of] orphans, menstruation, what is lawful, about the Hour, [distributing] spoils of war, the spirit, *Dhul-Qarnayn*, the mountains, and Judgement Day timing.[131]

In the same way, situations would arise requiring a ruling and revelation would come down accordingly, such as, "**Indeed, Allah has heard**"[132] in the incident between a husband and wife where the *fiqh* that prohibits describing one's wife as their mother (*dhihar*) was revealed. This was a way of divorce in the pre-Islam time of ignorance (*jahiliyah*), and we are required to refrain from. The verses also teach us to retract and the forms of "atonement" or "expiation (*kaffarah*) necessary to compensate.

The time of the Prophet☷ was the most important period. Not only because revelation was being sent *per se* or because he himself spread teachings of *fiqh*, bringing solutions to practical queries, but very importantly, he taught his companions the methodology of deriving rulings, interpreting text, and reaching sound legal opinion (*ijtihad*).[133] This was essential for the forthcoming generations. Scholars throughout the history of Islam and today now have the tools, knowledge, and expertise to deal with existing legal matters as well new legal matters to accommodate changing needs, situations, and incidents that arise over time.[134]

---

[130] The focus of this book is on the essentials of the key rituals.

[131] See Qur'an, 2:189, 2:215, 2:217, 2:219, 2:220, 2:222, 5:4, 7:187, 8:1, 17:85, 18:83, 20:105, 51:12, 79:42.

[132] Qur'an, 58:1.

[133] *Ijtihad* refers to the efforts and critical thinking needed to reach a sound and founded legal conclusion.

[134] You will recall at the start of this book it was mentioned: "the teachings and rulings of this message had to be fixed in matters that need to be fixed until the Day of Judgment and at the same time flexible in matters to accommodate changing times and circumstances".

The period of The Companions (*sahabah*)

After the death of the Prophet☪, the number of Muslims grew rapidly, and Islam spread widely. There were companions who were distinguished in their knowledge and understanding. They had the ability to exercise religious opinion and consultation (*shura*) on newly arising matters, to compliment the already established *fiqh* taught by the Prophet☪.

The same methodology was applied in many situations where companions showed they were highly qualified and senior scholars. This meant that at times of much needed judgement and opinion they were able to deal with complex matters, such as:

- Election of leaders (*caliphs*)
- Sayidna Abu Bakr dealing with those refusing to pay their *zakat* and compiling the Qur'an into book form
- Sayidna 'Umar dealing with changes to spoils of war and introducing state benefits
- Sayidna Ammar ibn Yasir appointed a governor
- Sayidna Ibn Masoud appointed a judge, resolving matters with a profound understanding of the social context

In addition, there was those sent to various parts of the world to spread this knowledge, including:

- Sayidna Ibn Abbas to Makkah
- Sayidna Abu Musa al-Ashari to Basra
- Sayidna Abdullah ibn Amr to Egypt
- Sayidna Muadh ibn Jabal to Syria

By this time, Schools of Law started to evolve, paving the way for the four *madhahib* we have today.

The generation of The Successors (*tabi'in*)

What happened to the companions was replicated with the generation of Successors. As the companions were taught and developed with knowledge and methodology, they taught and created expert scholars of this later generation. The input from scholars of both eras led to a rich legal heritage, creating several highly qualified experts of *fiqh*. The likes of the great imam Abu Hanifah and imam Malik. They applied their methods in addressing *fiqh* matters of their times, bringing it to a new advance.

The formation of Legal/*fiqh* Schools (*madhahib*)

Whilst Muslims are devoted to following the Qur'an and Sunnah, some may ask an important question: *how can this be achieved by reverting directly to the Qur'anic and Sunnah text bearing in mind Islamic law is very broad and complex?* And at the same time, for practicality, expect the text to be straightforward and explanatory.

As we have seen, scholars in the early days of Islam were qualified to derive from the Qur'an and Sunnah the rulings of *fiqh* and as a result have provided step-by-step guidance on how to practice the religion. They were the most qualified to understand Qur'an and Sunnah as they witnessed revelation and the spread of Islam. They were also close to the Prophet☪ taking from him directly. The later learned scholars continued to understand and extract rulings with the same methodology and scriptural interpretation as the companions. The expertise, strong abilities, and competencies they possessed made them worthy of this. Their work progressed until 'Schools of Law' or *madhahib*"[135] were developed. A *madhab* linguistically means 'a way'.[136] It is a method of interpreting scripture that brings scholars together as a group like a school.

Every act of worship and ritual you undertake should be based on the teachings of these schools/*madhahib*. They have slight differences according to the rulings they have reached which all fall in line with sound knowledge of Islam and acceptable opinions. It is useful to be familiar with them as you are likely to regularly hear the names of these schools and the renowned righteous scholars who founded them.

The Schools of Islamic Law are four, named after their founders:

(1) Abu Hanifah (80-150 A.H.) founder of the **Hanafi school/***madhab*.
Imam Abu Hanifah was an early scholar who lived in Iraq. Today his school is the most predominant in Turkey, Pakistan, India, Afghanistan, the ex-Soviet Muslim states and parts of the Middle East.

(2) Malik ibn Anas (93-179 A.H.) founder of the **Maliki school/***madhab*.
Imam Malik lived in Madinah, the city of the Prophet☺ throughout his life. Today, his school is widespread in North Africa and sub-Saharan Africa. For centuries it was the predominant school of Andalusia (Muslim Spain).

(3) Muhammad ibn Idrees al-Shafi'i (150-204 A.H.) founder of the **al-Shafi'i school/***madhab*.
Imam al-Shafi'i was from the Quraysh tribe (same tribe as the Prophet☺). He studied and lived in numerous places, finally settling in Egypt. Today his school is mostly in Malaysia, Indonesia, and parts of the Middle East and Africa.

(4) Ahmad Ibn Hanbal (164-241 A.H.) founder of the **Hanbali school/***madhab*.
Imam Ahmad lived in Baghdad and was known to be a great scholar of *hadith*. His school is most popular today in Saudi Arabia and other parts of the Arabian Peninsula.

It is important to understand there are many reasons scholars and jurists came to different conclusions. In this is great benefits and blessing.[137] The feature of 'difference' should be seen as something positive, an essential quality, and spirit of the religion.[138] The richness of opinions and conclusions offer wide scope to religious rulings and serves the varied needs of Muslims in all parts of the globe.[139]

For example, in a *hadith*, the Prophet☺ encourages Muslims to follow the month of fasting (Ramadan) with six voluntary days which are separate to the month of Ramadan: "***Whoever fasts the month of Ramadan and then follows it with six days of fasting from [the Islamic month of] Shawwal, it will be as if he has fasted for the entire year***".[140]

---

[135] Singular = *madhab*.

[136] Al-qamous al-muhit, al-mu'jam al-wasit, al-misbah al-monir, lisan al-arab, al-mawsou'a al-fiqhiyah al-Kuweitiyah.

[137] Al-Suyuti. J. Jazil al-mawahib fi Ikhtilaf al-madhahib, p.21.

[138] Qur'an, 2:178, 2:185, 2:286, 4:28, 5:6, 8:66. Al-Bukhari (39, 5673, 6463, 7235), Muslim (3).

[139] Al-Yafie. A. Al-tamadhub dirasa ta'seilia, p.174.

[140] Muslim (2758).

Considering Arabic is a rich language in terms of its complexity, it can be understood that scholars will reach different opinions, while agreeing on the fundamentals.

By looking at the *hadith*, the average person may already be asking a few questions:

Does "**follows it with six days from Shawwal**" mean follow immediately after Ramadan, i.e., the first 6 days of *Shawwal*? or follow it with any six days of *Shawwal*? or follows "**from Shawwal**" meaning starting from the month of *Shawwal*, so can be anytime over the following 11 months until the next Ramadan?

Clearly it is open to interpretation. The difference of opinion amongst the Schools of Law/*fiqh* ranges between the recommendation of fasting them immediately after Ramadan, fasting any 6 during *Shawwal*, consecutively or separately and even fasting after *Shawwal*.[141] They are all acceptable. The opportunities in these varied opinions means a person may choose from several options. Someone may fear falling ill so fasts them immediately in the first 6 days of *Shawwal* whereas another person falls ill and recovers the month after *Shawwal*. Everyone benefits.

One must remember that the Prophet was sent to "**the whole of mankind**"[142] and as "**a mercy to the whole of mankind**"[143] so "**relieves them from their burdens and shackles that were upon them**".[144] *Fiqh* is no different. How can it be when it is derived from the Qur'an and his Sunnah. It accommodates a wide range of needs and brings about ease.

There are many wisdoms in rules of *fiqh*. Some which may be clear and apparent while others may not be. You are not required to understand the wisdom or logic behind a ruling to practice it, you are required to worship your Lord sincerely and devotedly. Be a worshiper of Allah not logic and wisdom. Do not make your mental convince a condition to accept or be content with a ruling. A slave wholeheartedly compels himself to the command of the Master!

Do you have to commit to one *madhab* or is it enough that the acts of worship fall within the four *madhahib*?

There are two opinions on this. One opinion is that you should fully comply with only one *madhab* you choose to follow. The other opinion states you can revert to another *madhab* and this takes two forms:[145]

(1) To completely move from following one *madhab* to another one

- Someone ignorant of their *madhab*
  Where a person has no knowledge of a *madhab* and is attributed to it just by name. It is permissible for them to move to another *madhab* as they are new to acquiring knowledge of *fiqh* altogether. They are yet to properly study and committed to a *madhab*.

- Someone knowledgeable of their *madhab*
  Where a person does have knowledge of their *madhab* but wishes to change to another for a worldly pleasure/corrupt intention. This is prohibited and considered dishonouring the religion for worldly gains.

---

[141] Al-Dimyati, I. Mawsou'at al-fiqh 'ala al-madhahib al-arba'a (4/128-31).

[142] Al-Bukhari (438), Muslim (521).

[143] Qur'an, 21:107.

[144] Qur'an, 7:157.

[145] Al-Suyuti. J. Jazil al-mawahib fi Ikhtilaf al-madhahib, pp.32-5.

For a genuine, religious motive/reason:

- Someone ignorant of their *madhab*

  A person has been engaged in learning the particulars of their *madhab* but has not gained any real knowledge of it and has found another *madhab* to be easier to understand and adopt. This person is obliged to move immediately and is sinful if intentionally delays this move.

- Someone knowledgeable of their *madhab*

  Someone with scholarly/advanced level of knowledge and has found himself content with the rulings of another *madhab* based on its methodology and strength of evidence. It is obligatory for them to move.

(2) To partially revert to another *madhab* in specific matters while continuing to devote to the existing *madhab*

It is permissible if a person is unable to practice a matter or is experiencing difficulty and their *madhab* offers no fulfilling solution.[146] There are conditions to this:[147]

- To not be searching for easy options *per se* to satisfy one's egoistic desires
- Has not already started to action the ruling in their *madhab*
- Feels content with reverting to the other *madhab* and believes its imam to be of knowledge and virtue
- Cannot be in matters of judicial ruling and does not go against a judicial ruling
- If performing a ritual in the new *madhab* where another *fiqh* matter is dependant on, it must be fulfilled according to the conditions of the new *madhab*.[148]

Complying with the *madhahib*

Many scholars over the history of Islam warn of the danger in going outside *madhahib*.[149] The four imams were known to be at the highest level of *ijtihad*: *mujtahid mutlaq* or 'absolute *mujtahid*'.[150] Reaching this level is not easy and to date has not been reached despite claimants in the past and in present times.[151] As for the lower levels of *ijtihad* scholars, the *ummah* has been blessed with many and – Allah﷾ willing – will continue to.

While a person should hold firm to their *madhab*, intolerance towards other *madhahib* or their imams is sinful, rejected, and indeed immature. One should show high regard and respect to all *madhahib*. The renowned scholar Ibn 'Abdeen advises:

"Holding firmly on to a madhab is an obligation, and intolerance is prohibited. Holding firmly is to follow its teachings, believing it to be the truth and whereas intolerance is foolishness and that is to belittle other madhabs or the imams of those madhabs and this is rejected. They are great scholars of Islam who sought the truth and are correct and authentic".[152]

---

[146] *Fatawa Al-Subki* (1/147), Ibn Hajar in *al-tohfa* (3/256), *hashiyit al-Sharwani* (3/256).

[147] Al-Yafie. A. Al-tamadhub dirasa ta'seilia. p.212.

[148] For example, if you pray according to one *madhab*, you must fulfil the the purification rules according to that madhab as purification is a condition for the prayer to be accepted.

[149] The likes of, for example, sheikh al-Islam al-Kawthari, the former Grand Mufti of the Ottoman Empire in his book *Al-la madhabiyyah*.

[150] A *mujtahid mutlaq* is a scholar at the level of the four Imams Abu Hanifa, Malik, al-Shafi'i, and Ahmad. They are unrestricted in their highly qualified ability to apply legal reasoning, draw analogies, and infer rulings from the evidence due to the depth of their expertise in necessary sciences, and their linguistic and juridical proficiency.

[151] Al-Yafie. A. Al-tamadhub dirasa ta'seilia, p.84, 102.

[152] Ibn 'Abdin. Al-oqoud al-durriyah fi tanqeeh al-fatawi al-hamidiyyah (2/333).

Taharah literally means 'cleanliness'.[153]

Islamically, is 'the removal of ritual impurity'.[154]

Islam applies much emphasis on a person being pure both inwardly (the heart) and outwardly (the body/actions). There are many references to this in the Qur'an and Sunnah, "**Indeed, Allah loves those who constantly repent** (referring to inward purification) **and loves those who purify themselves** (referring to outward purification)".[155]

Ritual purification is important not just for maintaining a pure physical state *per se* but as *fiqh* is concerned with all physical actions, it is a means for readiness to performing certain rituals including prayer (*salah*). It is necessary, therefore, to understand what physical purification involves:

- Your body is in a pure ritual state – does not need to remove the condition of major or minor ritual impurity
- The clothes you wear is free from impure things
- The area prayer is being performed on is clear from impure things
- What is considered impure
- Levels of impurity and the methods of removing

Ritual purification is two-fold. To deal with something non-physical and something physical:

(1) Non-physical - the need to purify following a certain **action** (*hadath*) which creates a **condition**

For example, passing wind (the action). This *action* changes the condition from ritual purity to ritual impurity and prevents the person from praying until they return to the condition of ritual purity. There are two types of *hadath*, minor and major, each with their method of overcoming:

- Minor: by performing *wudu* (ablution or ritual/purificatory wash)
- Major: by performing *ghusl* (ritual/purificatory bath). Also known as full ablution.

(2) Physical - the need to purify by removing a certain impure **thing** (*najas*). Physical filth.

For example, urine (the thing) on the clothes, body or area being prayed on. This *thing* prevents from performing prayer until it is removed.

How do we reach ritual purification – in both cases (minor and major)?

- Use of water
- Reverting to dry ablution (*tayammum*),[156] the use of earth-dust

Since water is the primary source for purification, it is necessary to first know:

- Types of water
- Use of water/ruling on types of water

---

[153] Lasan al-arab, al-misbah al-monir.

[154] Al-Nawawi. *al-majmou'*.

[155] Qur'an, 2:222. Tafsir al-Qurtubi. Qur'an, 6:151 and 7:33.

[156] Which serves as an alternative to water when it is not available or cannot be used. To be discussed later.

Types of water

Water that can be used comes from the following:

- Rain **water**
- Sea **water**
- River **water**
- Well **water**
- **Water** of melting snow or ice
- **Water** of hailstones
- Spring **water**

It is water that falls from the sky or comes from the ground and has remained in its original natural condition, unchanged. Such that it continues to be called just *water*.

Use of water/ruling on types of water

What if something impure has fallen into the water? Or something pure mixed with it? Or the water has already been used? There are rules relating to water usage, divided into three categories:

Natural water, inherently pure (*mutlaq*)

Description: has remained in its natural original state[157]

Ruling: It is <u>pure</u> and is <u>purifying</u>

Usage: as it is purifying, it can be used to purify from the impure **action** (*hadath*) and impure **things** (*najas*)

Changed water (*mutaghayir*)

Description: something (pure) has been added to it. For example, lemon juice, which means it is no longer in its original state and no longer called just *water*

Used water (*musta'mal*)

Description: already used to overcome ritual impurity, *wudu* (ablution) or *ghusl* (bathing) or removal of filth (*nagas*)

Ruling: both are <u>pure</u> but <u>not purifying</u>

Usage: as they are not purifying, cannot be used to purify from the impure **action** (*hadath*) or impure **things** (*najas*)

Impure water (*najis*)

Description: contaminated by something impure entering it[158] making it impurified (*mutanajis*)

Ruling: <u>impure</u> and <u>not purifying</u>

Usage: as it is not purifying, it cannot be used to purify from the impure **action** (*hadath*) or impure **things** (*najas*)

---

[157] Even in the case of salty water. If it is sea water which is naturally salty it is permissible, but where salt is added it would changed it from its original natural condition.

[158] If the water amount is less than 216 litres and has come in contact or mixed with something impure, the water is impure and cannot be used.

If the water amount is more than 216 litres and has come in contact or mixed with something impure, the water is still pure and can be used. However, it becomes impure if one or more of its descriptions (colour, smell, or taste) has changed. You determine [roughly] 216 litres by just observing visually.

What is considered impure (*najas*/physical filth)

- Pig and dog[159]
- Alcohol or any liquid intoxicant
- What comes out of the two private parts:

    Excrement/faeces or urine of a human or animal

    Wadi and *madhi*[160]

- Vomit[161]
- Any dead animal[162] except:

    - all types of seafood and locusts
    - those who do not have flowing blood such as flies
    - those slaughtered correctly for halal eating

- Flowing blood and pus[163] of a human or animal

Levels of impurity and methods of removing

The method of removing impurities depends on its level. These are:

- Heavy impurity (*mughalladhah*)

    Pig and dog and their offspring lapping into a container.

Removing this requires the container to be washed seven times one of these times using dust.

- Light impurity (*mukhafafah*)

    Urine of a baby (boy) who is only fed on milk[164] and under 2 years old.[165]

Removed by sprinkling/spraying water over the urine. Do not need to pour water.

- Moderate impurity (*mutawasitah*)

    Anything other than the above.

Removed by washing with water once. More times if needed, until the *actual* impurity is removed.[166]

---

[159] And offspring of both or one of them with another animal, even if that other animal is pure.

[160] *Wadi* is thick white fluid that emits after urinating or carrying something heavy.

Madhi (pre-seminal fluid) is thin white sticky fluid which is discharged due to sexual stimulation.

Mani (semen/sperm) is thick white fluid emitted by male or female as a result of sexual ejaculation. This is pure.

[161] Only vomit that come from the stomach, not that coming from the chest and throat.

[162] Or parts of living animals which have detached such as broken limbs.

[163] A large amount that flows beyond the surface of the wound. Small amounts are excusable.

[164] Whether breastfed or animal milk.

[165] Performing the sunnah of *tahnik* (introducing the taste of a date into the mouth of a newborn baby) and medicine are exceptions to this ruling.

[166] The aim is to remove only the *actual* physical impurity itself. You are not required to remove the effect of it. For example, vomit on clothes, you only need to remove the vomit itself. Once removed and washed there may remain a stain, this is excusable.

These are manners that should be observed when visiting the toilet, and that related:

- Do not carry into the toilet anything with the name of Allah on it
- Enter with the left foot and seek refuge from Satan[167]
- Avoid urinating and releasing faeces in public areas and where people commute
- Do not to recite any part of the Qur'an or speak or reply to anyone unless in an emergency
- Do not urinate near a hole in the ground, in a shaded place or at a growing tree or plant[168]
- Do not urinate in stagnant non-flowing water or in open windy spaces[169]

While in the toilet/release of urine and faeces

- Do not expose your body parts where other people can see
- Be seated[170] tilted to the left side, leaning on the left thigh[171]
- Wait until the last trace of urine stops coming out
- Remove faeces by wiping the anus surface with stones, tissue, or something similar that is solid and pure, at least three times[172] followed by using of water
- Leave with the right foot and thank Allah Almighty[173]

Fitra actions

The word 'fitra' can be described with many words such as purity, innocence, origin, and natural. There are certain actions which ensures a person continues to be in the physically natural state they were created in.[174] These were practiced at the time of previous prophets, hence is considered instinctive and natural human habits.[175] Habits that bring about everyday-life and religious benefits such as beatification of one's image and presentation, thorough cleanliness of the body, and harm prevention towards one's self and others (the likes of odour and bad smell). It is also a manifestation of "**And He formed you and perfected your form**"[176] meaning Allah created mankind with what preserves their perfect form and beautifies their image, so do not spoil with what uglifies your image. Maintain cleanliness, hygiene, and beauty,[177] for "**Indeed, Allah is Beautiful,**[178]**and loves beauty**".[179]

---

[167] By saying "*Bismillah Allahumma innee a'oozu bika min a khubuthi wa alkhabaa'th*". "In the name of Allah. O Allah, I seek protection/refuge in you from the male and female Satans". The toilet is a place where they gather, so this is to seek protection from any harm they may inflict.

[168] The hole: to avoid harmful insects and bugs coming out and harming you. Under the shade: as people are likely to sit there. At a growing tree/plant: these creations should be left to grow and nurture with clean water not harmful body waste.

[169] To avoid the impurity of urine splash onto one's clothes and body.

[170] This ensures all traces of urine has left, preventing the clothes and body from becoming impurified with urine and so as much faeces has left the body as possible.

[171] Being the Sunnah of the Prophet, this position eases urinating and excreting.

[172] Or by using three sides of one of these.

[173] By saying "*Ghufranak*". "*Alhamdulillah illadhi adhhaba anni al-adha wa 'aafaaneé*". "(O Allah) I seek forgiveness and pardon from You". "All Praise be to Allah, who has taken away from me discomfort and granted me relief".

[174] Al-Dimyati, I. Mawsou'at al-fiqh 'ala al-madhahib al-arba'a (1/223).

[175] Al-'Asqalani. *Fath al-Bari sharh al-Bukhari* (10/32), al-Shawkani, M. *Nayl al-awtar* (1/109).

[176] Qur'an, 40:64.

[177] *Fath al-Bari sharh al-Bukhari* (10/351).

[178] Meaning has beautiful names and attributes and beautiful actions, all in line with His All-Perfection. Ibn al-Qayyim, *al-fawa'id*, p.323.

[179] Muslim (265). See also Muslim (2346).

These are:

- Male circumcision[180]
- Removing pubic hair
- Shortening the moustache
- Cutting/shortening nails
- Removing hair under the armpits

Use of containers (*aniyah*)

It is not permitted to use gold or silver containers, dishes, platters, cups, instruments, implements, utensils, devices, and the like. That is if the gold and silver metal is solid or plated. If concealed by another substance, it is permissible.

There are many wisdoms in this ruling which includes being considerate and sensitive to the feelings of poor people. Despite their poverty, they are aware that gold and silver have high-value-worth as opposed to other metals and stones which their worth is not apparent to every person.

Ritual/purificatory bath (*ghsul*) - major ritual purification

Ghusl linguistically means 'the running of water over something fully'.[181]

Islamically is 'passing water over the entire body in a certain way and intention of performing this ritual'.[182]

Before doing the minor purification of ablution/*wudu*, one needs to be in a state of major purification which means there are things if done a person needs to take a ritual/purificatory bath.

Things that make a ritual/purificatory bath obligatory are six:

(1) Ejaculation of sexual fluid[183] - whether awake or asleep

(2) Sexual insertion[184]

(3) Death – before burial[185]

For Women:

(4) Menstruation[186]

(5) Postnatal bleeding[187]

(6) Giving birth[188]

---

[180] Obligatory as per consensus amongst scholars. There is no consensus regarding female. Al-Dimyati, I. *Mawsou'at al-fiqh 'ala al-madhahib al-arba'a* (1/226-7).

[181] Lisan al-arab.

[182] Moghni al-mihtaj (1/68), Maraqi al-falah, p.52, kashf al-qina' (1/138).

[183] I.e., both male sperm and female sexual fluid or any fluid released during orgasm. Recognised by (a) follow sexual contraction (b) come with sexual gratification (stimulation) (c) can come from non-sexual activity or stimulation (while asleep). When moist, it smells like bread dough, and when dry smells like egg-whites.

[184] Insertion of part of or the full head of the penis into the vagina (or anus, although this is not permissible and is a great sin). Full sexual intercourse does not have to happen.

[185] Obligatory for all Muslims except martyrs.

[186] Periodic discharge of blood from the vagina.

[187] Blood discharged after giving birth. It does not include bleeding prior to or during giving birth.

[188] Ritual bath becomes obligatory even in the case of dry birth or miscarriage.

Obligatory actions of ritual/purificatory bath are two:

(1) Intention[189]

(2) To ensure water reaches the entire body and hair[190]

Recommended actions of ritual/purificatory bath are five:

(1) Saying "*bismillah al-Rahman al-Raheem*" at the beginning or at least "*bismillah*"

(2) Performing *wudu* before starting to wash

(3) Rubbing the hand over the body while washing[191]

(4) Wash the limbs consecutively[192]

(5) Begin with the right side then the left

Performing a ritual/purificatory bath, step-by-step:[193]

- Begin in the name of Allah☸ [194] by saying "*bismillah al-Rahman al-Raheem*" [195] or at least "*bismillah*"

- Remove any impure thing and dirt on the body[196]

- Perform *wudu* [197]

- Pour water over the right side of the body (3 times) doing the intention when starting to pour the first time

- Pour water over the left side of the body (3 times)

- Pour water over the head and the middle of the body (3 times)

- Ensure water reaches all areas, using the hand to rub the water against the body

- Perform these actions consecutively and in this order

Anything that prevents water reaching the obligatory areas (the whole body and hair) must be removed or moved, such as nail polish, tight accessories,[198] waterproof mascara, and head caps.

---

[189] To have the intention in the heart of removing the condition of major ritual impurity. You can have one bath to remove more than one major impurity.

Note: you cannot have an intention to remove a minor impurity (as the primary) and add to it major impurities (as secondary). Major must precede the minor.

Meaning of intention: to want to do something simultaneously with the action; its place is the heart (obligatory). It is not obligatory to utter verbally but is recommended as it assists in formulating the intention in the heart. *Tohfit al-mihtag* (2/12).

[190] Water must reach all the hair to the roots (the head) and all the skin including under the nails, the outward visible part of the ear canals, the foreskin for uncircumcised men, and the private part of a non-virgin women which gets exposed when squats to relieve herself.

[191] To ensure water reaches everywhere, including between the folds of skins and into cracks and completely penetrating the hair.

[192] One after another without stopping. Do not allow a limb to dry before starting the next limb (unless extreme hot/cold/windy weather has caused it to dry quicker than normal).

[193] This is the complete and perfect way. It encompasses both the obligatory and recommended actions.

[194] Every important action you do, start with the name of Allah☸. With His name comes great blessing and reward. Tafsir Abu al-Saud, tafsir al-Baydawi (Qur'an, 1:1).

[195] "In the name of Allah the Most Compassionate, the Most Merciful".

[196] Removing the impurity so that the body is free from impure things and the dirt to remove anything that prevents water reaching the skin.

[197] The same as the ablution performed for prayer. Details to follow.

[198] For example, a ring does not have to be taken off but can be moved while water runs on the finger.

Forbidden actions if in a state of minor or major ritual impurity:

Forbidden actions - <u>major</u> impurity condition are six	Forbidden actions - <u>minor</u> impurity condition are four
(1) Prayer	(1) Prayer
(2) *Tawaf*[199]	(2) *Tawaf*
(3), (4), (5) Touch, carry or recite the Qur'an	(3), (4) Touch or carry the Qur'an
(6) Sit in the Mosque	
Forbidden actions for a woman in a state of menstruation are ten:	
(1) Prayer	
(2) *Tawaf*	
(3), (4), (5) Touch, carry or recite the Qur'an	
(6) Sit in the Mosque	
(7) Fasting[200]	
(8) Divorce	
(9) Passing through the mosque for a woman who believes her blood may soil the Mosque	
(10) To take sexual pleasure in the area [specifically] between the navel and knees	

Occasions where a ritual/purificatory bath is recommended:

For Friday prayer[201]	Upon entering Islam	After recovering from loss of mind-soundness (insanity)
On the 2 *Eid* days[202]	For Solar Eclipse prayer	Entering the state of *Ihram* (pilgrim sanctity)
For Drought prayer	For Lunar Eclipse prayer	After washing a deceased person
For staying in *Muzdalifah*[203]	For performing *tawaf*	For standing on *Arafah*[204]
For throwing the pebbles (*jamarat*)[205]	For entering Makkah and Madinah[206]	For performing *Sa'i*[207]

---

[199] Circumambulating (the act of moving round) the *ka'ba* in Makkah.

[200] Whether obligatory (during the month of *Ramadan*) or any other recommended or voluntary fasting.

[201] Starts from the time of *fagr*.

[202] Starts from the time of *fagr* and is recommended for the day itself (not for attending the prayer). Therefore, the recommendation is also for those not visiting the mosque for the prayer and women in their state of menstruation, postnatal bleeding or irregular blood.

[203] Hajj (pilgrimage) related.

[204] Hajj (pilgrimage) related.

[205] Hajj (pilgrimage) related.

[206] The city of the Prophet ﷺ.

[207] Walking seven times back and forth between the hills of Safa and Marwah (in the *Ka'ba* area in Makkah).

Wudu linguistically means 'cleanliness'.[208]

Islamically is 'to wash certain parts of the body with water and an intention of worship'.[209]

Obligatory actions of ablution are six:

(1) Intention[210]

(2) Wash the entire face[211] (once). At the start of washing the face, the intension is to be done[212]

(3) Wash both hands and arms completely, from the fingertips up to and including the elbows joints[213] (once)

(4) Wipe [any] part of the head[214] (once)

(5) Wash the feet up to and including the ankles joint[215] (once)

(6) Perform these actions in this sequence[216]

Recommended actions of ablution are seven:

(1) Wash the limbs consecutively

(2) Wash/wipe the limbs and head a second and third time

(3) Begin with the right limbs then the left[217]

(4) To not be excessive/wasteful with water[218]

(5) Avoid 'slapping' the face when washing it[219]

(6) Not to ask another person to pour water for you[220]

(7) To not dry the limbs[221]

<u>Note</u>:

Wiping is to have water touch the limb and washing is to have water running along the limb.[222]

If one is unsure whether a particular limb or head has been washed/wiped or not, it must be done, then to continue in the normal sequence from that point onwards.

---

[208] Al-qamous al-muhit, lisan al-arab, al-mu'jam al-wasit.

[209] Moghni al-Mihtaj (1/74), al-Iqna' (1/39).

[210] An intention in the heart that you are performing this action to removing the *hadath* (minor ritual impurity) or to perform *wudu* to pray.

[211] The entire face, from the top of the forehead where the hairline usually begins down to the chin in length, and from ear to ear in width. It is obligatory to wash all facial hair from the inside and outside whether thick (moustache, eyebrows) or thin (small beard). As for thick beards, there is an exception to just wash the outside.

[212] Because the face is the first obligatory action.

[213] It is advisable to go slightly beyond the elbow (and beyond the end of any limb) to ensure it is fully covered.

[214] The minimum is to wipe one single hair, on the head (root of the hair) not hang down below the hairline.

[215] Water must also run between the toes for all areas of the feet to be covered.

[216] To observe the sequence is to ensure no limb precedes the one before.

[217] Except those limbs that would be done together simultaneously or using both hands together (e.g., washing the face, ears).

[218] As an indication, the Prophet used to perform *wudu* with the amount of a double-handful (using both hands) of water (*mudd*) which is approximately 0.51 litres and bath with the amount of 4 double-handfuls (*Sa*), approximately 2.03 litres.

[219] A person's face is honourable as the person himself is and should be respected. Qur'an, 17:70.

[220] Unless needs help and support.

[221] Unless there is an excuse such as illness or cold weather.

[222] Wet hands, a wet cloth would suffice. It is not necessary the tap runs over it or pouring a large amount of water on it.

Performing ablution, step-by-step (encompassing both obligatory/*fard* and recommended/*sunnah* actions):

- Begin by saying "*audhu billahi min al-shaytan al-rajim*"[223] then "*bismillah al-Rahman al-Raheem*"
- Wash both hands from the fingertips up to and including the wrists joint (3 times)[224]
- Rinse the mouth (3 times)[225]
- Wash the nose by throwing water into the nostrils using the right hand, blowing it out using the left (3 times)[226]
- Wash the entire face (3 times)[227]
- Wash both hands and arms completely, from the fingertips[228] up to and including the elbows joint (3 times)[229]
- Moisten both hands and pass along the front of the head, sliding the paired hands to the back (up to the neck nape) and return them to the point of start (3 times)[230]
- Wipe the ear, both together with the forefingers cleaning the inside and the thumbs the outside (3 times)[231]
- Wash the feet up to and including the ankle joint (3 times)[232]

Things that invalidate (nullifies/cancels) the state of ablution/minor ritual purification are six:

(1) Anything that exits from the front and back private parts[233]

(2) Anything impure leaving the body elsewhere[234]

(3) Loss of mind-soundness through sleep[235] or other causes[236]

(4) Skin-to-skin contact between adult[237] male and female[238] without a barrier[239]

(5) Touching the front and back private parts[240] with the palm or inner surface of the fingers

(6) Anything that invalidates the state of major impurity requiring a ritual/purificatory bath (*ghusl*)

---

[223] "I seek Allah's protection (refuge) from Satan, the accursed".

[224] Here all 3 times are recommended (*sunnah*), as this itself is *sunnah*.

[225] All 3 times are recommended (*sunnah*), as this itself is *sunnah*.

[226] All 3 times are recommended (*sunnah*), as this itself is *sunnah*.

[227] As this is obligatory (*fard*), only the first time is obligatory, the second and third are *sunnah*.

[228] Passing the fingers through each other (*takhlil*).

[229] As this is obligatory (*fard*), only the first time is obligatory, the second and third are *sunnah*.

[230] As this is obligatory (*fard*), only the first time is obligatory, the second and third are *sunnah*.

[231] All 3 times are recommended (*sunnah*), as this itself is *sunnah*.

[232] As this is obligatory (*fard*), only the first time is obligatory, the second and third are *sunnah*.

[233] The urethra (via the penis), vagina and anus. Whether it is solid (like faeces), liquid (like urine), or gaseous (like passing wind). Includes what typically exit from the private parts or that are uncommon such as worms and kidney stones. Includes what is ritually impure (like blood) as well as things that are pure (like babies, sperm).

[234] Such as blood and pus. A small amount is excusable, which oozes to the surface of a wound without flowing over the surface. Vomiting is excusable if it is less than a mouth full.

[235] Except sleeping while the buttocks are firmly seated on the ground/chair with no gap.

[236] Insanity and drunkenness. Excludes daydreaming and drowsiness (the inability to hear the words of those present, even if one cannot understand what is being said). The *wudu* becomes invalid as you are unaware of your state of ritual purification if/when it had been invalidated.

[237] Adults meaning the age that normally stirs up sexual desire in a person. *Wudu* is still valid if this is the case in only one of the two persons. For example, a mid-thirty year old male having skin-to-skin contact with a young 6 year old or an 80 year old whom both have no sextual desire.

[238] This ruling does not apply to two people of the same gender.

[239] Anything covering the skin (clothes etc). If there is no barrier and the skin-to-skin contacts takes place, the state of *wudu* becomes invalid whether that contact was with or without sexual desire and whether the contact was intentional or unintentional. If you have been touched by the other person the *wudu* is still valid, but not the case if you were the one who accidently or intentionally touched the other person.

It includes touching with the tongue or a malfunctional surplus limb **but does not include** contact with teeth, nails, or severed limbs (i.e., limbs that are separated, cut off or broken apart) or touching the hair of the other person.

[240] Of you or another person.

Why is it important to know the obligatory and recommended (*fard* and *sunnah*) actions?

Say for example you have little amount of water to perform *wudu*. By knowing what is obligatory you can do the minimum that is accepted using the limited amount of water available. You are aware you cannot revert to any alternative (dry ablution/*tayammum*) as the water amount is sufficient for fulfilling the obligatory actions.

Or say you need to pray *zuhr* and there is only a few minutes left for *asr*. By knowing and limiting to the obligatory *wudu* actions you save much needed time and pray before the new prayer time comes in. In summary, by knowing, you are better able to manage situations and ensure fulfilling your rituals correctly.

An example of a mistake some people do is reverting to *tayammum* because they do not have enough water to do the full *wudu* (including the *sunnah* actions). Their *tayammum* is invalid if they have enough water to do the obligatory actions and their prayer by default becomes invalid and unaccepted. Do we now see the importance of what was mentioned in the earlier pages of this book: *you cannot fulfil or progress in something you do not know about*, hence "**Seeking knowledge is an obligation upon every Muslim**".[241]

The use of toothstick (*miswak*)

The toothstick or *miswak* is a twig (like a toothbrush) used for oral hygiene from the time of the Prophetﷺ till today.[242] The best toothsticks come from the *Salvadora persica* tree.[243] Its use is recommended at all times - to maintain consistent hygiene and cleanliness of the mouth [244] - and strongly recommended during these four times:

(1) Upon waking up from sleep

(2) Before performing *wudu* and before performing prayer

(3) When the state of the mouth is changed (becomes stale) due to not eating or talking for a long period of time

(4) Before reading Qur'an and doing *dhikr* (Remembrance)

Wiping over the footgear (*khuff*)

Islam offers many opportunities to bring about ease, just as it advises Muslims to approach the religion with ease.[245] This includes wiping over a type of footgear called *khuff* instead of having to remove shoes and socks to wash the feet for *wudu*. A *khuff* is a thick leather sock or footwear made from material that is pure (e.g., boots).

Wiping, linguistically, is 'to pass the hand over something'.[246]

Islamically is 'to wet a certain type of *khuff* in a certain place for a certain period'.[247]

---

[241] Ibn Majah (224).

[242] Lisan al-arab, al-mu'jam al-wasit.

[243] Also known as toothbrush tree.

[244] Al-majmou' (1/272), hashiyat al-Jamal (1/119, 221), nayl al-awtar (1/126), al-moghni (1/95).

[245] Al-Bukhari (39).

[246] Al-Jurjani, Al-ta'rifat, Al-qamous al-muhit.

[247] Tafsir Al-dur al-manthur (1/174).

Conditions to wiping on the footgear are four:

(1) Made so it is possible to walk in[248] for a long period/distance without being torn[249] and is water repellent[250]

(2) Worn on both feet, the *khuff* covers the area that is obligatory to wash in *wudu*[251]

(3) Is worn when in a state of complete ritual purification[252]

(4) It is free from anything that is impure

Duration of wiping:

If travelling, a person can wipe on them for up to 3 days and nights (24 hours x three, so 72 hours).

If resident, can wipe on them for up to one day and night (24 hours).

The duration begins the moment a person loses their minor purification state after wearing the *khuff*.[253]

When *wudu* is required the normal actions are performed and when it comes to the feet, the *khuff* remains on and to just wipe once over the top of each one with wet hands. This way the *wudu* is considered complete.

Things that cancel/end the permissibility of wiping over the footgear are three:

(1) Taking one or both off, intentionally or unintentionally[254]

(2) The duration has ended

(3) Anything that invalidates the major purification state[255]

Dry ablution (*tayammum*)

Linguistically, *tayammum* means 'to revert to something'.[256]

Islamically is 'reverting to what is pure to remove an impure ritual state'.[257]

This is the use of pure dust (with debris) for just the face and hands, with certain conditions.

The reasons allowing *tayammum* are two:

(1) water is available but cannot be used

(2) no water available.

---

[248] Including outdoors.

[249] So it is not easily ripped or torn, exposing the feet that is supposed to be covered.

[250] Which prevents water entering or the foot feeling dampness. It does not have to be completely waterproof.

[251] The entire foot, up to and including the ankle bone. With movement, stretching, running etc, that area must remain fully covered.

[252] Before wearing, the person needs to be in a state of minor and major ritual purity, hence complete purification.

[253] I.e., having done something that requires *wudu*.

[254] You cannot re-wear them and continue the duration if you invalidate the minor or major ritual purity state. You must start again by wearing while in a state of complete purification and adhere to the conditions. The duration in such case starts from the beginning. If still in a state of *wudu* and have taken one or both off, you need to only wash the feet and re-wear them continuing with the same duration.

[255] Requiring *ghusl* or revert to *tayammum*.

[256] Al-Jurjani. *Al-ta'rifat*.

[257] Ibid.

		Comments/considerations
Water is available but cannot be used	Not enough water for a ritual bath (*ghusl*) or ablution (*wudu*)	Provided there is not enough water to even do the obligatory (*fard*) actions, you can revert to *tayammum*.
	Danger and health risk	If trying to get water poses a danger or risks loss of life. Or in the case of an injury whereby placing water on that limb could harm or need to place a plaster, bandage, plaster cast over its, you can revert to *tayammum* partially[258] or there is severe cold weather, you can revert to *tayammum* fully.
	Shortage	Water is available but is needed for drinking and if used could lead to severe thirst, illness, or death, you can revert to *tayammum*.
	Property	If water is available but does not belong to you and do not have permission to use, you can revert to *tayammum*.
No water available	Not visible	Cannot see any water in your surrounding and after asking people in the area, you can revert to *tayammum*.

General rules of *tayammum*:

- You cannot revert to *tayammum* until the time of the prayer has entered
- Each *tayammum* is valid only for one obligatory/*fard* prayer but unlimited *Sunnah* prayers
- *Tayammum* replaces both *ghusl* and *wudu* so serves as minor and major ritual purification combined
- If after doing *tayammum* water is found and have not prayed yet, water must be used for *wudu* otherwise the prayer becomes invalid. If water is seen after the prayer is completed and you are a traveller, the prayer is accepted. If you are resident and not on travel, the prayer should be repeated using water for *wudu*
- You cannot revert to *tayammum* if there is the presumption you can obtain water
- If any of the above reasons that allow reverting to *tayammum* is no longer the case, you cannot proceed[259]
- The reasons that invalidate the state of minor and major purification invalidate the state of *tayammum*

---

[258] The conditions to these:

- there is harm if removed

- to limit to the area needing to be covered or beyond only if necessary

- placed on the limb while in a state of ritual purification (if not, the prayers would need to be repeated as the purification element is absent)

- the remaining/uncovered parts of the limb is to be washed/wiped as normal

- can continue to wipe on it for as long as is necessary

Here you would do *wudu* as normal and when reaching that covered part of the limb do *tayammum* by running the hand on it with dust.

[259] As it is intended to replace water only in its absence or inability to use.

Conditions of *tayammum* are five:

(1) The use of earth dust[260]

(2) Dust must be free from any impurities

(3) Dust that is unused[261]

(4) The dust cannot be mixed with say flour or anything similar[262]

(5) Must first remove any impurities and dirt on the limbs

Obligatory actions of *tayammum* are five:

(1) Intention[263]

(2) Transfer of the earth dust onto the body[264]

(3) Wiping the face[265]

(4) Wiping the two hands, fingertips to and including elbows joints

(5) Follow this sequence

Recommended actions of *tayammum* are three:

(1) To begin in the name of Allah⸽ by saying "*bismillah al-Rahman al-Raheem*" or at least "*bismillah*"

(2) Wiping the right [limbs] before the left

(3) Performing consecutively

Performing *tayammum, step-by-step*[266]

- Begin in the name of Allah⸽ by saying "*bismillah al-Rahman al-Raheem*" or at least "*bismillah*"
- Tap the palm of both hands - with fingers wide apart - simultaneously on a surface that has pure dust and debris.[267] Then shake the hands to remove the debris
- Wipe the whole face once, starting from the top to the bottom
- While starting to wipe the face, do the intention of performing *tayammum* to enable you to pray
- Again, tap the palm of both hands in the same way
- Wipe the right arm, starting at the fingertips to and including the elbow joint and return back up to the fingertips covering any part not wiped
- Wipe the left arm in the same way

---

[260] It does not matter if the earth is red, black, yellow, or salty in which nothing grows but cannot be earth turned into ashes or clay that has been pounded and softened.

[261] Which has already been used on a limb or has been dusted off a limb.

[262] Such as saffron.

[263] To have the intention in the heart that you are performing *tayammum* to enable you to perform prayer i.e., making the prayer permissible – it will not suffice to make any other intention such as performing *wudu* because *tayammum* /dry ablution is not normal ablution but acts as a [substitute] means for the prayer to be accepted.

[264] It will not suffice to pass dust over the face and arms with dust already on them. The process must start by placing the hands on earth dust then placing onto the limbs.

[265] Covering all the face, as set out in performing *wudu*.

[266] The complete way, encompassing both the *fard* and *sunnah* actions.

[267] This can be a carpet, wall, or concrete which is dry and free from impurities.

There are three types of bleeding exiting from the vagina:

Menstrual blood[268] (*haid*)

Dark coloured and pungent[269] lasting a minimum duration of 24 hours and a maximum of 15 days (normally 6 or 7 days). The minimum duration of purity between each menstrual cycle is 15 days with no maximum limit (normally 23 or 24 days). The minimum age a women can start to menstruate is 9.

There are 8 things that are not permissible to do when going through menstruation.

(1) Prayer

(2) Fasting

(3) Performing *tawaf*

(4) Reciting the Qur'an

(5) Touching or carrying the Qur'an

(6) Entering the Mosque

(7) Sextual intercourse

(8) Sexual enjoyment in the area between the women's navel and knees

Postnatal bleeding (*nifas*)

Blood that exits after giving birth, lasting a minimum period of an instant and a maximum of 60 days (with an average of 40 days). It is not permitted to do the same eight things as in the case of menstrual bleeding.

Irregular blood (*istihada*)

Blood that exits outside the days of menstrual and postnatal bleeding and does not relate to them. It is light red coloured.[270] A women may still perform prayer and fasting and have intercourse although it does invalidate the state of minor purification requiring *wudu* and the area must be cleaned.

---

[268] Monthly period.

[269] A sharp smell.

[270] Its colour could vary from being in one country to another and due to the person's condition or any illness at the time.

Introduction

Prayer is the second pillar of Islam which literally means 'supplication'.[271]

Islamically, it is 'a set of actions and words that begin with saying "*Allahu akbar*" (*takbir*), ending with saying "*al-salamu alaykum*" (*tasleem*), and with certain conditions'.[272]

Islam is based on the belief that individuals have a direct relationship with Allah. Prayer is a vital means for remembering Him, expressing love, respect, glorification, and gratitude, and contributes to purification. A Muslim can get closer to their Lord and strengthen their connection through prayer. Performing them on time is one of the greatest deeds.[273] It also helps measure your level of obedience and good character. Allah says, "**Verily, prayer deters from immorality and wrongdoing**".[274] It can be concluded that if a person is uprightly obedient (Islamic teachings), it is likely their prayers are performed with a degree of perfection. If not, this is a warning to focus on perfecting them.

Prayer involves certain physical movements and postures, reciting Qur'an, and supplications. All done while facing the Sacred House of Allah, the *Ka'ba* in *Makkah*, referred to as 'facing the *qibla*'. As part of a deep connection between the slave and their Lord, everything in a person, physically, spiritually, intellectually, should be harmoniously involved in the prayer, with utmost submission and humility. This is why there are movements (physical), reading verses and passages while pondering (mental) remembrance/*dhikr* along with feelings and emotions (spiritual).

Prayer can be done anywhere. In the mosque, home, work, indoors, outdoors, and even aboard a vessel in the sea or a plane in the air, providing the conditions are being met. Just as a person can pray alone and in congregation. There are five obligatory prayers in every 24 hours. Each with a period to be completed within. It is highly recommended to pray immediately when the time of each one enters. You should aim to never delay a prayer, especially out of laziness or prioritising less important things. What on earth can be more important than prayer when the Prophet tells us in several *hadiths* the dearest deed to Allah is to perform your prayer on time.[275] The valid excuses for delaying obligatory prayers are: (a) oversleeping[276] (b) forgetfulness[277] (c) illness (d) when travelling (with pre-conditions); where it is permissible to combine some prayers by praying one at the time of the latter one.

---

[271] Qur'an, 9:103. Muslim (3520).

[272] Moghni al-mihtaj (1/120), kashf al-qina' (1/221).

[273] Al-Bukhari (7534), Muslim (252).

[274] Qur'an, 29:45.

[275] Al-Bukhari (527) and Muslim (254).

[276] When there is excessive tiredness it is recommended to rest to be able to concentrate when performing, but one must ensure every prayer is performed before the next one.

[277] Where a person forgets to perform a prayer and remembers when the time of the next one has entered. This should not be due to negligence.

A *rak'ah*[278] is a unit of the prayer. Each prayer consists of one or more units which is a combination of the specific movements (repetitive cycles of bows and prostrations) in addition to the recitations and supplications. So, for a prayer of 4 units/*rak'at*, the collection of movements and recitations would be repeated four times.

The obligatory/*fard* prayers are:

(1) Fajr - dawn prayer

(2) Zuhr - noon prayer

(3) *Asr* - mid-afternoon prayer

(4) *Maghrib* - sunset prayer

(5) *Isha* - night prayer

The number of units for each prayer:

Prayer	Fagr Dawn	Zuhr Noon	Asr Mid-afternoon	Maghrib Sunset	Isha Night
Units (*rak'at*)	2	4	4	3	4

There is an additional obligatory prayer for men:

Prayer	Friday prayer *Jumuah* prayer (prayed in a mosque or anywhere in congregation)
Units (*rak'at*)	2
Jummah replaces *zuhr* prayer. If a person is unable to attend due to illness etc, *zuhr* is prayed as normal. The *sunnah* prayers for *zuhr* are done for the *jummah* prayer i.e., 2 or 4 before and 2 or 4 after.	

There are other *sunnah* prayers. Some are associated with the *fard* prayers, performed before[279] or after, and others that are separate and standalone. The virtues of all these are broad and reward is immense.

The ones associated with the *fard* prayers are called *rawatib*. When performed before is called *qabliyyah* and when performed after is called *ba'diyah*. These are:

Prayer	Fagr Dawn prayer	Zuhr Noon prayer	Asr Mid-afternoon	Maghrib Sunset prayer	Isha Night prayer
Sunnah (before)	2	2+(2)	(4)	-	-
Sunnah (after)	-	2+(2)	-	2	2

---

[278] Plural = *rak'at*

[279] Before praying that obligatory prayer but after the time for that prayer has entered.

From these *sunnah* prayers, 12 are confirmed (outside the brackets) and 8 unconfirmed (in brackets). Out of transparency and clarity, scholars have split them into these categories.

Confirmed = the Prophetﷺ always used to perform, consistently.

Unconfirmed = the Prophetﷺ used to perform occasionally or inconsistently

The Prophetﷺ said: "***Whoever persists in performing twelve Rak'at from the Sunnah, a house will be built for him in Paradise: four before the Zuhr, two Rak'ah after Zuhr, two Rak'ah after Maghrib, two Rak'ah after the Isha and two Rak'ah before Fajr***".[280]

The *rawatib* not related to *fard* prayers:

Al-witr	Performed at night after *Isha*, ending all prayers and the day with.
(The odd number prayer)	Number of *rak'at* = minimum 1 and can be 3, 5, 7, 9, and 11.
Al-duha	Prayed after sunrise and before it has reached its zenith (i.e., 15 minutes before *zuhr*).
(Mid-morning prayer)	Number of *rak'at* = minimum 2, up to 12. In sets of 2.
Tahiyut al-masjid	Performed when entering a mosque.[281] The idea is to engage immediately with prayer.
(Greeting the mosque)	If when entering you pray any other prayer, that will suffice as the objective is fulfilled.
	Number of *rak'at* = 2 unless praying another prayer where it would vary.
Al-istikhara	To seek guidance and direction on a matter. Asking Allahﷻ to help make a right choice.[282]
(Seeking guidance)	Number of *rak'at* = 2. Followed by a specific supplication after completing the prayer.[283]

Separate/standalone *sunnah* prayers, the *nawafil* (supererogatory)[284] are:

Qiyam al-leil	The act of praying during the night. Starts after *Isha* and ends at *fagr* time.
(Night vigil prayer)	Number of *rak'at* = unlimited, in sets of 2.
Al-tarawih	Prayed each night during the fasting month of *Ramadan*, after *Isha* in congregation.
	Number of *rak'at* = minimum 2. To have completed is to pray its 20. In sets of 2.

---

[280] Al-Tirmidhi (416), al-Nisa'i (1796), Ibn Majah (1140).

[281] The only exception is the mosque of *ka'ba* in Makkah. The respect/greeting action of this mosque is to perform *tawaf*.

[282] For example, asking if one should choose a certain job, marry a certain person, undertake a certain action or venture. It is about [practically] affirming Allahﷻ knows what you do not and entrusting His perfect choice.

[283] **Transliteration**: "Allaahumma innee astakheruka bi'ilmika, wa'astaqdiruka biqudratika wa'as'aluka min fadhtik al-adheem, fa 'innaka taqdiru walaa 'aqdiru, wa ta'lamu, wala a'lamu, wa'Anta Allamul-Ghuyob, Allahumma in kunta ta'lamu 'anna haatha al-'amra [then mention the thing to be decided] khayrun lee fee dene wa ma'aashee wa'aqibati 'amre - or say, Aajilihi wa'aajilihi - faqdurhu lee wa yassirhu le thumma barik lee feh, wa in kunta ta'lamu anna haatha al-'amra sharrun lee fee deenee wa ma'aashee wa 'aaqibati 'amre – or say, Aajilihi waajilihi - Fasrifhu 'anne wasrifne anhu waqdur liy al-khayra haythu kana thumma ardhine bih".

Translation: "O Allah, I seek your counsel through your knowledge, and I seek your assistance through your might and I ask you from your immense favor, for verily you alone have power while I do not, and you know while I do not, and you alone possess all knowledge of the unseen. O Allah, if You know this matter (mention matter here) to be good for me in relation to my religion, my life and livelihood and the end of my affairs – or say, my present and future - then decree it for me and facilitate it for me, and then place blessing for me in it, and if You know this affair to be harmful for me concerning my religion, my life and livelihood and the end of my affairs, then move it away from me and move me away from it, and decree for me what is good, wherever it may be, and make me content with it". Al-Bukhari (7390).

[284] Its great merits include: gaining the love of Allahﷻ. Al-Bukhari (6502), makes up for any deficiencies in the obligatory prayers. Abi Dawud (864), al-Tirmidhi (413), al-Nisa'i (465).

Eid prayers (Al-fitr & al-adha)	This prayer is slightly different. In the in the first *rak'ah* the Imam/leader says *"Allahu akbar"* seven times and in the second *rak'ah* five times before starting to recite *al-Fatiha*. Those praying behind should follow. These exclude the *"Allahu akbar"* said to enter/start a prayer. The rest of the prayer is performed as normal with the sermon/*khutba* delivered after, unlike the *jummah* prayer, done before. Number of *rak'at* = 2.
Al-istisqa prayer (Drought prayer)	A community-wide prayer done in congregation for seeking water (rain) from Allah҈ during times of drought and low rainfall. The sermon/*khutba* is delivered after the prayer. Number of *rak'at* = 2.
Al-kusuf prayer (Solar eclipse prayer)	A community-wide prayer done in congregation during a solar eclipse. Number of *rak'at* = 2.
Al-khusuf prayer (Lunar eclipse prayer)	A community-wide prayer done in congregation during a lunar eclipse. Number of *rak'at* = 2.

While all prayers are important, there are those highlighted for certain reasons. Here are two examples:

Fard prayers: "**Maintain with care the [five obligatory] prayers and the middle prayer and stand for [the sake of] God, devoutly obedient**".[285] The middle prayer is *asr*.[286] It does not mean the others are less important. Look at the verse again, it says the prayers (the obligatory, all five) then states [in particular] the middle prayer. Therefore, all are important but the middle one has been highlighted twice for a reason: once mentioned with the five prayers and again separately. If a person is conscious and devoted to performing this on time and with perfection in the middle of a busy day when people are indulged in different activities and livelihood, they are likely to be conscious of and pray the remaining four prayers likewise.[287]

Sunnah prayers: "**The Prophet was never more regular and particular in offering a Nawafil [prayer] than the two rak'at (Sunnah) of the Fajr prayer**".[288] "**The two rak'at at dawn are better than this world and what it contains**".[289]

Through these *sunnah* prayers and along with the hundreds of other voluntary actions in Islam there is scope for countless reward and blessing. A great mercy from Allah҈ in offering all this to us. The oceans of love and opportunity He offers is beyond every worldly pleasure and above the worlds altogether, indeed, "**If you count the bounties of Allah, you will not be able to number them**".[290] This broad variety gives you choice. There may be times you may be full of energy and want to do more. Treat these as a great asset, but primary focus must be on performing on time the obligatory ones and perfecting

---

[285] Qur'an, 2:238.

[286] Tafsir al-Tabari. With other opinions stating it is other prayers, not Asr. Tafsir al-Qurtubi.

[287] Tafsir Abu al-Saud, al-tafsir al-wadih (Hijazi, M).

[288] Al-Bukhari (1170, 1687,1690).

[289] Muslim (1688).

[290] Qur'an, 14:34.

them. The wide variety of voluntary actions also creates humility and humbleness in a person. If you have done one or some of these, do not forget there are many more you have not done so be grateful and be with Allah﷾ a nobody.

Prayer is a magnificent grace. In a *hadith*, we see a remarkable portray of its virtue, "**Consider if one of you had a river by his door in which he bathed five times a day. Would any filth remain on him?**" They [the Companions] said, "No." Then the Prophet replied: "**Likewise, Allah wipes away sins with the five daily prayers**".[291] And in another, "**The parable of the five prayers is that of a river running at your doorstep in which one cleanses himself five times a day**".[292]

Think for a moment how Allah﷾ is imposing upon you a ritual five times a day so you can wipe your sins! Nothing surprising, for He is the Loving-kind (*Al-Wadud*), the all-Generous (*Al-Kareem*). And now this great *hadith* on how important *Sunnah* prayers can be when added to the obligatory ones: "**Indeed, the first deed by which a servant will be called to account on the Day of Judgement is his Salat. If it is complete, he is successful and saved, but if it is defective, he has failed and lost. So if something is deficient in his obligatory (prayers) then the Lord, Mighty and Sublime says: 'Look! Are there any voluntary (prayers) for my worshipper?' So with them, what was deficient in his obligatory (prayers) will be completed. Then the rest of his deeds will be treated like that**".[293]

Conditions for a Muslim to pray are two:

(1) Maturity[294]

(2) Mind-soundness

Conditions prior to performing prayer (prerequisites) are five:

(1) Absence of a ritual impure state (minor and major) and no inexcusable impurity on the body or clothes

(2) Covering the body's intimate parts (*awrah*)[295]

(3) Praying on something (or spot) that is free from impurities[296]

(4) Knowing the prayer time has entered[297]

(5) Facing the *qibla*[298]

---

[291] Al-Bukhari (528), Muslim (1522).

[292] Muslim (1523).

[293] Al-Tirmidhi (415), al-Nisa'i (466), Ibn Majah (1425).

[294] Once reached puberty, prayer becomes obligatory upon the Muslim. The same with fasting and all obligatory rituals and commands.

[295] It is parts of the human body which is customarily kept covered by clothing in public areas and in front of people. In prayer, the obligatory parts to be covered are:

For men: between the navel and knees

For women: the entire body excluding the face (the underside of her jaw and area behind the chin should be covered) and hands up to the wrist. The clothing worn must be:

      Thick enough to not expose the skin and hair

      Wide enough (baggy) to not reveal the shape of the body

      Free from openings, rips, and holes that reveals a part of the body

[296] This is the area where the forehead, hands, and knees come in to contact with the ground.

[297] Knowing the prayer times from:

- A printed/online timetable (from a local mosque etc) that is accurate. Be careful: times could differ from one place to another in the same city, especially large cities.

- Hearing the call for prayer (*adhan*)

- Knowing from someone you trust

[298] That is the direction of the *ka'ba* in Makkah. There are two situations where facing the *qibla* is not obligatory:

(a) If there is intense fear – such as in the middle of a battle, flood or around a tyrant

(b) Performing *sunnah* prayers while on travel (conditions of travel to follow) and riding a form of transportation: an animal (horse, camel etc) or vehicle (ship, train, airplane, car etc)

Prayer fundamentals *(arkan)* are eighteen:

In order of occurrence, there are 18 prayer fundamentals. Not doing without a valid reason can invalidate the prayer unless these are made up before ending the prayer. Each of them is obligatory whether praying behind an Imam, as an Imam, or alone. If the prayer ends without making up for them, the whole prayer must be redone.

(1) Intention[299]

(2) Standing while praying, if physically able to

(3) Saying the opening "*Allahu akbar*"[300]

(4) Reciting *al-Fatiha*[301]

(5) Bowing[302]

(6) Reposing therein[303]

(7) Rising and standing straight

(8) Reposing therein

(9) Prostrating

(10) Reposing therein

(11) Sitting between the two prostrations

(12) Reposing therein

(13) The final sitting (for *tashahhud*)

(14) Saying the *tashahhud*

(15) Saying the prayers upon the Prophet[304]

(16) Intention to end the prayer

(17) The first taslim, saying "al-salamu alaykum wa Rahmatullah" [305]

(18) Performing the above in this order

Greater recommended actions are four:

Prior to starting prayer: (1) the call to prayer *(adhan)* (2) the call for commencement of prayer *(iqamah)*

During prayer: (3) the first *tashahhud* [306] (4) the *qunnut* supplication[307]

---

[299] The place for the intention is the heart. It is not enough to just verbally utter, although it is recommended. *Tohfit al-mihtag* (2/12). All prayers must be named in the intention.

[300] Known as takbirat al-ihram.

[301] Chapter one of the Qur'an – the Opener. All seven verses, including "*bismillah al-Rahman al-Raheem*".

[302] Back to be straight and legs. As you descend, place the two hand palms on the knees. This position is called *ruku'*.

[303] To remain in this posture until calmness and stillness is attained, only a few seconds.

[304] What is referred to as the second/last part of the *tashahhud*.

[305] "Peace be upon you", when ending the prayer, turning to the right.

[306] Done after completing two *rak'at* of all prayers that have more than two *rak'at*. Any prayer with less has only the one *tashahhud* which is the final one.

[307] After standing from the final *rak'ah's* bow in every *witr* and *fagr* prayer only during the second half of the month of Ramadan.

Transliteration: Allahumma ihdini feeman hadayt, wa a'fini fiman afait, wa tawallani fiman tawallait, wa barik Li fima atait, wa qini sharra ma qadait, fa Innaka taqdi wa la yuqda Alaik, wa innahu la yadhillu man walait, tabarakta Rabbana wa ta'alait.

Translation: "O Allah guide me among those You have guided, pardon me among those You have pardoned, befriend me among those You have befriended, bless me in what You have granted, and save me from the evil that You decreed. Indeed, You decree, and none can pass decree, and none can pass decree upon You, indeed he is not humiliated whom You have befriended, blessed are You our Lord and Exalted".

Lesser recommended actions (*hay'at*) are fifteen:

(1) Raising hands simultaneously with saying the opening "*Allahu akbar*", before and when raising from bowing

(2) Placing the right hand over the left when standing

(3) Saying the opening supplication[308]

(4) Seeking refuge from Satan[309] by saying "*A'oothu billaahi min al-shaytan al-rajeem*"[310] before reciting *al-Fatiha*

(5) Reciting loudly *al-Fatiha* and Quranic verses in relevant prayers[311]

(6) Quiet recitation in relevant prayers[312]

(7) Saying "*ameen*" after completing *al-Fatiha*

(8) Reciting Qur'anic verses[313] after *al-Fatiha*

(9) Saying "*Allahu akbar*" when moving from position to another (except when raising from bowing)

(10) Saying "*sami'a Allahu liman hamidah*"[314] and "*Rabbana walak alhamd*"[315] when raising from bowing

(11) Saying "*subhana Rabbi al-'azim*" in the bowing position and "*subhana Rabbi al-'ala*" in prostration

(12) Placing both hands on thighs while sitting for *tashahhud*[316]

(13) The position of *iftirash*[317] in the first sitting for *tashahhud*

(14) The position of *tawarruk*[318] in the final sitting for *tashahhud*

(15) The second *taslim*, saying "*al-salamu alaykum wa Rahmatullah*"[319]

Each of the three categories of actions in the prayer have their own rule if missed:

Obligatory actions, the integrals	Greater recommended actions	Lesser recommended actions
Perform the missed action and continue from that point. Do two prostrations for forgetfulness.	Do not return to the missed action. Do two prostrations for forgetfulness.	Do not return to the missed lesser recommended action. Do not prostrate for forgetfulness.
If one loses count of how many *rak'at* they reached, they should rely on the lesser amount and do two prostrations. The prostrations are done at the end of the prayer. After the last *tashahhud* and the prayers upon the Prophet☉ prostrate twice then do the *taslim*: turning to the right and left saying "*al-salamu alaykum wa Rahmatullah*".		

---

[308] There are different formulars of supplication. Refer to books of *fiqh* or the Book *'Remembrance'* (*al-adhkar*) by imam al-Nawawi.

[309] Prior to reading Qur'an (chapter one, the Opener - *al-Fatiha*).

[310] "I seek refuge with Allah from the accursed Satan".

[311] The obligatory prayers being *fagr, maghreb, isha* and the recommended prayers being *qiyam al-leil, witr* prayers.

[312] The remaining prayers.

[313] This is only in the first two *rak'at* of any prayer.

[314] As you begin to rise from bowing.

[315] Once fully stood up in a straightened position.

[316] The fingers of the left hand stuck together and spread on the thighs. The right hand making a fist except the index finger which points outward during the *tashahhud*.

[317] To place the left foot on its side sitting on it, keeping the right foot vertical while resting on the bottom of the toes turning them towards the *qibla*.

[318] Sitting with the left buttock on the ground, right foot placed vertically with toes pointing towards the *qibla* and left foot on its side emerging from under the right foot.

[319] When ending the prayer, turning to the left.

Differences between men and women in prayer:

Men	Women
Spread their elbows out beyond their sides	Draws herself together in bowing and prostration
Raise stomach off their thighs in prostration	Lowers voice in the presence of a non-mahram[320]
Recite loudly, where relevant	Claps if an error or issue is observed
Says "*subhanAllah*" if an error or issue is observed[321]	Covers her entire body except the face and hands
Intimate parts (*awrah*) is between the navel and knees	

What causes the prayer to be invalidated are eleven:

(1) Intentional speech[322]

(2) Excessive moment[323]

(3) Ritual impurity[324]

(4) Impurity (*najasa*) on the body or cloths[325]

(5) The Intimate parts (*awrah*) are exposed

(6) A change in intention[326]

(7) Turning away from the direction of the *qibla*[327]

(8) Eating[328]

(9) Drinking

(10) Crackling or loud laughter

(11) Apostasy

---

[320] Mahram is an Arabic word derived from "Haraam," which means something that is prohibited or sacred. A mahram for a woman is someone she is not permitted to marry and are allowed to see her without a headscarf (*hijab*) and can touch. Mahrams are divided into the following three categories. Tafsir al-Qurtubi, tafsir al-Razi (Qur'an, 4:23):
(a) Mahram by blood/kinship:
Ascendants (parents, grandparents, great grandparents), descendants (children, grandchildren, great-grandchildren), siblings of parents (mother and father's sisters and brothers including half-sisters and half-brothers), siblings (including half-sister, half-brother), children of siblings (nephews and nieces).
(b) Mahram by marriage:
Ancestors of the spouse (parents, grandparents, great-grandparents), descendants of spouse (daughter-in-law, son-in-law, wife, or husband of your grandchildren), wife/husband of your ancestors (father's wife, mother's husband, wife of grandfather, husband of grandmother), descendants of your spouse in your care/guardianship (stepdaughter, stepson).
(c) Mahram by breastfeeding:
The mother breastfed by, and her children (breastfeeding siblings).

[321] Alerting the imam of an error he may have made or granting permission for a visitor to enter or warn a blind person or anyone of potential harm and danger.

[322] A minimum of a single letter that conveys a meaning (for example, "O!") or two consecutive letters that do not convey a meaning (for example, "Ba!"), but there are exceptions:
a) The prayer remains valid if there is intentional speech that occurs as part of a supplication
b) If it was unintentional speech (for example thought the prayer was over and started to speak) unless it is a lot of speech, of more than six consecutive words

[323] For example, jumping or several consecutive motions.

[324] Where the prayer is started while being in a pure ritual state and then becomes invalidated, e.g., a person passes wind.

[325] Such as excessive blood or pus released and flows unless is removed immediately. For example, a bird soils on a person's jacket while praying but removes the jacket immediately.

[326] Such as intending to leave the prayer.

[327] The chest moving away from the direction of the *qibla*.

[328] Whether a small or large amount, including any food left over in the mouth from eating before entering the prayer.

Inability to pray

Whoever is physically unable to perform their prayer standing is permitted to sit. If unable to pray seated may do so lying down or on their side. This shows how important prayer is as a divine command. Concessions can be made but it cannot be missed. Specific circumstances should be discussed with a qualified scholar or authentic fatwa organisation.[329]

Times when it is not permissible to pray are five:

This is a prayer that '*has no reason*' or '*without a cause*' meaning you just get up to perform a prayer. Your intention is just to pray, not intending a *fard* or *sunnah* prayer. An example is to pray 2 *rak'at* just for reward.

(1) After *fagr* prayer until the onset of sunrise

(2) After *asr* prayer until the onset of sunset[330]

(3) Sunrise until its completion and the sun has risen one spear-length above the horizon

(4) When the sun is at its zenith[331]

(5) From the onset of the sunset until its completion

There are exceptions when prayer can be performed during these times:

(1) If the prayer has a reason or cause

(2) Inside the Haram Mosque in Makkah

(3) When the sun is at its zenith on Fridays, if observing *jummah* prayer

In this next section we see how to perform the prayer in a complete way which encompasses both the *fard* and *sunnah*. Aim to have all *sunnah* actions including in all prayers, not just the obligatory.

If you are new to prayer and feel there is much to remember, this is normal. You can work to include the *sunnah* actions gradually over time. However, it is best to become accustomed to the complete way from the start. Be assured if you persevere, are committed, humble yourself and have patience Allah✹ will support you. What may start as a struggle will become eased, "**And seek help through patience and prayer. Indeed it is a burden except for the humbly submissive and devout [to God]**".[332]

---

[329] Who abide by the four *madhabs*.

[330] When a person has actually performed their *asr* prayer not necessarily after the time/call of prayer for *asr*.

[331] Except on Fridays when praying in the *ka'ba* in Makkah.

[332] Qur'an 2:45.

Performing the prayer, *step-by-step.*

Part one - preparing for prayer

Purification:

- Ensure you are in a state of major purification. Perform *ghusl* if needed.

- Perform ablution/*wudu* if needed.

- Or perform *tayammum* if necessary, ensuring the conditions are met.

- Ensure the body and clothes are free from inexcusable impurities.

- Use a prayer mat or clean cloth. If you have nothing to spread, look at the spot for any likely impurities. If it seems free from impurities,[333] go ahead and pray.[334]

Ensure the prayer time has entered.

Face the *qibla*. The direction of the *Ka'ba* in Makkah.

Be prepared to say the prayers in Arabic. This is a must. The language of the Qur'an.[335]

Cover yourself (the *awrah*). Whatever needs to be covered must be covered during the pray and during any movements and change in posture. For example, when prostrating your lower back cannot be exposed.

Part two - performing the prayer

First empty your heart. You are about to enter the prayer by declaring "*Allahu akbar*" (Allah is the Greatest). Before saying this feel it in your heart. Disregard your surroundings, leave behind any thoughts, and ignore any distractions.

While standing straight, raise the hands up next to the ears and shoulders, saying "*Allahu akbar*".

Make the intention in your heart. At the same time of raising your hands.

Place the right hand over your left hand. Both between your chest and navel with eyes focused on the ground.[336]

Say the opening supplication.

Seek refuge from Satan. Saying "*a'oothu billaahi min al-shayta al-rajeem*".

---

[333] Keyword here is '*seems*'. Islam does not burden an individual to examine extensively if there is any impurities or traces of it. Vigilance and attentiveness are enough. Look for things like the smell of what could be impure. Is this spot hidden and isolated where someone or an animal may have urinated? And so on.

[334] Remember: pure and clean are two different things. You can aim for the mosque. If not, a hospital, airport etc where there is likely to be a prayer room. This way you can be sure the place is free from impurities, is quiet, and an opportunity to pray with someone in congregation (*jama'ah*) for greater reward.

[335] Ask someone who is competent to teach you, and practice regularly.

[336] It helps to keep focused and undistracted. Do not let your eyes wander.

Read surah al-Fatiha. To be recited in all *rak'at* of any prayer

بِسْمِ ٱللَّهِ ٱلرَّحْمَٰنِ ٱلرَّحِيمِ ①

Bismi l-lāhi r-raḥmāni r-raḥīm(i)

ٱلْحَمْدُ لِلَّهِ رَبِّ ٱلْعَالَمِينَ ②

'alḥamdu lil-lāhi rab-bi l-'ālamīn(a)

ٱلرَّحْمَٰنِ ٱلرَّحِيمِ ③

'ar-raḥmāni r-raḥīm(i)

مَالِكِ يَوْمِ ٱلدِّينِ ④

Māliki yawmi d-dīn(i)

إِيَّاكَ نَعْبُدُ وَإِيَّاكَ نَسْتَعِينُ ⑤

'iy-yāka na'budu wa'iy-yāka nasta'īn(u)

ٱهْدِنَا ٱلصِّرَاطَ ٱلْمُسْتَقِيمَ ⑥

'ihdinā ṣ-ṣirāṭa l-mustaqīm(a)

صِرَاطَ ٱلَّذِينَ أَنْعَمْتَ عَلَيْهِمْ غَيْرِ ٱلْمَغْضُوبِ عَلَيْهِمْ وَلَا ٱلضَّالِّينَ ⑦

Ṣirāṭa l-ladhīna 'an'amta 'alayhim, ghayri l-maghḍūbi 'alayhim wala ḍ-ḍāl-līn(a)

Note: if when reciting you stop at the end of a verse do not pronounce what is between brackets. If reciting a verse and the following one together, do pronounce.

Say "*ameen*" after completing al-Fatiha.

Recite any other verses from the Qur'an:[337] Another chapter/surah or part of one (only in the first 2 *rak'at* of *fard* prayers and in all *rak'at* of *sunnah* prayers).

Move slowly to bowing down (*ruku*) position. The back and neck as straight as possible parallel with the ground, eyes focused on the ground, fingers and palm on the knees. Body should be relaxed, reposing therein, saying "*subhanna Rabbiy aladheem*" (three times).[338]

Return to the upright standing position (raise from *ruku*). As starting to rise say "*sami' Allahu liman hamidah*"[339] raising the hands to the side of the face, as done at the start of the prayer.

While standing upright, say "*Rabana walak al-hamd*".[340] Keep arms straight down the side, reposing therein.

Say "*Allahu akbar*" while going down to prostrate. In prostration, ensure there are seven limbs fully touching the ground including the forehead. Both knees, both palms, the nose and the portion under the toes of both feet.

When positioned fully in prostration (*sujood*) say "*subhanna Rabbiy ala'la*" (three times).[341]

---

[337] For those who are new to prayer or have not memorised several verses/chapters of the Qur'an, is it permissible to read in every prayer and every *rak'ah* the same verses. Gradually build on memorising some more verses.

[338] "Glorious is my Lord the Greatest". This can be said also 5, 7, 9, and 11 times.

[339] "Allah hears those who praise Him".

[340] "Our Lord, all praise is for you". You can also add: "*hamdan katheeran tayyiban mubaarakan feeh*" (praise which is abundant, excellent and blessed).

[341] "Glory be to my Lord Almighty." This can be said 5, 7, 9, and 11 times.

Rise from *sujood* saying *"Allahu akbar"* and sit on knees. Place the left foot from ball to heel on the floor. The right foot toes only on the floor with hands placed flat on the thighs[342] in the position of *iftirash*, saying, *"Rabi-ighfir lee, Rabi-ighfir lee"*.[343]

Return to prostration saying *"Allahu akbar"*. When fully in the prostration position say *"Subhanna rabbiy ala'la"* (three times), reposing therein.

Raise from prostration sitting on the knees.

One *rak'ah* is now complete. Depending on the prayer, it will either end here or continue.

If continuing for more *rak'at*, the above is repeated the relevant time of times. After the second *rak'ah* of every prayer more than two, the first part of the *tashahhud* is recited. If the prayer is only one or two *rak'at* it is said once at the end with its continued part, the Prayers upon the Prophet ﷺ:[344]

The first part:
> At-tahiyyaatu Lillaahi was-salaawaatu wat-tayyibaat
> As-salaamu 'alayka ayyuhan-Nabiyyu wa rahmatullaahi wa barakaatuhu
> As-salaamu 'alayna wa 'ala 'ibaad-illaah-his-saaliheen
> Ash-hadu al-aa ilaaha ill-Allah wa ash-hadu anna Muhammadan 'abduhu wa rasooluhu

The continued part (or second section), Prayers upon the Prophet ﷺ:[345]
> Allaahumma salli 'ala Muhammad, wa 'ala aali Muhammad
> kama sallayta 'ala Ibraaheem, wa 'ala aali Ibraaheem
> Wa baarik 'ala Muhammad, wa 'ala aali Muhammad
> Kama baarakta 'ala Ibraaheem, wa 'ala aali Ibraaheem
> Fil aalameen innak hameedun majeed

Return to the standing position. Say *"Allahu akbar"* as starting to move from the sitting position. This is now the start of the second *rak'ah*.

Ending
Remain seated on knees saying the *tahsahhud* and Prayer upon the Prophet ﷺ placing both hands on thighs, sitting in the position of *tawarruk*. Intend to end the prayer with *taslim*, saying *"al-salamu alaykum wa Rahmatullah"* turning to the right and the same to the left.

---

[342] Top of the thigh where the knee joints are.

[343] "O Allah, forgive me".

[344] "All compliments, prayers and pure words are due to Allah. Peace be upon you, O Prophet, and the mercy of Allah and His blessings. Peace be upon us and upon the righteous slaves of Allah. I bear witness that there is no god except Allah and I bear witness that Muhammad is His slave and Messenger".

[345] "O Allah, send prayers upon Muhammad and upon the family of Muhammad, as You sent prayers upon Ibrahim and the family of Ibrahim, You are indeed Worthy of Praise, Full of Glory. O Allah, bless Muhammad and the family of Muhammad as You blessed Ibrahim and the family of Ibrahim, You are indeed Worthy of Praise, Full of Glory".

Friday prayer

Conditions obligating Friday prayer upon a Muslim are six:

(1) Maturity

(2) Mind-soundness

(3) Free

(4) Male

(5) Sound health

(6) Resident

Conditions for performing are three:

(1) The location is a city or town[346]

(2) A congregation of at least 40 who are required to attend

(3) Within its designated time (after *zuhr* and before *asr* prayer times)

Obligatory elements are three:

(1) Two sermons[347] with the Imam/leader standing while delivering the two sermons and sits in-between

(2) Praying two *rak'ats*

(3) Doing the above in a congregation

Lesser recommended actions are four:

(1) Perform a *ghusl* prior to prayer

(2) Wearing white clothing

(3) Trimming of fingernails and toenails

(4) Apply perfume

It is also recommended to:

(a) listen attentively during the delivery of the sermons

(b) even during the sermons, to pray two *rak'at* upon entering the mosque before sitting.

Congregational/group prayer (*jama'ah*)

Congregational or group prayer is a great Islamic practice that carries 27 times more reward than praying alone[348] and has a great social and spiritual impact. This can be done in a mosque, house or anywhere. The minimum number of persons is two, one of whom will be the Imam/leader.[349]

---

346 Not prayed in a camp site or non-permanent dwellings.

347 Five essential elements: (1) to praise Allah (*hamd*) (2) Prayers upon the Prophet (*salah*) (3) to give the advice to be mindful of Allah (*taqwa*) (4) recite at least one Qur'anic verse in one of the two sermons (5) supplicating/*duaa* for the Muslims in the second sermon.

348 Al-Bukhari (645), Muslim (1477), Ahmad (5332).

349 The leader does not necessarily have to be a scholar, mosque imam or someone who has studied Islamic sciences extensively.

Conditions for leading a prayer are four:

(1) Those being led are not aware of anything the imam/leader has done that would consider the prayer invalid[350]

(2) The Imam/leader cannot be following someone else in the prayer. They should be the ones followed, leading

(3) Can recite the Qur'an correctly

(4) Knowledgeable of the *fiqh* of prayer and is able to perform correctly

Conditions for those being led, the followers are five:

(1) The intention. Must intend to follow the imam/leader

(2) To stand in a row behind the imam/leader unless only one other person is praying, so would stand to their right

(3) Aware of their movements to be able to follow. Knowing when to move from one position to the next

(4) The imam/leader and followers are in the same place[351]

(5) Women can only lead other women, men can lead everyone

Shortening and combining prayers (*jam' and qasr*)

A traveller is entitled to shorten and combine some obligatory prayers. This is to give ease to the traveller who may experience tiredness and exhaustion. Shortening and combining are two different things. You can choose to do one or both or neither.[352] A person is considered a traveller if:

- The travel is not for a sinful purpose
- The distance of travel is at least 81 kilometres (50.4 miles)[353]
- The person is travelling for 3 days or less (excluding the departure and return travel days)
- The person has left their city's residential areas and have become at least on the highway/motorway

Shortening: this is specific to prayers consisting of 4 *rak'ats* which become 2.

Combining: all prayers (except *fagr*) can be prayed together at the time of the earlier or the time of the latter one. *Zuhr* and *asr* go together, *maghreb* and *isha* go together. You cannot combine say *asr* and *maghreb*. *Fagr* is not combined with any prayer. Therefore:

Prayer	Normally	Shortened to	Combining
Fagr	2	remains 2	Prayed alone
Zuhr	4	2	Combined
Asr	4	2	Combined
Maghreb	3	remains 3	Combined
Isha	4	2	Combined

---

[350] Not being in a state of ritual impurity, lacks mind-soundness or any of the conditions for prayer.

[351] If in a mosque: it must be in the same building. It is permissible to be in a separate room to where the imam is leading the prayer providing the followers are aware of the movements (which can be inferred by hearing recitation, hearing "*Allahu Akbar*" when moving from a position to another, etc).

Praying in separate buildings: providing there is a row of followers that runs through the two buildings. It is permissible even if there is a wall separating them.

[352] It is not obligatory to shorten and/or combine, but a reason for ease that Muslims are advised to benefit from. Qur'an, 2:185, 5:6. Al-Tabarani in *al-kabir* (11880).

[353] You do not have to wait until you reach 81km. As long as the travel itself is more than 81km and have left the city's residential area, you can shorten and combine.

If you decide to combine the first (*zuhr*) at the latter time of the second (*asr*) you should do the intention to combine and delay during the time of that first one and before the time of the second enters. When starting to pray, the intention to combine and shorten is to be done at the point of intention for every prayer when saying "*Allahu akbar*". When combining the second at the earlier time of the first, the intention when praying to shorten and combine is also to be done. The same for *maghreb* and *isha*.

If you are being led by an Imam/leader in a pray who is praying normally (not travelling/shortening), you cannot shorten the prayer. You must follow and imitate them all the way by praying the full number *rak'at* they pray. If you are leading the prayer as a traveller, they can pray with you 2 and when you end the prayer, they get up to complete the remaining *rak'at*.

The Deceased

"***Remember often the destroyer of pleasures [i.e., death]***"[354] and be reminded that "***Every soul will taste death. And you will only be given your [full] reward on the Day of Judgement. Whoever is spared the Fire and admitted to Paradise [will] indeed triumphed and the life of this world is no more than a deceptive enjoyment***".[355]

Remembering death moves the individual far from deception that he shall remain in this worldly-life forever. Rather, it makes them conscious of the reality of their full life journey which does not stop here, creating a worldly life-Hereafter balance.

Nothing will accompany a person in their grave and there will be no luggage to take. There is no pre check-in, just a sudden end of life. One moment seeing the things you are used to seeing and the next minute seeing an angel assigned to detach the soul from the body and execute your departure. You cannot ask to extend your stay, negotiate a late check-out, or say goodbye to loved ones. Only your actions will join you. No wealth, children, status, or any worldly gains, "***When death comes to one of them, he says, 'My Lord, send me back that I might do righteousness in that which I left behind'. No! It is only a word he is saying and behind them is a barrier until the Day they are resurrected***".

Death helps overcome arrogance by reminding that whatever a person holds onto they will end up leaving behind. For the thoughtful believer death is humbling and for the ignorant, arrogant, egotistic, and boastful is a reminder, "***No one will enter Paradise who has even a mustard-seed's weight of arrogance in his heart***".[356] It also instils hope, knowing that peace and eternal happiness comes with Paradise. The real permanent life that is filled with delight and endless bounties, "***(such things) as no eye has ever seen, nor an ear has ever heard nor a human heart can ever think of***".[357]

---

[354] I.e., Death. Al-Tirmidhi (2460), Ahmad (7925), al-Nisa'i (1825), Ibn Majah (4258).

[355] Qur'an, 3:185.

[356] Muslim (266), Ahmad (3913), Ibn Majah (4173).

[357] Al-Bukhari (7498).

Obligations towards a deceased Muslim are four:

(1) **Washing**: handling the body with care and dignity, gently washed an odd number of times (once, three, five times etc.) covering every part of the body. *Lote tree leaves (sidr)* is used for the first wash and the last rinse using camphor.

(2) **Wrapping in a shroud**: in a covering that conceals the body of the deceased called *kafan*. The least is to cover the *awrah* area. For men three sheets is to be used and for women five sheets.

(3) **Funeral prayer (*janazah*)**: performed in congregation, standing (no bowing or prostrating). The Imam/leader will say "*Allahu akbar*" four times and the followers repeat after him:

- After the first, read *al-Fatiha*
- After the second, read the second part of the *tashahhud* (prayers on the Prophetﷺ)
- After the third, pray for the deceased
- After the fourth, pray for all fellow Muslims

(4) **Burial**: lowering the deceased gently into the grave, laying on their right side positioned facing the *qibla*.

This is the end. Everyone looking the same. The rich and the poor all buried in the same way. Just as one was bathed and wrapped in a cloth when they arrived into this world, shall be bathed and wrapped after departing. The only thing that remains is good deeds and righteousness. Then moves onto the next stage, "***The Day when neither wealth nor children will help. Except the one who returns to Allah with a pure sound heart***".[358]

Fasting (*sawm*)

Linguistically means 'abstinence'.[359]
Islamically, is 'to abstain from certain things that invalidate the fast, with certain conditions, from the break of dawn until sunset with the intention of worship'.[360]

Fasting is the fourth pillar of Islam, performed during the holy month of *Ramadan,* the ninth month of the Islamic (*hijri*) calendar. Beginning with the sighting of the new moon, Muslims who meet certain conditions are required to abstain from eating, drinking, and sensual pleasures from dawn to sunset, and which continues for 29 or 30 days (depending on the moon sighting of the new month).[361] As *Ramadan* moves back every year approximately 10 days, it comes in different seasons throughout the course of a person's life where there are months when the breaking of fast[362] is earlier in the day than other seasons.

---

[358] Qur'an 26:88-9.

[359] Al-Jurjani. *Al-ta'rifat.*

[360] Moghni al-mihtaj (1/420), al-ta'rifat.

[361] By the sun the days are known and by the moon the months are known. Tafsir Ibn Kathir (4/248).

[362] A term used for ending the period of fast during the day, i.e., at the time of *maghreb* prayer.

Fasting is a means to developing devoutness, "***so that you may attain taqwa***".[363] The idea is if a person can persevere and abstains from lawful things such as food and drink to please Allah☬, exercising self-control, they can devote to abstaining from what is prohibited. Attaining taqwa, i.e., becoming God-conscious is by overcoming egoistic desires and fasting helps control desires.[364]

Conditions for a Muslim to fast are three:

(1) Maturity

(2) Mind-soundness

(3) Ability to fast[365]

Obligatory actions of fasting are four:

(1) Intention[366]

(2) Abstaining from eating and drinking

(3) Abstaining from sexual intercourse

(4) Abstaining from vomiting intentionally

What invalidates the fasting are eight:

(1) Anything intentionally reaching the body's cavity[367] or head through an orifice[368]

(2) Insertion of something into the anus, urethra, or vagina

(3) Vomiting intentionally

(4) Sextual intercourse, intentionally

(5) Ejaculation resulting from [sextually desired] skin contact

(6) Menstruation

(7) Postnatal bleeding

(8) Loss of mind-soundness

What does not invalidate fasting:

(1) What reaches the body cavity out of forgetfulness, force, or ignorance[369]

(2) What is in-between the teeth mixed with saliva if unable to discharge[370]

(3) Dust of the road, sifted flour or flies reaching the body cavity

---

[363] Qur'an, 2:183.

[364] Tafsir al-Jalalin. See also al-Bukhari (1905, 5065), Muslim (3398), Ahmad (3592).

[365] Physically able and with no health conditions restricting.

[366] Non-obligatory fasting (Mondays, Thursdays etc): the intention can be done up to the time of *zuhr* prayer provided anything that invalidate fasting was not done (eating etc). Obligatory fasting (Ramadan etc): intention is to be done before *fagr*. For Ramadan, in the Maliki *madhab* (and a view in the Hanafi *madhab*) you can do one intention for the whole month (done before *fagr* of the first day). Al-Dimyati, I. *Mawsou'at al-fiqh 'ala al-madhahib al-arba'a* (4/35). If your *madhab* states it must be done every day of Ramadan, it is advisable to do one intention for the whole month and again for each day. In the case of missing the intention for any day, you are covered by the initial one for the month.

[367] This is the fluid-filled space in the body that holds and protects its internal organs. In this context, includes the brain, chest, and abdomen.

[368] Opening to the body.

[369] Deliberate intake of anything besides air or saliva into the body invalidates the fast.

[370] Such as food. Provided this is after having cleaned in-between the teeth using a miswak, a toothpick, toothbrush, or something similar.

Sunnah/recommended actions of fasting are four:

(1) Rush to break the fast[371]

(2) Break the fast with certain dates called *Rutab*, or any dates or water

(3) Delay the pre-dawn meal[372] to as late as possible

(4) Avoid repulsive and unpleasant speech

Days fasting is not permissible are five:

(1) The two Eid days

(2) The three days immediately after Eid al-adha (the days of *tashriq*)

It is undesirable to fast the *Day of Doubt* (*yaum al-shakk*)[373] unless it coincides with a regular habit to fast. Such as a person used to fasting Mondays and Thursdays and this day falls on one of them.[374]

Making up for fasting and expiations

Anyone who intentionally violates the restrictions of fasting must repent for committing a great sin. There are rules for making up unlawful breaking of fast, missing days in Ramadan, and those who are permitted not to fast.

Making up:

- Whoever intentionally does not fast Ramadan without a valid reason must make up these days before the following Ramadan. Whoever breaks their fast during the day without a valid reason must contune their fast and make up that day.

- If a person is ill, they are allowed to not fast and need to make up for the missed days. The illness does not have to be to the extent they are physically unable to fast. Even if with fasting there is likely to be hardship the person is unable to bear, they can not fast. Likewise, if a person starts the day fasting then falls ill or fears hardship, they can break their fast.

- A traveller is permitted to not fast and must make up the days. Travel must start before the time of *fagr*.

- Woman on menstruation, postnatal bleeding or giving birth are not allowed to fast and are to make up the days.

- A pregnant woman who fears for her health can break her fast and make up the days. If she fears only for her child, she can also not fast, makes up for those days, and has an expiation of one *mudd* of food (approximately 0.6kg) to donate.

---

[371] As soon as the *maghreb* prayer time enters.

[372] Known as *suhur*. It has blessings in it and does not have to be a full or substantial meal. Any small amount of food or water is sufficient.

[373] The 30th day of the previous month of Shaban, given this name as there is no certaintly regarding the number of days in Shaban as it depends on the moon sighting.

[374] Regarding this, Prophet Muhammadﷺ said: "None of you should fast a day or two before the month of Ramadan unless he has the habit of fasting (Nawafil) (and if his fasting coincides with that day) then he can fast that day". Al-Bukhari (1914), Muslim (2518).

Expiations:

- Whoever is expected to make up breaking their fast/not fasting in Ramadan (without a valid reason) and has not done so before the following Ramadan while able to, has an expiation of one *mudd* of food to donate for each missed day.

- Whoever intentionally has sexual intercourse (both parties) during the time of fasting must make up the day and fulfil the expiation; to set free a Muslim slave. If a slave is not found, to fast consecutively for two months, if unable to do so, to feed 60 poor people with each receiving one *mudd* of food.

- A deceased who has not completed their days of Ramadan fasting, one *mudd* of food is to be donated on their behalf for every missed day.

- Inability to fast; someone elderly or with an ongoing medical condition or long-term illness is to donate one *mudd* of food for each missed day.

Spiritual Retreat (*itikaf*)

Linguistically, means 'to prevent or commit to something'.[375]
Islamically, this is 'to take up residence in the mosque in a specific way for a specified period and a certain intention'.[376]

During the month of Ramadan there is the ritual of *itikaf* or Spiritual Retreat which is *sunnah*. This can be done outside the month of Ramadan as well. The same conditions apply and can be for any amount of time in a mosque. Imam al-Nawawi states: "*it is recommended to perform itikaf regularly. It is most recommended while fasting, during the month of Ramadan, and especially in its last ten days*".[377]

Conditions for *itikaf* are two:
(1) The intention
(2) To remain in the mosque[378]

As a person's intention to commit to *Itikaf* in the last ten days of Ramadan is considering a vowe,[379] they should not leave the mosque throughout the whole duration except in the case of:

- A genuine need such as going to the lavatory, to perform *wudu* or *ghusl*
- A genuine excuse such as sickness or menstruation (which prevents from remaining in the mosque)
- Sexual intercourse, as this invalidates the person's *itikaf*

---

[375] *Al-misbah al-monir.*

[376] *Al-moghni* (2/183), *fath al-qadir* (2/305), *al-fatawi al-hindiyah* (1/211), *al-bijirmi ala al-manhaj* (2/591).

[377] *Al-majmou'* (6/501, 514).

[378] As it is a ritual/worship specifically based in the mosque, one should remain in it throughout.

[379] A *vowe* is when a person commits to performing an action that would have been voluntary. This is different to an *oath* which is to affirm something that may occur in the future using a name or attribute of Allah Almighty, such as saying "*I swear by Allah I shall......*" or "*I swear by the Lord of the worlds I shall......*"

The word *zakat* means 'growth and purification'.[381]

Islamically, is 'taking from a particular property in a particular way of a particular description and distributed to a particular group of people to fulfil an obligation and to purify, increase, and bless one's wealth'.[382]

It also has a humanitarian and social importance, aiming to spread a spirit of unity and oneness, just as it is a means for developing self-discipline, detaching from stinginess, greed, and attachment to worldly gains. It allows redistribution of wealth, relief of poverty, safeguards a fair and dignified living standard for society, instils social responsibility, and develops humility and compassion.[383] Other benefits include:

- Accepting that nothing is truly ours but all given by Allah۞ so we can share and show gratitude
- Remembering that as we have entered this world with nothing, we shall leave with nothing
- Affirms that what we possess in wealth and otherwise is not by chance, it is the choice of Allah۞

There are two types of *zakat*:

Zakat of fast-breaking (*zakat al-fitr*)

This is to be paid by every Muslim as soon as Ramadan enters i.e., as of *maghreb* of the day prior to fasting, up until the end of Eid day (by *maghreb*). Its amount is the weight of a *saa'* (approximately 2.4kg) of the food people typically eat in their region. It can be donated as food or its equivalent in money. The greater benefit today in fulfilling the needs of poor people is to donate in money.[384]

Conditions for a Muslim to pay *zakat al-fitr* are two:

1. Ramadan has started
2. The person's own provision needs are sufficed and that of their dependents

Zakat al-fitr is payable for every person and every one of their dependents or under their care (spouse, children etc).

---

[380] *Zakat* is a broad subject with much detail. For the purpose of this book the important thing is to know there are two types. More information can be found books of *fiqh*.

[381] Lisan al-arab.

[382] *Al-majmou'* (6/94), *al-hawi* 4/3, Muslim (6592).

[383] Hojat Allah al-baligha, pp.139-41.

[384] *Al-majmou'* (5/295), *moghni al-mihtaj* (1/368), *al-hawi* (4/425).

Zakat on wealth (zakat al-mal)

An obligation to pay annually a percentage of 2.5% of excess money. And extents to other assets such as livestock, excess jewellery, and trade goods.

Conditions for a Muslim to pay *zakat al-mal* are three:

(1) The person is free

(2) Possesses the minimum amount. This is called the *nisab*, meaning the threshold

(3) A lunar/*hijri* year (354 or 355 days) has passed, known as the *hawl*

Distribution of the *zakat*: types of people to receive (the beneficiaries) are eight:

(1) The poor[385]

(2) The needy[386]

(3) Those employed to collect the *zakat*[387]

(4) For hearts to be reconciled[388]

(5) To free slaves and captives

(6) Support those in debt

(7) Spent in the cause of Allah؎

(8) The wayfarers[389]

Hajj and umrah

Linguistically, *hajj* is 'aiming for something great'.[390]

Islamically, 'aiming for a certain place (the *ka'ba* and *Arafah*) at a particular time to perform particular actions (standing on the mountain of *Arafah*, *tawaf* and *sa'i*) with conditions'.[391]

Linguistically, *umrah* means 'to visit'.[392]

Islamically, is 'to visit the *ka'ba* to perform a particular ritual with certain conditions'.[393]

They are both rituals which involved travelling to the city of *Makkah* (Saudi Arabia) where the *qibla* is directed to and the *ka'ba* situation. They tend to be mentioned together and associated with one another as *umrah* is seen as a mini *hajj*. They differ according to way they are observed. *Umrah* is not a pillar of Islam, whereas *hajj* is the 5th pillar.

---

[385] Those with no or little money and income that does not fulfil their needs.

[386] Someone in difficulty. Unable to suffice their needs and that of their dependents. This is a person in less need than the prior (the poor).

[387] Such as charity organisation employees.

[388] For example, new Muslims requiring extra support and compassion.

[389] Those who are stranded in a place or traveling with no/little resources.

[390] Al-mawsou'a al-fiqhiyah al-kuweitiyah (17/23).

[391] Moghni al-mihtaj (1/459), al-ta'rifat.

[392] Lisan al-arab.

[393] Al-majmou' (7/7), moghni al-mihtaj (1/459), Al-hawi (1/459).

There is no consensus amongst scholars that *umrah* is obligatory[394] but they agree it is a blessed ritual with much reward and spiritual benefit.[395]

Umrah can be done any time of the year and takes approximately 2-3 hours to complete depending on how busy the area is. *Hajj* is performed in the 12th (and last) month of the Islamic calendar (*Dhul Hijjah*).[396] It involves more ritual actions and is done over several days and in different locations.

They are both not everyday rituals, hence not relevant to everyone. This next section will focus only on giving a generic idea of their broad activities.

Normally those who travel for *umrah* and *hajj* also visit the city of Madinah. This is not part of those rituals but without a doubt visiting the Prophet☺ who is buried in his mosque there is an absolute honour and pleasure, peace and blessings of Allah☺ be upon Him.

Objectives and benefits of *hajj*

The gathering for *hajj* is a great Islamic conference and grand show of faith and diversity of the Muslim population. Hundreds of nationalities all in one place harmoniously declaring their servitude to Allah☺ alone, freeing themselves from anything and anyone but Him.

In this experience lies many social, spiritual, educational gains and development, "***That they may witness the benefits for themselves, and remember the name of Allah***"[397] such as instilling humility. One method is by removing the outer differences where men clothe into the same garment kept simple and free from stitches, just as it strengthens one's determination in maintaining good manners, sacrifice, patience, charity, generosity, and being mindful of Allah☺.[398]

Hajj helps engrave humbleness, equality, and oneness of the Muslim nation. All artificial boundaries are removed and there is no sense of geographic divide, national superiority, or ego.[399] Foul language, debate, and argument is forbidden and can lead to the ritual not being accepted.[400] Only harmonious brotherhood and empathy is expected. A bond develops through showing consideration of each other's affairs by exchanging information, concerns, and deepened understanding of one another's country and society, as one well-bonded nation, one entity, "***The believers in their mutual kindness, compassion and sympathy are just like one body. When one of the limbs suffers, the whole body responds to it with wakefulness and fever***".[401] The devotion and support towards one another is to be solid and unconditional, "***The believer is to the believer like parts of a building, each one of them supporting the other***".[402]

---

[394] The Shafi'i and Hanbali *madhahib* say it is obligatory to perform once in a lifetime for those who are able to (conditions to follow).

[395] Such as exerting effort and strive (al-Nisa'i, 2626), expiation of one's sins (al-Nisa'i, 2629) and the honour of being the guest of Allah☺ (al-Nisa'i, 2625).

[396] *Ihram* can start from the first day of Shawwal. Qur'an, 2:197. Tafsir al-Tabari, tafsir al-Qurtubi.

[397] Qur'an, 22:28.

[398] Al-Khin. M and Al-Bugha. M., Al-fiqh al-manhaji ala al-madhab al-Shafi'i, p.376.

[399] *Ibid*, pp.374-5.

[400] Qur'an, 2:197.

[401] Al-Bukhari (6011), Muslim (6586).

[402] Al-Bukhari (2446), Muslim (6585), al-Tirmidhi (2041).

Conditions for a Muslim to perform *hajj* and *umrah* are five:

(1) The person is free

(2) Maturity

(3) Mind-soundness

(4) Physical and financial ability (sufficient funds)[403]

(5) The passage and journey to *Makkah* is safe

Umrah fundamentals *(arkan)* are five:

(1) Entering state of *Ihram* with intention

(2) Circumambulation of the *ka'ab* (*tawaf*)

(3) Walking between the hills of *Safa* and *Marwah* (*sa'i*)[404]

(4) Shaving or trimming the head (*halq/taqsir*)[405]

(5) Maintaining this sequence (*tartib*)

Impermissible things while in the state of *Ihram* are ten:

(1) Men wearing sewn/stitched garments

(2) Men covering their head, women covering face and hands

(3) Combing hair

(4) Shaving, trimming, or plucking hair

(5) Trimming nails

(6) Use of perfume

(7) Killing a game animal[406]

(8) Marriage or contracting a marriage[407]

(9) Sexual intercourse

(10) Engage in sextual foreplay

---

[403] Provision, transportation, and related costs. To also ensure the needs of the family/dependants is sufficed while away.

[404] Seven times, the first begins at the *Safa* and ends at the *Marwah,* the second from the *Marwa* to the *Safa* etc.

[405] The minimum is to remove three hairs from the head. It is impermissible for women to shave their head and suffices to just trim a little bit from the ends.

[406] Directly or indirectly by ordering it to be done.

[407] For one's self or anyone else.

Performing *umrah*, step-by-step:

- Wear the *Ihram* clothing[408]
- Prepare the intention for performing *umrah* before reaching the *miqat*[409]
- Pray 2 *rak'at*
- Constantly observe *talbiyah*
- Perform *tawaf*: anti-clockwise direction (*ka'ba* to the left), engaging in reciting Qur'an, *dhikr*, and supplication
- Pray two *rak'at* at the 'Station of Ibrahim' (*maqam Ibrahim*)
- Drink from the water of Zamzam
- Perform *sa'i*: complete 7 circuits starting with the *Safa* (will end at the *Marwah* on the 7th circuit)
- Shave or trim hair (men).[410] Women only trim a little bit from the ends

Hajj fundamentals *(arkan)* are six:

(1) Entering state of *Ihram* with an intention

(2) Spending time in the boundaries of *Arafah*[411]

(3) Perform the *tawaf* of *ifadah*[412]

(4) Walking between the hills of *Safa* and *Marwah* (*sa'i*)

(5) Shaving or trimming the head (*halq/taqsir*)

(6) Maintaining most of these in a certain sequence (*tartib*)[413]

Hajj obligatory (*fard*) actions are five:

These are obligatory but not the same as the fundamentals (*arkan*):[414]

(1) Entering the state of *Ihram* from the point of *miqat*

(2) Adhering to *Ihram* restrictions

(3) Stay the night in *Muzdalifah*

(4) Spending nights in *Mina*

(5) Throwing the stones at the three pillars (*al-jamarat*)

---

[408] For men is two pieces of white sheets free from stitches with no other clothing under or over. For women, any clothing which is loose-fitting, covering the whole body.

[409] These are five points distanced from the Holy City of Makkah which pilgrims must not cross before they are in a state of *Ihram*, if intending to enter for *umrah* or *hajj*. Each *miqat* depends on the direction the pilgrim is entering from. These are:

    1) *Dhu'l Hulaifah* (also known as *Abbyar Ali*) - 18 kilometres (11 miles) southwest of the Prophet's Mosque (al-Masjid al-Nabawi) in Madinah and 438 kilometres (272 miles) north of Makkah.

    2) *Al- Juhfah* (also known as *Rabigh*) - 191 kilometres (118 miles) northwest of Makkah.

    3) *Qarn al-Manazil* (also known as *al-Sayl*) - 80 kilometres (50 miles) east of Makkah.

    4) *Dhat Irq* - 92 kilometres (57 miles) northeast of Makkah.

    5) *Yalamlam* (also known as al-*Sadiah*) - 105 kilometres (65 miles) south of Makkah.

[410] Minimum of three hairs, providing is on the head (root of the hair) not hang down below the hairline.

[411] Being present there even for a single instant between *zuhr* prayer time (*zawal*) of the 9th of *Dhul Hijjah* (the day of *arafah*) and dawn of the 10th of *Dhul Hijjah*.

[412] Performed after the time spent in *Arafah*.

[413] Intention comes before everything, standing in *Arafah* before the tawaf, shaving/trimming, and performing Sa'i. There is no required order between *tawaf* and shaving/trimming.

[414] Fundamentals/ *arkan* are essentials that must be done. If not done, the ritual is not considered valid whereas these actions, if not done, can be made up or compensated.

Hajj recommended (*sunnah*) actions are six:

(1) Perform *hajj* before *umrah* (*ifrad*)

(2) *Talbiyah*[415]

(3) Perform the *tawaf* of arrival (*tawaf al-qudum*)

(4) Stay the night in *muzdalifah*

(5) Pray two *rak'at* at the 'Station of Ibrahim' (*maqam Ibrahim*)

(6) Perform the farewell tawaf (*tawaf al-wada'*)

Types of *hajj* are three:

This choice falls in line with the general principle in Islam of ease and being able to fulfil rituals without being overburdened, accommodating needs and abilities that varies from one person to another, "**God intends for you ease and does not intend for you hardship**".[416]

(1) *Ifrad*: to perform *hajj* alone (no *umrah*). Pilgrims enter Makkah in a state of *Ihram* and remain in it until they perform *hajj*.

(2) *Tamattu*: upon entering Makkah, *umrah* is performed before starting the ritual of *hajj*. Pilgrims are not required to remain in the same *ihram*. They enter the state of *Ihram* with the intention of performing *umrah* only. Once this is completed, they come out of that *Ihram* and re-enter a new one to perform *hajj*. This way, in-between, they are relieved from the *Ihram* restrictions. There is sacrifice of a *shah* [417] for this.

(3) *Qiran*: to perform both *hajj* and *umrah* as one. Pilgrim must enter the state of *ihram* with the intention to perform both then go onto performing *hajj* only, which encompasses the *umrah*. There is a sacrifice of a *shah* for this type.

Performing hajj, *step-by-step*:

Before arriving in *Makkah*

- Pilgrim needs to first decide on the type of *hajj* they shall perform
- Take a ritual bath (*ghusl*)
- Wear the *Ihram* clothing
- Prepare the intention before entering the *miqat*
- Pray 2 *rak'ats*

---

[415] A devotional prayer uttered by pilgrims:

Transliteration: "Labbaik Allahumma labbaik. Labbaik la sharika laka labbaik. Innal-hamda wa-nimata laka wal-mulk, la sharika laka".

Translation: "I respond to Your call O Allah! I respond to Your call. You have no partner. I respond to Your call. All praise, thanks and blessings are for You. All sovereignty is for You. And You have no partners with You".

[416] Qur'an, 2:185.

[417] This can refer to either a one year old sheep (*shah jadha'ah*) or a two year old goat (*thaniyyah*).

Arrival in *Makkah*

Perform *umrah*, depending on the choice of *hajj* type. Observe constant *talbiyah*.

On the 8th of *Dhul Hijjah* everyone proceeds to Mina.

Mina,[418] 8th of *Dhul Hijjah*

Pilgrims make their way to Mina after *fagr*, to remain until the next morning, praying there *zuhr*, *asr*, *maghreb*, *isha*, ending with the *fagr* prayer.

Arafah,[419] 9th of *Dhul-Hijjah*

On the morning of the second day pilgrims start to make their way to *Arafah*, to stay within its boundries for a period of time between *zuhr* and *fagr*. Usually, pilgrims leave straight after *maghreb*. The prayers of *zuhr* and *asr* can be combined and shortened. *Sunnah* actions to be observed:

- Perform a *ghusl*
- Face the *qibla*
- Attend the *Arafat* sermon *(khutbah)*
- Supplication and *dhikr* with emphasis on repentance and seeking forgiveness
- To be there during the day and night i.e., to remain for some time after *maghreb*

Muzdalifah,[420] 9th of *Dhul Hijjah*

Pilgrims spend the night in *Muzdalifah* under the open sky, combining the prayers of *maghrib* and *isha* and shortening, remaining until *fagr*. *Sunnah* actions to be observed:

- Maintain calmness and tranquillity[421]
- Regular *dhikr*, *talbiyah* and supplication[422]
- Collect 70 pebbles of similar sizes for the ritual of *rami* (stoning of the devil).

Tawaf al-ifadah and *sa'i*, 10th of *Dhul Hijjah*

Pilgrims return to *Makkah* to perform *tawaf* of *ifadah* and *sa'i*.[423] Once complete, then go back to *Mina*. From this point they perform the stoning of the devil *(rami)*, slaughtering *(nahr)*, and shaving or trimming *(halq/taqsir)*.

---

[418] A small town approximately 6 km away from Makkah.

[419] Located 14.4km (8.9 miles) from Mina, where Prophet Muhammadﷺ delivered the final sermon.

[420] A small town between *Mina* and *Arafah*, approximately 7km (4.4 miles) from *Arafah*.

[421] Al-Bukhari (1587), Muslim (1218, 1282).

[422] Qur'an, 2:198.

[423] It may also be done later, combined with the farewell *tawaf*.

Rami (stoning the devil) 10-13th of *Dhul Hijjah*

There are three stone structures/pillars where stoning is performed in *Mina* using the 70 pebbles collected.[424]

These are, in sequence (which must be followed):

The first/small pillar - *al-Jamarah al-sughra*

The second/middle pillar - *al-jamarah al-wusta*

The third/large pillar - *al-jamara al-kubra (jamrat al-aqabah)*

Stoning is divided into two phases:

(1) Stoning at the largest pillar on the day of slaughtering (*nahr*)[425] on 10th of *Dhul Hijjah*.
On this day there it is only this one pillar, with 7 stones.

(2) Stoning on the three days of *tashriq*: 11th, 12th, and 13th of *Dhul Hijjah*.
The 63 remaining pebbles are thrown: 7 at each pillar.

Therefore:

First day - 11th *Dhul Hijjah* - throwing 7 pebbles on each pillar = 21 pebbles

Second day - 12th *Dhul Hijjah* - throwing 7 pebbles on each pillar = 21 pebbles

Third day - 13th *Dhul Hijjah* - throwing 7 pebbles on each pillar = 21 pebbles

<u>Note:</u> *If the pilgrim is only staying in Mina for two days which is acceptable, this is done in the same manner excluding day three. Only 49 pebbles are thrown in total.*

Slaughtering (*nahr*)- pilgrims can purchase sacrifice coupons in advance in *Makkah* where it is done on their behalf.

Shaving or trimming (*halq/taqsir*) - men pilgrims are advised to completely shave their head or can revert to only trimming. While forbidden to shave their head, women are only required to trim a little from the ends.

Mina, staying the days of *tashriq*: 11th, 12th and 13th

Pilgrims stay in *Mina* tents for 3 days (or 2), each of these days spending most of the night-time, between maghreb and fagr i.e., beyond halfway. A great seclusion opportunity to engage in prayer, Qur'an, supplication, *dhikr*, and contemplation,

"Celebrate the praises of Allah during the Appointed Days. But if anyone hastens to leave in two days, there is no blame on him, and if anyone stays on, there is no blame on him, as long as they are mindful of God. Be mindful of God, and remember you will be gathered to Him [in the Hereafter]".[426]

---

[424] It is advisable to collect more than the 70 required in case the target is missed while throwing or any of them are lost. Pebbles can also be collected from anywhere in Mina.

[425] The first day of *Eid al-Adha*.

[426] Qur'an, 2:203.

Tawaf al-wada' (farewell tawaf) and *sa'i*,

Performed as the last thing before leaving *Makkah*. Those remaining for a period of time or engaging in shopping etc should leave this to the very end. No *sa'i* is to be performed after it unless *tawaf al-ifadah* has not been done. In this case, both these *tawafs* are combined as one and *sa'i* done once.

The experience and details of *hajj* is broad. Give yourself enough time before travelling. Study it well to avoid the burden of having to remember every detail while there. This will allow you to focus on the ritual itself, connect with Allahﷻ and gain the fruits. And know there are 'educational objectives' in the many of its actions and commands. This way you are not just doing what is expected but aim to seize every opportunity to develop and refine as well.

What are educational objectives?

These are goals a person expects to reach through what they experience; the interactions, commands, preventions, restrictions, and the learning extracted from these which has an impact on the person and develops them. Its impact is greater when one is determined to change and refine so has the mindset and attitude in line with the goals.[427]

Examples of educational objectives of *hajj*:

Self-discipline and self-restraint:

Amongst millions of people, it is crowded, hot, sweaty and can be tiring at times. At the same time there is consequences to bad manners and there should be "**no misconduct, nor quarrelling during the Hajj**".[428] This requires patience and self-control. Requires consideration for others and empathy; devoted to help them in these conditions to also succeed, just as it requires one has disregard for luxuries or the expectation they can maintain a comfort zone.

Instilling humility and a worldly-Hereafter life balance:

In *Muzdalifah*, sleeping under the open sky, on the dusted ground. Reminding of a reality no person shall hide or run away from. From this dust we were created, in this dust we shall be buried and from this dust we shall resurrect. Let not this worldly life distract or deceive you, and "**Remember often the destroyer of pleasures [i.e., death]**".

Through these experiences and strives, the person is conscious of and practically exercising self-disciplined, self-restraint, and humility. Then, throughout the duration of the *umrah* and *hajj* and with regular practice they persevere in strengthening these to first becoming a habit then embedded characteristics, helping the person refine. By not being conscious of educational objectives and development potential, one misses out on valuable opportunities to fine tune their behaviours and traits. Do remember, everything in this religion and on this path is about attaining righteousness. About persevering to better yourself, progress in piety, and advance in obedience, "**O people! There has come to you advice from your Lord, and healing for what is in the hearts, and guidance**".[429]

---

[427] This is the same in anything we learn in Islam. Being a Qur'anic verse, a hadith, name of Allahﷻ etc.

[428] Qur'an, 2:197.

[429] Qur'an, 10:57.

CHAPTER SIX

The Book of Eman
Aqidah
(Principles of Faith/Belief)

Knowledge, our limitations, and Allah Almighty

Here the focus is on understanding how we obtain information and knowledge of things and our limitations as human being, as creations.

It is important that before we speak about matters of *aqidah*/principles of belief we get to know how far a person's ability can go in knowing or comprehending the reality of things. Underestimating our ability could lead to not fulfilling our religious duties or perfect as required, while overestimating could lead to indulging into matters that are not meant to be comprehended, are beyond our remit and limitations. If it is beyond our capacity, then we are not required to know or be concerned with, "**Allah does not burden a soul with more than it can bear**".[430]

There are three means for gaining knowledge: [431]

- The [sound] mind
- The [sound] senses
- Authentic news

All three are closely related and rely on one another. The senses need the mind to be able to perform their intended role just as the mind relies on the senses to feed it with what it requires and correct it if it goes wrong. Authentic news requires the mind to analyse, understand and prove its authenticity and the mind relies on authentic news to feed it with information that is absent and beyond its ability and capacity to know.[432]

The mind referred to is not the subjective mind which differs from person to person in terms of mental abilities, it is the mind which carries 'established principles' that are 'commonly accepted'. What is fixed and decisive in the human mind such as the submission that two is greater than one and a part is less than the whole. These are principles and essential 'built-in' knowledge every sound mind agrees on and cannot – by its very nature – be opposed or denied.

How we comprehend things:[433]

Every human being has the ability to reach realisation.[434] However, the information gathered in order to reach the realisation of something does not initiate from within but comes from the outside world through the five senses (touch, sight, hearing, smell, and taste).[435] The more the senses feed in information of things, the more a person is able to understand, analyse, imagine, come up with ideas, concepts, theories etc. Other than that, would not be able to. This is the person's [limited] remit and ability. A blind person who has no sense of seeing, no matter how clever they are would never know the reality of the colour red or green. Why? Because their sense of seeing has never fed this information in. The same with a deaf person, can never imagine the reality of a loud noise.

---

[430] Qur'an, 2:286.

[431] Al-Samarqandi, N. Al-aqaa'd al-nasafiyah.

[432] Al-Hussein, A. Al-zubda al-haniyah fi sharh al-khareeda al-bahiyah, p.24.

[433] Al-Maydani. A. Al-aqidah al-islamiyah wa osossiha, pp.15-6.

[434] Meaning the ability to develop an understanding of something, suddenly or by a process starting.

[435] Which are connected to internal senses (anger, love, pain, balance, hunger, desires etc).

They lack prior experience and exposure. The same goes for every person. Everyone's realisation of something depends on what they have experienced of it. Just like a person who has full [sound] senses cannot imagine the taste of a certain food if they have never experienced it or any of its ingredients.

The conclusion here is that if it was not for these senses, we would not be able to comprehend anything and would remain in total ignorance and unaware. The link between the use of senses and realisation is mentioned in several verses in the Qur'an, such as, "***indeed, the worst of living creatures in the Sight of God are those who are [wilfully] <u>deaf</u> and <u>dumb</u>, who do not <u>reason</u> [i.e., the disbelievers]***".[436]

<u>Limitation of senses:</u>[437]

Even with the number of senses we have, we are limited. There is no sense to tell us our body temperature like a thermometer or a sense to tell the speed we are walking and running at, a sense recording altitude or one to measure our weight like a scale. If Allah﷾ had willed He would have given us more senses to grasp more realities, but He determined we are given only the ones we have, as these are all we need to fulfil the purpose (and scope) of our creation hence are limited in numbers. Also, they are limited in ability. You could be in a room insisting there is no noise, but a technical device proves you wrong and there is in fact sound which is not apparent to you. A woman can deny she has anything unusual happening in her body when all it takes is a device to prove she has an embryo developing in her womb. And the list goes on. So, a person cannot deny something exists just because they cannot sense it.

Limited also in capacity and extent. Seeing requires the distance of things to be close enough and the same with the sense of hearing. Touching has a greater condition where there must be direct physical contact.

<u>Imagination:</u>

Likewise, our imagination relies on experiences of the senses. No matter how imaginative a person can be or how creative they are, all they are doing is putting together components of the outside world to form a mental picture. These components were already known through the senses in past experiences. [438] For example, someone imagines a new flying vehicle stationed on residential rooftops, can fly from city to city and country to country, fitted with a TV and goes into autopilot mode from the moment it takes off. While this is not a vehicle we have today, all that was done was put together things that do exist around us and we know and have already experienced; flying, distance, altitude, take-off, landing, autopilot, and a TV, all helped form this imaginary object.

---

[436] Qur'an, 8:22. See also 2:171.

[437] Al-Maydani. A. Al-aqidah al-islamiyah wa osossiha, p.17.

[438] *Ibid,* p.19.

Limitations of the human mind:[439]

The mind is governed by senses. It does not operate in the world of the unseen or reach conclusion in isolation. Our mental activities such as connecting dots, forming pictures, analysing, and concluding are a result of what the senses feed into the mind. As our senses are limited, so is the mind. No one can form a mental picture of the Hereafter as none of our senses have experienced it or any part of it. The same with angels and all matters of the unseen (*ghayb*). This is where revelation comes in to tells us about what is beyond our mind, our imagination, senses, and is not visible, hearable, or touchable. This is the role of authentic news through the means of revelation.

Therefore:

It is crucial a person understands that all creations are limited. Even humans who are honoured with the mind. Knowing how different types of knowledges are acquiring needs to be clear to avoid confusion and corruption in the view of things and create barriers to mature understanding and pure belief. The mind, for example, is not the means to feeling if something is hot or cold nor are the senses made to know something of the unseen. Do not allow ignorance to pull you back.

Conclusion

Allah knows best. This needs to be clear and firm in our hearts. He is the all-Knowing, the all-Wise, all-Seeing, and all-Hearing. We are not talking about a specialist or a scholar who are all limited. We are talking about the Unlimited. Yet there are those who question Him and give themselves the right to approve or disapprove His actions and commands. Or want to understand fully why He decided something to accept it. Or thinking we have everything figured out, **Say, "Are you going to teach Allah about your religion, when Allah knows everything in the heavens and the earth, and Allah is aware of all things?"**[440]

Our test is to consistently submit to the command of our Lord. This is the trait of a true believer. How can the limited understand or comprehend the Unlimited, how can the limited question the Unlimited, and how can the limited grasp the wisdom behind the rules and commands of the Unlimited! **"The guidance of Allah is the [true] guidance; and we have been commanded to submit to the Lord of the worlds"**.[441] The end of this verse is very fitting and alerting: "**Lord of the worlds**". Anything and anyone else are flawed and lack in capability and perfect attributes. Including you and me.

---

[439] *Ibid,* p.20.
[440] Qur'an, 49:16.
[441] Qur'an, 6:71.

What is *aqidah*?

Aqidah is an Arabic word which means to 'tie, fasten and bind something firmly'.[442]
Islamically, is 'to develop belief that is firm in the heart, undoubtful and tightly knotted'.[443]

It is a set of beliefs a Muslim adheres to and becomes tight in the heart. But is about first developing knowledge and understanding in the mind, which then penetrates the heart with certainty and affirmation, becoming unshakable and irreversible.[444]

What does the knowledge of *aqidah* cover?

Referring to the hadith of Jibril mentioned earlier, the Prophet's response to Eman was:

- Belief in Allah
- His Angels
- His Books
- His Messengers
- The Last Day
- In Fate (*qadar*)

Also known as the *principles of belief*, scholar have put these into three categories. The knowledge of:

(1) Everything that relates to Allah (*al-illahiyat*)
(2) All matters relating to **prophets & messengers** (*al-nabuwwat*)[445]
(3) All matters relating to the **unseen** (*ghaybiyyat* or *sam'iyyat*). These are matters we would not have known about except from 'hearing' or a 'heard source'[446] i.e., the Prophet.

The knowledge of *aqidah* guides us to understand:

Allah	Prophets & messengers	The unseen
Necessary: what must be attributed to Allah	Necessary: what must be attributed to them	What can only be known through revelation
Impossible: what cannot be attributed to Allah	Impossible: what cannot be attributed to them	
Possible: what can and cannot be	Possible: what can and cannot be	

Examples:
Allah – the principles of *aqidah* teaches us it is <u>Necessary</u> that God is self-Sufficient. You cannot imagine a god that needs help to achieve something. He would not be a god if he is limited in ability. It is therefore <u>Impossible</u> a sound mind would accept God is not self-sufficient. And similarly, understanding what is <u>Possible.</u> For example, He can choose to create something or not, possible to make someone in a certain image, shape and size or not.

---

[442] Lisan al-arab, al-qamous al-muhit.

[443] Al-misbah al-monir.

[444] Al-Maydani. A. Al-aqidah al-islamiyah wa osossiha, p.31.

[445] Which includes Divine Books and Scripture mentioned in *hadith* Jibril.

[446] Including angels, the Last Day and Fate/Qadar referred to in the hadith.

Prophets and messengers – it is <u>Impossible</u> they are inflicted with contagious diseases. This would hinder their duty to connect with people in spreading the message. They cannot be sent to be amongst people and at the same time people are obliged to stay away from them. Therefore, while it is <u>Possible</u> they can fall ill as they are human, it is <u>Necessary</u> they are able to spread their message fully meaning there cannot be any obstacles or reasons that prevent this, including a disease that is contagious.

The unseen – we would not know, for example, that angels existed or know their names and duties without being told through revelation by the means of prophets and messengers and revelation.

These will be detailed below, but do you start to see how *aqidah* works on the mind, develops sound understanding and corrects perceptions. Think of the contradictions and problematic ideas a person could develop about Allah﷾ and prophets and messengers if the principles of *aqidah* was not studied or understood. Think of how limited the understanding of the world and religion would be if we were unaware of unseen matters beyond the remit of the physical world. Islam is about purity of the heart, actions, and through the knowledge of *aqidah*, purity of the mind.

Belief in Allah﷾ (*al-Illahiyat*)

How do we believe in Allah﷾ (in general)?
That He is described will all attributes of perfection, "***The highest description is for Allah. And He is the Almighty***".[447]

How do we believe in Allah﷾ (in detail)?[448]
When referring to Allah﷾ this relates to:

1. His Essence or Being (*dhat*) - the essence of Allah﷾ no one can know. Exalted He is, "***No vision can comprehend Him, but He comprehends all visions***".[449] This being the case, the Prophetﷺ teaches us to focus on where our ability and remit lies, "***Contemplate on the creation, not on the Creator***".[450] And one must not assume what he does not know and cannot have knowledge of, for indeed will be accountable for what he claims or assumes.[451]

2. His Attributes (*sifat*) - knowing how to describe Allah﷾ is a pillar to glorifying and connecting with Him. He introduced Himself through prophets and His Book. There is emphasis in the Qur'an and Sunnah on the importance of having sound knowledge and correct understanding about Him, just as He does not approve engaging in any corrupt thoughts about Himself. Because of this, everyone should stand firm in knowing Him as He has described Himself.[452] To know what must be attributed to Him as is **Necessary**,[453] what is **Impossible** as cannot be, and what is **Possible** out of His Choice and Will.

---

[447] Qur'an, 16:60.

[448] What is obligatory upon every Muslim to know.

[449] Qur'an, 6:103.

[450] Tafsir al-dur al-manthur (Qur'an, 53:42), al-Tabarani in *al-awsat* (6319). Al-Bayhaqi, *al-asma' wa al-sifat* (2/162), p.37. Al-'sqalani, *Fath al-Bari sharh al-Bukhari* (13/383)

[451] Qur'an, 17:36.

[452] Qur'an, 48:6, 41:23, 7:169, 9:65, 6:91.

[453] These are the essential and principal attributes not all of them.

Necessary	Impossible	Possible
What absolutely MUST be	What absolutely CANNOT be	What MAY be

Necessary	Impossible	Possible
Existence	Nonexistence	Anything that is possible
Pre-eternity	Originating	(can be and cannot be)
Ever-living	Ending	according to Allah's Will
Self-subsisting	Incapable	and Choice
Unlike created things	Similar to created things	
Oneness	Has partners	
Life	Death	
Knowledge	Lacks knowledge	
Power	Powerless	
Will	Lacks will	
Speech	Non-speaking	
Hearing	Non-hearing	
Seeing	Non-seeing	

The Necessary

1. Existence (*al-wujud*) – aqidah does not examine the nature of God's existence, rather it is a study of the existence of things that are proof of the existence of their Maker. In other words, His existence is known to be Necessary from the existence of everything else. Nothing existed at one point in time and there must have been a creator to bring uncreated things into existence. This creator must have always existed and cannot have depended on anything for His own existence. Not in need of a cause, a reason, force, or any influence, "**Allah, the Self-sufficient**".[454] Unlike the existence of created things which He Himself caused to exist, His existence is self-existing.

A man was once asked to prove the existence of God, He replied, *"O, glory be to Allah! The camel's dung (droppings) testifies to the existence of the camel, and the track (a mark or line of marks) testifies to the fact that someone was walking. A sky that holds the stars, a land that has fairways and a sea that has waves? Does not all of this testify to the existence of the Subtle, Knowledgeable [God]?"*[455] Just as no sound mind will accept there be a painting without a painter, a building without a builder, or a book without a writer. All things that He created are proofs of His existence.

2. Pre-eternity (*al-qidam*) – as all creations rely on God to bring into existence, He must have always existed. And like everything is created, so is 'time'. Therefore, His existence was "before" time. The concept of "before and after" cannot relate to Him as He cannot be governed by something He created and has control over, "**He is the First**"[456] without a beginning. Our witnessing of created things existing around us points to the pre-eternity of its Maker.

---

[454] Qur'an, 112:2.
[455] Tafsir Ibn Kathir (Qur'an, 2:21).
[456] Qur'an, 57:3.

3. Ever-living (*al-baqa*) – His existence is Necessary and He cannot be subject to death. Death is a created phase which He initiated and executes for creations. He is the One who creates life, enables continuation of life, bestows upon us everything needed in life, removes life, and resurrect for the Next life. He cannot be the creator of something that has powers over Him! As there is no start to His existence there can never be a time He does not exist. He is not bound, confined or affected by time, and has dominance over everything. If time was to end, His Necessary existence would not be affected in any way, "*Everyone on earth will perish, But will remain the Presence of your Lord*". *[He is] the Last*".[457]

4. Self-Subsisting (*al-qiyam bilnafs*) – Allah is not dependant on anyone or anything. Being space, place, time, or organs.[458] How can He be in need of created things that at one point were nothing and He made into something! These and every created thing depend on Him and indeed, "*God is free from need of all beings*"[459] rather, "*When We intend for something to happen, We say to it, "Be," and it becomes*".[460]

5. Unlike created things (*al-mukhalafah lilhawadith*) – all things other than Allah have flaws and deficiencies. He is free of any imperfections so is unlike any created thing. Not in a body form, shape, mass, dimensions, or colour. Nor can be attributed to Him movement or stillness or any created thing, "*There is nothing like Him*"[461] Partially or fully. And whatever one imagines Him to be, He is not. His attributes and actions are likewise perfect, flawless, unlimited and need nothing to assist or compliment.

6. Oneness (*al-wahdaniyyah*) – He is One without division, parts, composes or elements,[462] has no equivalent, "*Nor is there to Him any equivalent*"[463] and unique without a similar, "*Exalted is He; the One, the All-Mighty*".[464]

7. Life (*al-hayah*) – His life is not like the life of creations. His life is not causative, i.e., does not relate to anything that affects it, nothing whatsoever. It is inconceivable He be described with power, will and all His attributes unless there is life. Although for creations life comes before their chacteristics and attributes, for Allah, there is no prior or latter, His attributes have no beginning, are pre-eternal.

8. Knowledge (*`ilm*) – He has knowledge of all things. Every detail. All that existed, exists, yet to exist, and will not exist. Complete or partial lack of knowledge is Impossible. "*And with Him are the keys of the unseen; none knows them except Him. And He knows what is on the land and in the sea. Not a leaf falls but that He knows it. And no grain is there within the darknesses of the earth and no moist or dry [thing] but that it is [written] in a clear record*".[465] "*We created man – We know what his soul whispers to him: and verily we are closer to him than his jugular vein*".[466] This knowledge is not acquired nor

---

[457] Qur'an, 55:26-7, 57:3.
[458] The creed of imam al-Tahawi (line 48).
[459] Qur'an, 29:6.
[460] Qur'an, 16:40, 36:82.
[461] Qur'an, 42:11.
[462] Al-Bayhaqi. *Al-asma' wa al-sifat*, p.151.
[463] Qur'an, 112:4.
[464] Qur'an, 39:4.
[465] Qur'an, 6:59.
[466] Qur'an, 50:16.

does any of it come after not knowing, as in the case of humans and creations. Rather, "**God has [always] encompassed all things in knowledge**".[467]

9. Power (*qudrah*) – He is All-Able and with ultimate influence, infinite, unlimitedness and absolute power. Nothing can deter, limit, or delay it, "**God has power over everything**".[468] "**But God is not restricted by anything in the heavens or on the earth. Indeed, He is ever all-Knowing and all-Powerful**".[469]

10. Will (*iradah*) – whatever He wills shall happen and whatever He wills not to be will not be, "**Allah does whatever He wills**".[470] Nothing can prevent, delay, alter or compel. He has authority over all that happens and determines how every creation carves out in size, shape, colour, lifespan, and functionality, "**And your Lord creates what He wills and chooses**".[471]

11. Speech (*kalam*) – Allah speaks, "**To Moses God spoke directly**".[472] As His Being is '*unlike created things*' so are His attributes and actions. His speech is not similar or have anything in common with the speech of creations. It does not rely on created things such as organs, voice, and letters. We need tools and instruments such as sounds, vocal cord, and air, He needs no full or partial intermediary or intervention. He is perfect and self-standing, "**And it is not for any human being that Allah should speak to him, except by revelation or from behind a veil, or by sending a messenger [i.e., Angel] to reveal by His permission whatever He wills**".[473]

12. Hearing (*sam`*) – He hears all sounds without a need for organs, sound waves or anything. His hearing is limitless and unrestricted. What is apparent, "**God has heard your dialogue**" with the verse ending "**indeed, God is Hearing**"[474] or hidden, "**[God] said, "Fear not. I am with you both; hearing and seeing everything**".[475]

13. Seeing (*al-basar*) – He sees all things without light waves and organs. Even a black ant on a pitch-black night, "**Indeed, God is all-Hearing and all-Seeing**".[476] Nothing is an obstacle. The creator of all things sees it all.

---

[467] Qur'an, 4:126.
[468] Qur'an, 2:20.
[469] Qur'an, 35:44.
[470] Qur'an, 22:14.
[471] Qur'an, 28:68.
[472] Qur'an, 4:164.
[473] Qur'an, 42:51.
[474] Qur'an, 58:1.
[475] Qur'an, 20:46.
[476] Qur'an, 58:1.

The Impossible

The Impossible are what cannot be attributed to Allah﷾ as they cannot exist in the first place. These are the opposite of the Necessary ones mentioned:

1. Nonexistence – for God to not exist would mean nothing else would come into existence. Reality proves otherwise, "**Have they been created from nothing, or are they the creators of themselves?**"[477] This concludes it is Impossible for Him to be non-existent.

2. Originating - to have a beginning means at one point He was non-existent. And if there was a beginning then would have needed something to bring Him into existence which is Impossible. How can the self-standing creator be created![478]

3. Ending - He cannot be self-existing then at a later point become non-existing like creations who die. That would mean He is not self-standing and an external force is able to dictate Him and control His destiny. It is Impossible He could end.

4. Incapability - the One everyone and everything relies on for initial and continued existence and supply of provision cannot Himself be incapable and have a need. Incapability is a deficiency, a lack, and shortage meaning would need a greater power to complete the incomplete, top up the shortage and assist with what is lacking. God is above this. To be incapable is unacceptable and is Impossible. He cannot be the creator of things then rely on them to compliment His ability, "**O People, it is you who stand in need of God – God needs nothing, the Praiseworthy**",[479] hence throughout the Qur'an a constant reminder of His ability, "**Indeed, that was [always] easy for Allah**" or "**Indeed, that is [always] easy for Allah**".[480]

5. Similar to created things - if He was like His creations, He would carry attributes similar to them and if He were similar to them He would be weak like them, limited in power like them, in need like them, declines in ability like them, and time-bound like them. All created things carry flaws and deflects. His essence (Himself), His attributes and His actions are perfect and flawless. It is Impossible He could be like His creations.

6. Has partners - partners or associates complete or assist one another. If He is unique and is self-sufficient, if He is self-reliant then it is Impossible He has or needs any partners or assistant. His attributes are complete and self-dependent.

---

[477] Qur'an, 52:35.

[478] Then that creator would need another creator to create him and that creator needing another before him to create him and this would be never ending. For it to be never ending would mean there would never be a first creator and therefore there would be no creations. Reality proves there is creations so there must be a creator meaning He always existed.

[479] Qur'an, 35:15.

[480] See Qur'an, 4:30, 4:169, 22:70, 29:19, 33:19, 35:11, 57:22, 64:7.

7. Death - everything dies and perishes except He who created them. He is not temporary or governed by time. He has ultimate control of all things. To end means He lacks full control and can be controlled, which is <u>Impossible</u>.

8. Lacks knowledge - if you were to see a beautiful drawing or piece of art and claim this was done randomly or by chance and not made by someone of knowledge, would be insane. So how about these complex creations around us? The skies, sun, stars, plants, rivers and all the unusual and astonishing things. What about the knowledge and ability needed for these? The mastering and perfection put into their existence, function, and harmony. Can this all be without knowledge? The Creator and Sustainer of all this to lack knowledge is <u>Impossible</u>.

9. Powerless - to lack power means limited influence. Limited in what He wills and limited in the ability to action what is Possible. That would mean there is inconsistency in the scope of what He can achieve. It is <u>Impossible</u> to attribute any level of powerlessness to the One with all-Power and is limitless.

10. Lacks will - there cannot be anything that restricts the Will of God. Absolute authority, Power, and domination is the ability to will what He chooses, and action what He wills. To lack will means power and dominance becomes limited, interrupted, or denied, and so for the all-Powerful Almighty is <u>Impossible.</u>

11. Non-speaking - the divine Books revealed to His prophets is a clear proof of His speech. Had there not been speech they would not have been sent to carry a message nor would we be guided, "***And if anyone of the polytheists asks you for protection, give him protection so that he may hear the <u>Word of Allah</u>***".[481] Nor would His angels be tasked and given instructions, "***They do not disobey Allah in what they are <u>commanded</u>***"[482] or His messengers have been spoken to, "***And Allah <u>spoke</u> to Moses directly***".[483] So the fact this all occurred makes attributing to Him non-speech <u>Impossible</u>.

12. Non-hearing - He is aware of everything. As no name or attribute of His contradicts another, He cannot be all-Knowledgeable yet is absent from the sound of anything! Non-hearing is <u>Impossible</u>.

13. Non-seeing - it is <u>impossible</u> things happening in the worlds of God without God seeing them, in full detail with no limitations. Such ability and attributes are associated with His Being and does not require or rely on there being something to see. He always has this attribute regardless.

---

[481] Qur'an, 9:6.
[482] Qur'an, 66:6.
[483] Qur'an, 4:164.

The Possible

It is possible for Him to do or leave anything. To do something in one way or do in another way. He chooses what He does and how He does it, from whatever is possible. It cannot be from what is Necessary or is Impossible. Because what is Necessary, there is no choice, it itself must be and always is and what is Impossible there is no choice, it itself cannot be and will never be.

He may have chosen to created humans and was possible to not create them. May have chosen the sun to be round or another shape. All entirely His choice. This person be tall or short, black or white, rich or poor, "**And your Lord creates what He wills, and chooses**".[484]

"***Say, "O Allah, Owner of Sovereignty. You grant control to whom You will, and You take sovereignty away from whom you will. You honour whom you will, and You humiliate whom you will. In Your hand is all goodness. You are over all things Capable and Competent. You cause the night to enter the day, and You cause the day to enter the night; and You bring the living out of the dead, and You bring the dead out of the living; and You provide for whom you will without account [i.e., limit or measure]***".[485]

What is the meaning of *shirk* (polytheism)?

Shirk is to associate something or someone with Allahﷻ or any of His attributes. This is a grave sin like no other.[486] Allahﷻ forgives any sin and permits the person to enter Paradise except those who return to Him with *shirk*.[487] Imam al-Qurtubi explains there are three levels of *shirk*:[488]

(1) Major Shirk (*al-shirk al-akbar*) - to consider a person or thing (idols etc.) to be worthy of worship. This type is the worst form and was most widespread during the pre-Islam period of Ignorance (*jahiliyah*).

(2) Attributing ability and actions independently from Allahﷻ - to consider any creation to have any ability without Allahﷻ in doing or creating anything, even if the person or thing is not perceived to be a god. An example of this form was the words of *Numrud* at the time of Prophet Ibrahamﷺ who claimed, "***I too have the [self] power to give life and cause death***".[489]

(3) Hidden Shirk (*al-shirk al-khafi*) - this is insincerity in worship, referred to as *riya'*. When a person's worship is done for showing off and not purely for the sake of Allahﷻ. While this is forbidden and serious, it is the least severe form and whoever commits this or indulges in it is not declared non-Muslim.

---

[484] Qur'an, 28:68.

[485] Qur'an, 3:26-7.

[486] Qur'an, 4:48.

[487] Qur'an, 5:72. See also Qur'an, 4:48, 4:116 and tafsir al-Tabari, tafsir al-Qurtubi, tafsir Ibn Kathir, tafsir al-Jalalin.

[488] See tafsir al-Qurtubi (Qur'an, 4:36).

[489] Qur'an, 2:258.

The meaning of 'There is no Lord but Allah: La ilaha ila Allah'

He alone is worthy of all acts of worship and submission, to be devoted to with truthfulness and sincerity while associating nothing with Him, "**And your god is one God. There is no deity [worthy of worship] except Him**".[490] "**That is because God is the Truth, and that what they call upon other than Him is falsehood**".[491]

'There is <u>no</u> Lord <u>but</u> Allah' is to negate/deny and affirm/instil
The first part 'There is no Lord' denies (negates there are any gods)
The second part 'except Allah' instils (affirms there is only the One God, Allah﷾)

Essentially you are removing any doubt and affirming truth. Removing darkness and replacing with divine light, removing heart attachments and replacing with the one firm rope, "**And hold firmly to the rope of Allah**".[492]

'**There is no Lord but Allah**' is not just a heart belief or a verbal statement but a way of life, "**Say, "Indeed, my prayer, my devotions, my living and my dying are for God, Lord of the worlds**".[493] In a *hadith*, "**the one who dies knowing there is No Lord but Allah, shall enter Paradise**".[494] "**Know that there is no god but Allah**".[495] 'Knowing' is beyond knowledge of the mind. To return to Allah﷾ not associating with Him anything[496] and interpret into action and manifestations.[497]

Misinterpretations and misconceptions

In this section we look at a few Quranic verses and hadiths which may seem to have meaning that contradicts or is inconsistent with the way we glorify Allah﷾ and attribute to Him absolute magnificence, flawlessness, and perfection and which do not [seemingly] fall in line with the principles of *aqidah* already discussed. Firstly, there are two key verses one must be very clear on. They are essential for knowing how to describe Allah﷾:

"**There is nothing like Him**"[498] and "**Nor is there to Him any equivalent**"[499]

Due to the importance of this and danger of it not being settled in the mind and heart of every person, we reaffirm:

Allah﷾ is not like anything. He is without body, substance, or otherwise. He is a Creator, not made of created things. He, His actions, and attributes do not resemble anything He created and nor can in any way be imperfect. He is free from any attribute which may be assumed or imagined. He is beyond every perception, instinct, or conscience. He has no equal, no opposite, and no peer.

---

[490] Qur'an, 2:163.
[491] Qur'an, 31:30.
[492] Qur'an, 3:103. Hold firmly to the means of reaching your Lord, His religion, Divine Book, and His ways. The use of 'rope' referring to safety and salvation, as the religión is the reason/means for salvation. This is an Arabic languuage method called *isti'arah* (a metaphorical expression). See tafsir al-Qurtubi, tafsir Ibn Kathir, tafsir al-kashaf, tafsir al-Baydawi.
[493] Qur'an, 6:162. Tafsir al-Qurtubi, tafsir Abu al-Saud.
[494] Muslim (136). Ahmad (498).
[495] Qur'an, 47:19.
[496] Muslim (270).
[497] Tafsir al-Qurtubi, tafsir al-Baydawi, tafsir al-Baghawi, tafsir al-Sha'rawi.
[498] Qur'an, 42:11.
[499] Qur'an, 112:4.

Some people understand the attributes of Allah﷾ incorrectly and regrettably books, articles and websites do exist with wrong information. For example, in describing 'hand'[500] and 'self'[501] they wrongly interpret to be a physical form. As for the knowledgeable and qualified scholars, they have taken two approaches to such verses. Both are correct, accepted and adopted from the early days of Islam, referred to as *tafwid and ta'wil*.[502] Take the 'hand' for example:

(1) Scholars and Muslims of early generations did not engage themselves with interpreting the meaning of 'hand'. They confirm the text of the Qur'an and stop there, abiding still by what is Impossible to attribute to Allah﷾ so firmly reject it can take a physical form. This was the initial approach in the Muslim *ummah* for decades and still exists, referred to as *tafwid'* (accepting that only Allah﷾ knows its meaning).

(2) Other scholars found they needed to interpret it to avoid people misinterpreting to a meaning that is unacceptable, especially in parts of world where Islam spread, and Arabic is not their first language. They describe the 'hand' as being blessing or power. In chapter 48, verse 10, "**the hand of God is above their hand**" meaning the power of God is above their power/ability.[503] In our human-to-human usage we even say, "*let us put our hands together and make this a success*" i.e., let us put our efforts together. This approach is called *ta'wil*. They needed to revert to *ta'wil* because the intended meaning of some of these verses (and hadiths) is not obvious or expressed explicitly.[504] Arabic is a rich language where a single word could have several meanings.[505] This required scholars derive from the text correct choice of meaning that is in line with Allah﷾'s Perfection and Majesty.

While the physical form is one of the meanings of 'hand', it cannot be a choice for this context. On one hand, it would contradict core verses that describes Allah﷾ and which their understanding is clear, apparent, and confirmed through *ijma'* (consensus) amongst scholars[506] such as, "**There is nothing like Him**".[507] On the other hand, it would contradict the principle of *aqidah:* He is *'unlike created things'*, hence cannot have a physical hand like creations do. It all goes back to usage of the Arabic language for interpretation that is both fitting and acceptable.

The complexity and richness of the Arabic language should encourage the average person to seek clarification and not attempt to understand the text through their own intellect and opinion, and to have the humility to "**ask the people of knowledge if you do not know**"[508] especially if their knowledge of the language is limited and are not qualified.

---

[500] "The hand of God is above their hand". Qur'an, 48:10.

[501] "You know what is [hidden] within myself, but I do not know what is within Yourself". Qur'an, 5:116.

[502] See sharh al-Nawawi 'ala sahih Muslim (5/25) and (17/129). Also in *fath al-Bari sharh al-Bukhari* (13/411).

[503] Tafsir al-Tabari, tafsir zad al-masir, tafsir al-muharrar al-wajiz.

[504] Referred to as *mutashabih* verses.

[505] Rich and distinct in conveying meanings of a phrase and has a unique and complex method of constructing words from a basic root. A single word may need to be described using many styles of articulation, meaning, and definition. This is one reason why the Qur'an is a miracle, because it is in a language which is broad and profound.

[506] Referred to as *muhkam* verses.

[507] Qur'an, 42:11.

[508] Qur'an, 16:43 and 21:7.

Definitions of *ta'wil*.

Imam Firuzabadi: 'moving a verse away from a meaning that is not acceptable and fitting to one that is'. [509]

Al-Jurjani: the linguistic meaning, 'to give importance to an option over another, to consider it weightier'. [510]
Islamically, 'to divert a verse away from its apparent meaning to another possible meaning, if this meaning is aligned with the Qur'an and Sunnah'.[511]

The importance of *ta'wil*

There are two important considerations:

(1) As mentioned in the introduction of this book, *"since the early days of Islam, the preserving and spreading of Islamic knowledge has been an ongoing activity, revealing the truth, serving the seekers, opening the eyes of humanity to realities, and accommodating changes"*. One must accept that people and minds have changed over time which had to be dealt with (and accommodated). Scholars adopted this approach because it is authentic and not one they innovated themselves. The method of interpretation goes back to the time of the Prophet☺, the companions, and righteous scholars of Islam in a range of matters. In taking this approach, they are still governed by the teachings of the religion. Their interpretations are not standalone choice nor goes outside its remit. The methodology of *ta'wil* is merely a process of confirming the text through text, linking what is not clear (*mutashabih*) to [principal] verses that are clear-cut (*muhkam*) where scholars follow a process governed by the Qur'an and Sunnah and not in isolation.

(2) The historical context. The need to cleanse and enroot minds with clarity and religiously-sound understanding by dealing with the growing 'material thinking culture'. Over time people developed a habit of understanding and explaining everything materialistically, interpreting even the attributes of Allah☺ and His Being to be of a physical form.[512] So although the original position of scholars was *tafwid* (to refrain from interpreting), the reason why they did not interpret at the time must be clear. There was no need to interpret. No one then adopted a crooked or corrupt understanding of their Lord. No one attributed to Him physicality. They perfectly glorified Allah☺ and were careful to describe Him as He described himself.

Many people will end up following the *Dajjal*. By attributing to God physicality there will be no surprise they accept a [proclaimed] god that comes to them in a body form. Especially when he does things such as ordering rain to come down, and it does (by the Will of Allah☺). Do we see the danger of this flawed mindset, and how correct *aqidah* works to purify the mind. As for those who understand He is '*unlike created things*' they will never fall into the trap of the *Dajjal* (Anti-Christ). They already dismiss attributing to God physicality. It was therefore essential for scholars of *ta'wil* to not leave people adopt these corrupt thoughts and help them return to a sound and flawless perception of their Lord. Islam is not a religion that is static. It is comprehensive and all-embracing.

---

[509] In Basa'ir dhawi al-tamyiz fi lata'if al-Kitab al-'Aziz.

[510] In Al-ta'rifat.

[511] Ibid.

[512] Has a physical hand or interpreting "**The Most Merciful; on the Throne He settled**" (Qur'an, 20:5) as physically sitting on the Throne. Glory to Allah Who is unlike creations, sitting.

An example of the practice of interpretation at the time of the Prophet ﷺ is when some companions interpreted an unobvious instruction of the Prophet ﷺ and did not rely on the apparent meaning. Ibn 'Umar narrated:
"Upon our return from Al-Ahzab (The Confederates) the Prophet said, "None of you should perform the asr prayer but at Banu Quraiza's place." The asr prayer became due on the way. Some of those said, "We will not offer it untill we reach it (the place of Banu Quraiza)," while others said, "No, we will pray [now], for the Prophet did not mean that for us." Later this was mentioned to the Prophet, and he did not berate/disapprove any of the two groups".[513]

The first group interpreted according to the apparent meaning, to only pray *asr* in Banu Quraiza, whereas the second group interpreted as the need to speed up their walking pace to reach quicker in time to pray *asr* there and did not take it literally. The Prophet ﷺ accepted both. Those who reverted to the apparent and those who interpreted.

Going forward, practically,

The idea of this next section is not to just list several verses and *hadiths* but for the reader to develop a 'sense of filter' when coming across such text; instinctively rejects anything that suggests imperfection and refute unfitting interpretations. The Qur'an has attributed to Allah ﷻ for example face, eyes, side, and hand. If we were to rely on the apparent meaning, we would be describing Allah ﷻ as an unpleasant person with a face, hands, and several eyes. Who would be willing to describe their Lord ﷻ in this way! Have the courage to seek proper knowledge and remember *aqidah* is about correcting perceptions and mindset. It is your responsibility to ensure you are feeding your mind with the right information and able to differentiate between what is acceptable and what is corrupt.

"Allah ﷻ is the Light of the heavens and the earth"[514]

And in a *hadith*: "**O Allah! All the praises are for you, You are the Light of the Heavens and the Earth**".[515]
He cannot be like light coming through the walls or from the sun. It would be extraordinary to accept He be physical light. The reader should reject this meaning after knowing Allah ﷻ is '*unlike created things*' rejects any apparent meaning that contradicts the principles of *Aqidah*, then reverts to understanding the verse through qualified scholars.

This verse refers to Allah ﷻ being the cause and reason for light in heavens and earth and organising the affairs and guides those in it.[516] The verse goes on to say, "**His light is like...**" which shows light is a metaphor[517] to describe. Then concludes, "**Allah guides whoever He wills to His Light**", i.e., light is what He creates, not Himself.[518] People even use expressions like "*she is an absolute star*" or "*his investigation has brought to light new details*". Surely no one means physical light or star.

---

[513] Al-Bukhari (4119), Muslim (4602).

[514] Qur'an, 24:35.

[515] Al-Bukhari (7499), Muslim (1808).

[516] Tafsir zad al-masir.

[517] Abdel Salam, E, *Majaj al-qur'an*, p393. One of the rich Arabic language methods the Qur'an uses. See for example Qur'an, 8:1, 12:82. The use of metaphor in the Qur'an gives expression greater meaning and strength. Al-Jurjani, known as a 'master of Arabic grammar', gives the example, "I saw a lion" explaining, lion comes to mean 'brave to an extreme extent', but also retains its literal meaning. Al-jurjani, *dal'il al-i'jaz*, pp.70-1 and his *asrar al-balagha*, p.33. Imam al-Suyuti says, "If metaphor was removed from the Qur'an, it would remove its goodness and beauty element" Al-Suyuti, J. *Al-itqan fi 'oloum al-quran* (3/94).

[518] Tafsir al-Tabari.

"And We are closer to them than [their] jugular vein"[519] and **"And He is with you wherever you are"**[520]

Meaning He can hear and see everything you do, He knows what is apparent and what is hidden. He is with us with His knowledge and His power, not close in a physical sense.[521] Indeed, Allah is not in a body form to become physically closer after being physically distanced or vice versa.

A person can express closeness towards another in many ways. Stands beside them with sincere emotions or by doing prayers (*duaa*) for them or paying off their debts on their behalf etc. None of these are physical closeness. Again, the Arabic language offers choice of meanings to a single word for various contexts.

"And your Lord has come and the angels, row after row"[522]

Our Lord will not physically come anywhere. The verse means His Will and Command has come. What He wills will be actioned, describing the events of the Day of Judgement where He commands the angels will stand in rows behind one another.[523]

"Everything is bound to perish except His face"[524]

Allah is One, is unique, and His being is not made up of parts that make a whole. This verse cannot mean he has a physical face nor means His face shall remain whilst other parts can perish! He does not have a physical face, nor does He perish. His existence is never ending. This verse states everything shall come to an end except Allah Himself.[525] Again, the Arabic language is rich, and its ways of expressing is profound. The use of face comes with several meanings in the Qur'an. It would mean Himself in some verses and in other verses His acceptance.[526]

Even in our everyday usage we say, *"off the face of the earth"*. No one would be referring to a physical face.

"For you are truly under Our eyes"[527]

No physical eyes! It means under His watchful eyes i.e., His guard and protection.[528]

Again, in our everyday speech, a person may say "keep an eye on your child" or "I have my eyes on him". Definitely no one expects a physical eye physically placed on their child!

---

[519] Qur'an, 50:16.

[520] Qur'an, 57:4.

[521] Tafsir al-Tabari, tafsir al-Qurtubi, tafsir Ibn Kathir, tafsir zad al-masir, tafsir al-Baydawi, Tafsir al-Jalalin.

[522] Qur'an, 89:22.

[523] Tafsir al-Baghawi, tafsir al-Jalalin.

[524] Qur'an, 28:88.

[525] Tafsir al-kashaf, tafsir zad al-masir.

[526] Qur'an 18:28, 30:38, 92:20.

[527] Qur'an, 52:48.

[528] Tafsir al-Tabari, tafsir Ibn Kathir, tafsir al-Jalalin, tafsir hashiyat al-Sawi ala al-Jalalin, tafsir al-Baydawi.

"Allah descends every night to the lowest heaven when one-third of the first part of the night is over and says: I am the Lord; I am the Lord: who is there to supplicate Me so that I answer him? Who is there to beg of Me so that I grant him? Who is there to beg forgiveness from Me so that I forgive him?"[529]

In no way physically descends. Movement and actions like that of creations is refuted. It means His mercy comes down and accepts the prayers of those supplicating during the night and the repentance of those seeking it.[530]

"..and if he comes one span nearer to Me, I go one cubit nearer to him; and if he comes one cubit nearer to Me, I go a distance of two outstretched arms nearer to him; and if he comes to Me walking, I go to him running"[531]

Not literally. Meaning whoever draws close to Allah﷽ with worship and rituals He will be close to them with His mercy and support, and if the person increases in devotion and worship, He will increase in mercy and support.[532]

"My mercy excels and precedes My Anger"[533]

Anger is a feeling of annoyance and displeasure. Allah﷽ does not get angry, annoyed, or displeased as creations do. With creations, anger is a change of mood following an incident or change. Allah﷽ has no changes. Change means a person did not know then knew and when they knew their emotions changed accordingly. Allah﷽ is all-Knowing. Here mercy and wrath mean His Will. When it is His Mercy, it is His Will to forgive and anger is His Will to punish.[534]

"Allah created Adam to His image"[535] and in another hadith **"Allah created Adam to His image, sixty cubits in height"**[536] Allah﷽ has height! 30 meters and Adam was created to the same height! Indeed not. There are two opinions to this:

(1) "**To his image**" i.e., to Allah﷽'s image. Attributing it to Him does not mean He has an image! it means to the Image He chose to create him in.[537] Such as attributing to Allah mosques as 'Houses of Allah' does not mean He lives in houses. Or created Adam to his image meaning Adam has knowledge, life, speech, and hearing which Allah﷽ has,[538] whilst there is no comparison between those attributes of the Creator and that of even prophets and messengers.
(2) "**To his image**" meaning the image of Adam not Allah﷽. He will bring Adam and the people of Paradise back to their original image i.e., everyone will be of this height as this is the original height of mankind.[539] Over the course of time the size of people and creations became smaller.[540] Or Adam was created to his image meaning he was always to this height. He did not go through the process of developing from a sperm-drop to a clinging clot [of blood] etc.[541]

---

[529] Al-Bukhari (1145), Muslim (1772), Ahmad (7592).

[530] Sharh al-Nawawi 'ala sahih Muslim.

[531] Al-Bukhari (7405), Muslim (6805). A Qudsi Hadith.

[532] Sharh al-Nawawi 'ala sahih Muslim.

[533] Al-Bukhari (3194), Muslim (6970).

[534] Sharh al-Nawawi 'ala sahih Muslim.

[535] Muslim (6655).

[536] Al-Bukhari (6227), Muslim (7163).

[537] Al-Jawzi. A., Daf' shobhit al-tashbih, p.30, sharh al-Nawawi 'ala sahih Muslim.

[538] *Fath al-Bari sharh al-Bukhari*, Al-Jawzi. A., *Daf' shobhit al-tashbih*, p.30.

[539] Sharh al-Nawawi 'ala sahih Muslim.

[540] *Fath al-Bari sharh al-Bukhari*.

[541] Al-Jawzi. A., *Daf' shobhit al-tashbih*, p.30.

Introduction

Prophets and messengers were sent as a crucial link between Allah﷾ and His creations. Without them people would be left lost and with no real means of knowing Allah﷾, His commands, and prohibitions. It is not clear exactly how many there were. The common scholarly opinion is 124,000 prophets and 313 messengers[542] with only 25 mentioned in the Qur'an: *Adam, Idris, Hud, Salih, Ibrahim* (Father of the prophets), *Lut, Isma'il, Ishaq, Ya'qub, Yusuf, Ayyub, Shu'aib, Harun, Musa, Al-Yasa', Dhul kifl, Dawud, Sulayman, Ilyas, Yunus, Zakariyyah, Yahya, 'Isa, and Muhammad*ﷺ.

As they are chosen by Allah﷾, no one could know who was worthy or likely to be or not be a prophet or messenger, "***Allah knows best where [i.e., with whom] to place His message***".[543] They themselves had no control over matters and fall into the remit of Allah﷾'s Destiny and Will just like every other creation, "***Say, "I possess no power to do you harm or benefit you."***"[544] They have no choice to accept or reject revelation or prophethood, "***And I [Allah] have chosen you [for the message], so listen to what is revealed [to you]***"[545] nor have control over who believes and who does not, "***You surely cannot guide whoever you like [O Prophet], but it is God Who guides whoever He wills***".[546]

Many passages in the Qur'an respond to people of poor and naive judgement when they question why revelation was not sent to a specific category of people, tribe or nation saying, "***Why was this Qur'ān not sent down [i.e., revealed] to a powerful [wealthy] man, from [one of] the two cities?***"[547] Prophethood is not something that can be compromised or is open for negotiation, "***God chooses messengers from among the angels, and from among the people***".[548]

There are prophets and messengers greater than others, "***These messengers: We caused some to exceed others***"[549] and "***We have given some prophets advantage over others***".[550] This does not contradict, "***We make no distinction between any of His messengers***"[551] because here "***no distinction***" refers to the message. We make no distinction in believing in them all, as one ongoing message. Unlike other nations who believed in some prophets and messengers and rejected others. Those distinguished prophets are the ones who exceeded in patience and determination in dealing with their people. Known as *ulu al-'azm,* are Prophets Ibrahim, Musa, 'Isa, Nuh, and Muhammadﷺ, "***So be patient, [O Muhammad], as were those messengers with resolve and determination***"[552] and the greatest of them is the Seal of Prophets, Muhammadﷺ.[553]

---

[542] Imam al-Siyuti in tafsir al-dur al-manthur (2/746): Narrated by Abd Bin Hameed and al-Tirmidhi in *Nawdir al-Usul,* Ibn Hibban in his Sahih (2/79), tafsir Ibn Kathir (2/471).

[543] Qur'an, 6:124.

[544] Qur'an, 72:21.

[545] Qur'an, 20:13.

[546] Qur'an, 28:56.

[547] Qur'an, 43:31. The two cities being Makkah and Ta'if, the two main cities of the region.

[548] Qur'an, 22:75.

[549] Qur'an, 2:253.

[550] Qur'an, 17:55.

[551] Qur'an, 2:285.

[552] Qur'an, 46:35.

[553] Al-Bukhari (3535), Muslim (5961), Ahmad (9167).

The difference between a prophet (*nabi*) and messenger (*rasul*)

A Prophet is a human individual chosen to be given prophethood, an honourable status[554]and given revelation, although may not be ordered to preach it and would continue preaching the existing message (revealed before him). Also, through their actions and conduct those around them would learn and be guided, observing many lessons, manifestations of the message, and disciplines.

Once a prophet is ordered to spread revelation sent to him, he becomes a messenger as well. Therefore, every messenger is a prophet but not every prophet is a messenger. Prophets and messengers have miracles,[555] while messengers have divine books and scripture.[556] The Qur'an makes clear they are human, reiterating that everyone can follow and implement their teachings, "***Their messengers said to them, "We are [indeed] only humans like you***"[557] unlike a human following an angel, for example.

Miracles

A miracle is defined Islamically as a 'unique and supernatural act (or event) contrary to the laws of nature, at the hands of a claimant of prophethood, in line with their message, and is impossible to be imitated or copied'.[558] The conditions and characteristics for something to be a miracle are:[559]

(1) To be verbal (e.g., Qur'an), actions (e.g., the stick of Musa) or prevention (e.g., Ibrahim not burnt by the fire)
(2) Is extraordinary i.e., contrary to the norm and beyond the ability of people[560]
(3) Occurs from a claimant of prophethood
(4) Is of the same nature. For example, Musa challenged the magicians with a stick that turned into a snake and Prophet Muhmmad challenged his people's Arabic language through the miraculous [Arabic] verses of the Qur'an
(5) Must be impossible to debate and contradict

The wisdom from showing miracles is to confirm their legitimacy and truthfulness of their claims as any claim not proven will be rejected. Those who rejected the message and subjected prophets and messengers to mockery, insult, and denial had to be proven wrong. They were granted miracles that went against the 'Laws of Nature' people were accustomed to such as the Qur'an being something extraordinary and miraculous that it could only have come through the intervention of Allah. Miracles confirm the true prophets and exposes the liars.

---

[554] Qur'an, 18:110, 2:130, 3:33, 6:124, 19:58, 22:75, 28:68, 38:47.
[555] Al-Bukhari (7274), Muslim (152).
[556] Qur'an, 57:25.
[557] Qur'an, 14:11. Other verses include: 3:79, 18:1, 18:110, 19:30, 38:30.
[558] Al-Sharfawi, A., Sharh al-aqidah al-nasafiyyah, p.292.
[559] Tafsir al-Qurtubi, pp.59-60.
[560] See Qur'an, 10:15, 14:11, 52:34.

The difference between a miracle and other events or actions

There are actions or events people may confuse with miracles but do not carry its conditions:

Magic: is not unique and extraordinary/beyond the norm. The same steps can be followed reaching a same outcome.

Karamat:[561] this is the appearance of something that is difference in its nature to the customary way of things. Saints are gifted with this. No one, however, attributes to them prophecy or claim they are infallible.[562]

How do we believe in prophets and messengers (in general)?

To believe Allahﷻ sent prophets and messengers out of His mercy and generosity, "**The Messenger has believed in what was revealed to him from his Lord, and [so have] the Believers. All of them have believed in God and His angels and His books and His messengers, [saying], "We make no distinction between any of His messengers**",[563] to relay glad tiding to the disciplined believers and warning to those who go astray and deviate from the truth, "**[We sent] messengers as bringers of good tidings and warners; so that people may have no excuse before Allah after the sending of messengers**",[564] assigned with the duty to spread the message and clarify its teachings to all people, "**And We did not send any messenger except [speaking] in the language of his people to explain to them clearly**".[565]

The first of them was Adam[566] and the last was Muhammadﷺ.[567] It is upon every Muslim to believe they are infallible. They do not neglect what is obligatory nor commit what is prohibited and are described with high moral characteristics as they are the greatest examples, sent to portray righteousness and noble character. It is Allahﷻ Himself who has guaranteed their infallibility, "**For you are truly under Our eyes**"[568] i.e., under His the care, guidance, and protection, and assured, "**It is not [attributable] to any prophet that he would act dishonestly and unfaithfully**".[569]

How do we believe in prophets and messengers (in detail)?

To know what must be attributed to them as is Necessary, what to negate as is Impossible and that there are Possible things attributed to them. Knowing how to describe prophets and messengers in our mind is essential to avoid corrupt and crocked thoughts about those whom Allahﷻ raised in status and entrusted as carriers of His revelation. Because of this, everyone should stand firm in knowing them as He has described them.

---

[561] Pious people can have *karamat* (Singular: *karama*); supernatural ability which Allahﷻ grants to some of his righteous slaves. It is sometimes referred to as miracles which is obviously a non-prophetic miracle. See Qur'an, 3:37.

[562] Al-Sharfawi, A., Sharh al-aqidah al-nasafiyyah, p.312.

[563] Qur'an, 2: 285. See also 2:136.

[564] Qur'an, 4:165. See also 6:48, 6:130, 35:24.

[565] Qur'an, 14:4. See also 7:59, 10:47, 57:25.

[566] Ahmad (21546).

[567] Qur'an, 33:40.

[568] Qur'an, 52:48. See also 20:39.

[569] Qur'an, 3:161. Tafsir al-Kashaf

Necessary	Impossible	Possible
What absolutely MUST be	What absolutely CANNOT be	What MAY be

Trustworthiness	Betrayal of trust	
Truthfulness	Committing sins	What can and cannot be
Delivering the message completely	Not delivering the message	
Superior intelligence and wisdom	Inferior intelligence and wisdom	

The Necessary

1. **Trustworthiness** (*sidq*) – it is upon every Muslim to believe they were trustworthy; a clear sign of perfect coherence between their words and actions, one of their core and essential characteristics. They were infallible and divinely protected from inward and outward major or minor sins and disobedience. They do not betray and are entrusted with the duty to receive the message, convey in its original form, not holdback, add or speak from any whims or desire, "**Indeed, I am to you a trustworthy messenger**".[570] They were honourable people of integrity and morality in society even before receiving revelation and prophethood. Prophet Muhammadﷺ, as an example, described as the '*trustworthy*', was highly regarded, spread goodness, served people's needs and maintained strong family ties.[571]

2. **Truthfulness** (*amanah*) - they are characterised with reliability and truthfulness in accomplishing their mission and in all other aspects of their lives, immune from wrongdoing, of outstanding character, highly valued, and greatly appreciated amongst people. Prophet Muhammadﷺ, for example, called the '*truthful*,' even by the pagans of Makkah in the period of ignorance (*jahiliyah*).[572] If they were to be untruthful that would mean the message would be flawed and inaccurate. Their truthfulness confirms the truthfulness of the message, and the truthfulness of the message necessitated it is from God, "**This is what Allah and His Messenger had promised us, and God and His Messenger spoke the truth**".[573] "**Nor does he speak out of [his own] desire. It is not but a revelation revealed**".[574] They were truthful in their speech whether in serious matters, joking or entertaining, "**Verily, I do not say anything but the truth**".[575]

3. **Delivering the message completely** (*tabligh*) - they delivered the message totally, as it is, without concealing any of it, without detracting, and without adding to it other than revelation, as the primary and most sacred duty they had been tasked with. They transmitted the message in full to whom they were ordered to convey to, "**O Messenger, Convey that which has been revealed to you from your Lord**" then the verse continues, hypothetically speaking, "**and if you do not, then**

---

[570] Qur'an, 44:18. See also 3:161, 12:33, 38:47, 53:3-4, 81:21.

[571] Al-Bukhari (28), Muslim (160).

[572] Muslim (508).

[573] Qur'an, 33:22. See also 7:105, 12:46, 12:51, 19:41, 19:54.

[574] Qur'an, 53:3.

[575] Al-Tirmidhi (2108).

you have not conveyed His message"[576] and in another verse, "*I convey to you the messages of my Lord and advise you; and know from Allah what you do not know*".[577] Their integrity, trustworthiness, truthfulness and infallibility all prove their honesty, credibility, and attentiveness in delivering the message while being divinely guided, "*Had We not made you steadfast, you probably would have inclined to them a little*".[578]

4. Superior intelligence, and wisdom (*fatanah*) – prophecy is a great responsibility. If they did not have excellent capabilities they would have been unable to fulfil this. They were well able and equipped to grasp the divine message and resolve people's problems, queries, and needs. They had extraordinary intelligence, were sharp-minded, alert, with high-level logic, and ability to convince. If they lacked all this, they would not be qualified to relay the message in a persuasive manner, debate, and evidence with logical proof, or refute misconceptions and respond to the arguments of those who opposed, "*Invite to the way of your Lord with wisdom, good advice and warning, and debate them in a way that is best and most dignified*".[579] The interaction between Prophet Ibraham﷽ and Numrud is an example of their ability to debate even those filled with arrogance and stubbornness, "*He [Numrud] was left overwhelmed by astonishment and dumbstruck!*"[580]

Further evidence of their infallibility and immunity from sin

Whilst there are many verses, hadiths, events, and admissions from even non-believers that prove they had highly regarded traits and far from negative (inward or outward) influence, we refer to Qur'anic passages confirming this:

- In the story of Adam and Satan, Satan declares war on people, promising to deviate. He did however exclude a category of people, "*except Your chosen (guided) slaves from them*",[581] admitting he is unable to mislead such believers. Without a doubt, prophets and messengers are the greatest of believers, the closest to their Lord, the chosen, divinely guided, and perfect examples of servitude.

- Prophet Muhammad﷽ revealed to his companions everyone has assigned to them a *jinn* (*qarin*[582]) that attracts and tempts evil, and an angel that encourages good. His companions then queried if this included him as well. He replied, "*even me, except that Allah assisted me so the jinn has submitted and only orders me to do good*".[583]

- Muslims are commanded, by the order of the Qur'an, to not accept news of wrongdoers without verifying, "*if there comes to you a wrongdoer with information, investigate*".[584] By verifying they are able to validate or invalidate news. If prophets and messengers were able to sin, deceive or withhold information, then according to the Qur'an itself their news and reports should not be accepted at face value. This would hinder their duty as 'delivers of important news'.[585]

---

[576] Qur'an, 5:67. See also 7:61, 7:79, 7:93, 11:57, 16:35, 36:17, 46:23.

[577] Qur'an, 7:62.

[578] Qur'an, 17:74.

[579] Qur'an, 16:125. See also 6:83, 11:32, 2:251, 6:83, 12:55.

[580] See Qur'an, 2:258.

[581] Qur'an, 15:40.

[582] Qur'an, 50:27-9.

[583] Muslim (7108). See sharh al-Nawawi 'ala sahih Muslim.

[584] Qur'an, 49:6.

[585] This is the linguistic definition of a messenger. See *lisan al-arab* and *al-ta'rifat*.

The Impossible

What is Impossible is the opposite of the Necessary mentioned. Therefore:

1. Betrayal of the trust - while they are entrusted and attributed with trustworthiness, guaranteed divine protection and guidance, to be characterised with betrayal of the trust is <u>Impossible</u>. They were required to draw people towards them for what they represent, not draw them away. A corrupt trait such as dishonesty or betrayal of trust would drive people away which defeats the whole purpose of their sending.

2. Dishonesty/committing sins - to believe it is <u>Impossible</u> they would sin, be wrongdoers, egoistically driven or lack Infallibility at any moment. It cannot be imagined they have flaws that deprives them reliability and be worthy of carrying a divine message. Their immunity from sins means they are worthy of being followed, as we are commanded to follow their footsteps. If they were able to commit sins, this means – by default – their followers are too permitted to sin which contradicts the teachings of the Qur'an itself. Nor would it be fitting for Allah Almighty's perfection and Wisdom to choose carriers of his divine message who are sinful or immoral.

3. Not delivering the message completely - limiting their commitment/responsibility in delivering all divine revelation, to tamper, holdback, tweak, or anything that gets in the way of accuracy and honesty is <u>Impossible</u>. It would undermine their integrity and create mistrust causing their prophethood to be in doubt and their message rejected.

4. Inferior intelligence and wisdom - It is <u>Impossible</u> they can lack necessary mental qualities, abilities, and intelligence as this would hinder the very duty they have been sent for. If they lacked inferior intelligence and wisdom, they would be unable to deal with objection and stubbornness or succeed in preaching the message, leaving people with unanswered questions and unresolved concerns about their purpose in life yet remain accountable on the Day of Judgement!

The Possible

Although they had special attributes and were infallibility, they had human features just like ordinary people, "***Say, "I am only a human being like you***".[586] They were subject to all human conditions but in no way that would degrade their high rank. Those who knew them and interacted closely even before prophethood, observing them as an active and integral part of society, were able to verify their human-like traits, as opposed to being non-human or supernatural, unable to relate to them. Connectivity, integration, and relatedness were essential, "***Nothing prevented the people from believing, when guidance has come to them, except that they said, "Did Allah send a human messenger?" Say, "If there were angels on earth, walking around in peace***[587], ***We would have sent down to them from heaven an angel [as a] messenger***".[588] Should this not be the case, there would have been disconnection and disengagement between the message conveyers and the recipients, the 'teachers' and the 'students', leaving room for confusion, frustration, and genuine excuses.

---

[586] Qur'an, 18:110. See also Qur'an, 3:144, 5:75.
[587] Were settled and established there, as with human beings.
[588] Qur'an, 17:94-5.

Their bodies and structure were as the rest of humankind. They experienced the same symptoms and circumstances. Eating, drinking, sleeping, marriage, sexual activity, fell ill, and died.[589] They even at times experienced hunger, poverty, high-wealth, and were afflicted harm from others but only to an extent that did not prevent them from continuing to spread the message. They can faint for a short time which is different to short or long-term mental illness or instability. As for sleeping, Prophet Muhammadﷺ, his eyes sleep but the heart always remains awake.[590]

Misinterpretations and misconceptions

Here we look at Qur'anic verses and hadiths which [seem to] have meaning inconsistent with how we believe prophets and messengers to be infallible, although when understood agrees fully with the principles of *aqidah* set out earlier. It is essential they are understood the way Allah﷾ described them and to observe balance and objectivity when attempting to understanding their stories. There is danger in referring to your own intellect for understanding instead of referring to the Qur'an itself and qualified commentators of it. Context and detail are essential for clarity, balance and objectivity.

"Magic was worked on the Prophet" [591]

Prophet Muhammadﷺ was exposed to magic (*sihr*). However, the effect of this was limited to his body and in no way affected his heart, mind, or soul. When an average person is inflicted with magic there are several effects to this. As for prophets and messengers, it is important to remember they are protected for what they represent, carriers of revelation. Even if they share the same human-like experiences, this does not necessarily mean in the exact same way or to the same extent. They are under the watchful eyes of Allah﷾, His guard and ongoing protection. [592]

"He frowned and turned away. When the blind man approached him"[593]

Prophet Muhammadﷺ was sitting amongst leaders of Quraysh who were non-believers, fulfilling his duty to convey the message and guide to the truth. He always hoped they would believe considering this would impact also their many followers, devoted to saving every possible soul from disbelief and the trauma of the Hereafter. At times he would overburden himself and be reminded his role is to merely preach and deliver the message and is not accountable for anyone's choice,[594] *"But [O Prophet] are you going to worry yourself to death over them if they do not believe this message"*.[595]

While speaking to them, a companion named Abdullah Ibn Um Maktoum, who was blind, kept interrupting the Prophetﷺ asking him to teach him while being persistent. Although his blindness prevents him from seeing who he was speaking to, he was able to hear the serious conversation and should have shown patience. It was fitting for the Prophetﷺ to disapproved of him interrupting.[596] In chapter 49, we learn that the companions are ordered to show respect in the presence of the Prophetﷺ, *"O you who believe! Do not raise your voices above the voice of the Prophet, and do not speak*

---

[589] Al-Tattan, A., al-Kilani, M. *'Awn al-murid sharh jawharit al-tawhid,* p.766.

[590] Al-Bukhari (3304).

[591] Al-Bukhari (3268) and Muslim (2189).

[592] Tafsir al-Tabari, tafsir Ibn Kathir, tafsir al-Jalalin, tafsir hashiyat al-Sawi ala al-Jalalin, tafsir al-Baydawi.

[593] Qur'an, 80:1-2.

[594] Qur'an, 88:21-2.

[595] Qur'an, 18:6.

[596] Tafsir al-Razi.

loudly to him, as you speak loudly to one another"[597] with the next verse elaborating, "***Those who lower their voices before Allah's Messenger—those are they whose hearts Allah has tested for piety***" and the following two verses describing how the companions should conduct themselves, "***Indeed, those who call you, [O Muhammad], from behind the chambers - most of them do not use reason. And had they been patient until you [could] come out to them, would have been better for them. But God is Forgiving and Merciful***".

The Prophet ﷺ was ordered to discipline the companions, "***I have been sent to bring good manners to perfection***".[598] There was no fault on his part in frowning or being disappointment. There is even context to the way he frowned. He just turned his head away.[599] There is no way he could have offended the blind man as he could not have seen this. He did not, for example, condemned him with strong words, so even in frowning he showed mercy.

An important question remains. Why then was the Prophet ﷺ corrected for moving his head away. Why did revelation come down to say "***But how do you know? Perhaps he was seeking to purify himself or be reminded, and the message would benefit him***".[600] That is because he has high standards to maintain. To ensure nobody feels less than the another and to reflect high Islamic morals where every person feels valued regardless of social, political, or economic status. Here Allah ﷻ is emphasising that the Prophet ﷺ cannot afford to even give the impression that anyone is more important or superior above the other. This is despite the fact the companion was a believer, was around the prophet ﷺ and has access to him, whereas bringing those non-believing leaders to the truth is not an everyday opportunity. Allah ﷻ referring to Abdullah Ibn Um Maktoum as "**the blind**" was to show there was more of a reason to have focused on him as a matter of priority.[601]

But still, this can be argued for the leaders. For them it could also have been they were seeking to purify themselves. Here Allah ﷻ Himself ends this argument giving priority to the believer over the *elites of Quraysh*. The verses go on to criticise those leaders, saying "***as for the self-satisfied. To him you give attention. Though there is no blame upon you if he does not attain purity***".[602] Described as being 'self-satisfied' out of arrogance. They believed to be above the need for reminding and guidance, and with a feeling of great self-worth due to their status and wealth.[603] The Qur'an is drawing attention not to what they showed in their outer but how they felt in their inner, whereas Abdullah Ibn Um Maktoum was outwardly showing interest in learning and "***Perhaps he was seeking***" inwardly. Then comes a firm instruction, "***Never again! Indeed [in these verses] is a reminder***".[604] This was not reproach against the Prophet ﷺ but rather in his favour, for several reasons:

1. Out of the two options the Prophet ﷺ had, he chose the harder one in trying to bring [arrogant] leaders to the truth whereas the companion was actively seeking, persistently. Dealing with such eagerness and commitment is an easier task compared to those who require more time and effort in explaining, convincing and perhaps going as

---

597 Qur'an, 49:2.

598 Ahmad (8952), Malik (1733), al-Bukahri in *al-adab al-mufrad* (274). Islam gathers in the one religion all manners and brings it to the highest level as it provides the link between human virtues and Allah ﷻ's acceptance and reward.

599 Tafsir al-Tabari, tafsir al-Razi, tafsir al-Qurtubi.

600 Qur'an, 80:3-4.

601 Tafsir al-Razi.

602 Qur'an, 80:5-7.

603 Tafsir hashiyat al-Sawi ala al-Jalalin, tafsir al-Qurtubi, tafsir Ibn Kathir, tafsir al-Nasafi, tafsir zad al-masir.

604 Qur'an, 80:11.

far as debating and refuting, and on top of that the anticipated outcome is never guaranteed. It is clear the Prophetﷺ did not choose out of desire or convenience.[605]

2. Although, in the sight of the Prophetﷺ, this was a matter of judgement and priority (a thin line) and not a matter of right and wrong, the lesson for the Prophetﷺ was that he should not strain himself for bringing people to the truth, "*so whoever wills - let him believe; and whoever wills - let him disbelieve*".[606]

3. He knew the companion Abdullah Ibn Um Maktoum had belief and therefore some degree of knowledge of the religion while the non-believers require more guidance and teaching, but still, he cannot allow even an assumption that Islam places leaders over individuals or allows status to dictate importance or priority, even though everyone falls under his responsibility in delivering the message. This is an example of Allah﷾'s support and guidance for His prophets and messengers in ensuring a fine balance is always maintained.

Prophet Muhammadﷺ always represented the truth and honoured it. He showed, practically, his gratefulness for being corrected. Every time he used to see Abdullah Ibn Um Maktoum he would happily greet him with praise, saying "***greetings to the one on whose behalf I was admonished by Allah***".[607]

"***...and his eyes became white***"[608] [i.e., he lost his sight]

In the story of Yusuf (chapter 12), Prophet Ya'qub lost his eyesight. There is an opinion it was not total blindness, but his eyes became clouded limiting his sight.[609] Even if he had lost his sight completely, this was temporary due to sadness over the absence of his son Prophet Yusuf, but then, "***he regained his sight***".[610] In-between, it did not affect his duty as a prophet. As for the claim that Prophet Shu'aib was blind, this is unfounded.[611]

Moreover, prophets and messengers are free from contagious diseases as this would hinder them fulfilling their duty. If there was a disconnection between their ability to fulfil their duty in spreading the message and ability to connect with people (who will distance themselves to avoid being infected), then surely the message will not be spread, so there becomes no purpose or wisdom in sending that prophet or messenger in the first place. However, the reality according to the Qur'an in several passages was that they were closely connected with people. They were not speaking from high podiums, nor did they set up monthly surgeries for when people had questions can visit them for answers. They were amongst the people, serving people, guiding people, and devoted to the happiness and salvation of people. There were no barriers separating them. Several verses confirm they were not far from them, rather were 'with' them:

Prophet Muhammadﷺ: "***that the Messenger and those who believed <u>with him</u> said, "When is Allah's victory?"***".[612]
Prophet Hud: "***And when Our decree came, We saved Hud and those who believed <u>with him</u>***".[613]

---

[605] Tafsir al-Sha'rawi.

[606] Qur'an, 18:29. See also Qur'an, 2:137, 3:20.

[607] Tafsir al-Qurtubi.

[608] Qur'an, 12:84.

[609] Tafsir al-Alusi.

[610] Qur'an, 12:96.

[611] Al-Tattan, A., al-Kilani, M. *Awn al-murid sharh jawharat al-tawhid*, p.766.

[612] Qur'an, 2:214. See also Qur'an, 9:88 and 66:8.

[613] Qur'an, 11:58.

Prophet Salih: "**Then, when Our command came, We saved Salih and those who believed <u>with him</u>**".[614]

Prophet Shu'aib: "**And when Our command came, We saved Shu'aib and those who believed <u>with him</u>**".[615]

Prophet Musa: it was the disbelievers (Pharaoh, Hamaan, and Quaroon) who confirmed this, having said, "**kill the sons of those who have believed <u>with him</u>**".[616]

Just as they were attributed to their people not as fellow citizens or members of the community, but 'brothers' as mentioned in chapter 23: "**Their <u>brother</u> Noah said to them**" (verse 106), "**When their <u>brother</u> Hud said to them**" (verse 124), "**When their <u>brother</u> Saleh said to them**" (verse 142), "**When their <u>brother</u> Lut said to them**" (verse 161).

"And they ate from it…Thus Adam disobeyed his Lord"[617]

Reading this at surface level can be misleading. A prophet "**ate from it**" when told not to, and "**disobeyed his Lord**"!

One important consideration when attempting to properly understanding stories of the Qur'an, of prophets or any religious matter, is to bring together all verses and hadiths relating to the subject matter and understand in context. This is how scholars of Islam deal with text, gaining thorough understanding and deep insight. When we put together verses of prophet Adam's story, we can start to gather much needed information and context. But only if is [methodical] approach is taken.

Firstly, many people think Adam was supposed to remain in Paradise but because he ate from the tree, was punished by being sent down to earth. This is not correct. When Allah﷾ informed the angels of His new creation of humans (starting with Adam), He also mentioned where they would be placed to reside, "**I am placing a successor**[618]**on earth**".[619] So while the verse we are discussing: "**And they ate from it**" is in chapter 20, the part of his story mentioning he would reside on earth is in chapter 2. In is essential both are put together (for that part of the full story at least).

Adam was told regarding the tree, "**Live with your wife in Paradise and eat as freely as you please, but do not approach this tree**".[620] And later "**they ate from it.**" What happened in-between is where lessons are being taught. Satan whispered to Adam saying, "**O Adam! Shall I direct you the Tree of eternity and a kingdom that does not fade away?**"[621] although Allah﷾ promised Adam eternal bounties in Paradise,[622] warning "**Indeed this is an enemy to you and to your wife. Then let him not remove you from Paradise**". Whilst it was already destined Adam would leave Paradise, it was at the same time of his interaction with Satan he was made to descend to earth, intended to be a learning experience that showed how Satan can be a reason for destruction and suffering hence the verse concludes, "**for you [O Adam] would then suffer**".[623]

We are being taught there are deceptions in life. Feeling of everlastingness, true happiness, and comfort, that can be portrayed in many ways and decorated. One must be conscious of two important principles:

---

[614] Qur'an, 11:66.

[615] Qur'an, 11:94.

[616] Qur'an, 40:24-5.

[617] Qur'an, 20:121.

[618] The word used in the Qur'an is *khalifah*: successor, or generations of mankind, one following another.

[619] Qur'an, 2:30.

[620] Qur'an, 2:35.

[621] Qur'an, 20:120.

[622] Qur'an, 20:118-9.

[623] Qur'an, 20:117.

(1) How Allah﷾ describes something is the reality of what it is. So, "**do not let the present life deceive you**"[624] for it is temporary, perishable and its [supposed] pleasure are merely symbolic.

(2) Ultimate power lies in the hand of Allah﷾ alone. No matter how much a person, the self (*nafs*) or Satan try to beautify something, they have no self-power to action or guarantee you gaining it. They are simply shifting between hope and deception. The command of Allah﷾ is where real success and happiness is and one must be careful of their ways and choices, "**Did I not command you, O Children of Adam, not to follow Satan, for he is truly your sworn enemy, but worship Me [alone]? This is the Straight Path**".[625]

Prophets and messengers do not sin. So how do we understand this if Adam still ate from the tree?
The Qur'an clarifies, "**we once made a covenant with Adam, but he <u>forgot</u>, and We found <u>not in him determination</u>**".[626] A sin is considered one when there is deliberate intent to commit. Adam had no intent. In a *hadith,* the Prophetﷺ makes this distinction, "**Allah has forgiven my nation for mistakes and forgetfulness, and what they are forced to do**".[627]

We must also know that Adam interacted with angels just like he interacted with Satan.[628] To know that angels are the righteously obedient and Satan is disobeying and transgressing. Angels will support you[629] and Satan will obstruct you. We can relate to the angels who will protect and reassure us[630] but Satan will attempt to demolish and deviate us. Allah﷾ says, "**and do not follow the footsteps of Satan**"[631] but does not leave us. He exposes to us through this story his tactics and strengthens our conscious that, "**Indeed, he is to you a clear enemy**"[632] whereas angels "**glorify the praise of their Lord and seek forgiveness for those on earth**".[633]

Adam's experience in Paradise was temporary and purposeful. One of the Qur'an's methods in instilling its teachings is through stories and illustration which helps draw the reader's mind close to understanding the revelation purpose and objectives. These incidents are meant for our learning and refining. "**Indeed, in that is a lesson**" is repeated throughout the Qur'an as an ongoing reminder.[634] Adam's interacting with Satan is mentioned in several passages and chapters, with each giving detail and new dimension. Once all pieces of the picture are put together, a story or event can be understood in an objective and coherent way.[635]

---

[624] Qur'an, 35:5.

[625] Qur'an, 36:60-1.

[626] Qur'an, 20:115.

[627] Ibn Majah (2045).

[628] Qur'an, 38:71-4.

[629] Qur'an, 3:124-5.

[630] Qur'an, 41:30.

[631] Qur'an, 2:168, 33:56.

[632] Qur'an, 2:168.

[633] Qur'an, 42:5.

[634] See Qur'an, 12:111, 16:66, 23:21, 24:44, 79:26.

[635] This coherence (*nazm*) can be verses in a single chapeter and extend to pared chapters, and a group of chapters. Mir, M. *Coherence in the Qur'an*, p.5.

"Two disputants; one of us has wronged the other; so judge between us fairly, and do not be biased"[636]

This is the story of Prophet Dawud with the Angels who came to him seeking judgment over a supposed dispute. The idea was to test Dawud and draw our attention to several considerations through this story of the Qur'an. These real-life examples guide the reader to better understand the message in its practical manifestation, increases the knowledge of high principles and encourage everyone to embrace the truth and justice with balance and attentively.

Two angels came to Prophet Dawud in the form of humans, taking him by surprise climbing over the wall into his prayer chamber at night despite requesting not to be disturbed, so [637] **"he took fright."** [638] They assured him, **"Do not be afraid"** explaining they came unexpectedly seeking a resolve to a dispute: **"This brother of mine has ninety nine ewes, and I have just one ewe, and he said, 'Let me take charge of her,' and he pressured me overpowering with words"**.[639] i.e., my brother had no regard for my poverty and despite his wealth wants to take charge of my only ewe.

Two questions may already come to mind:

(1) How can one of the angels be at fault when angels **"do not disobey their Lord"**?[640]

(2) If they are both not at fault, how can they claim to have a dispute when there is none? Is this not a lie and a sin?

Here they were not talking about themselves but posing an example using themselves as two parties. [641] Like saying, for example, "*if someone hits my car, what should I do.*" This does not necessarily mean the person's car was hit. It could relate to someone else or this person is questioning how people should react in such situations or just wanting a different opinion on the matter. So, they did not have a dispute amongst themselves, nor did they claim to. Another thing to bear in mind, what was the purpose of one of them mentioning the small number of ewes he had (just one) versus the ninety-nine his brother had? The focus should be on whether he has the right to take it or not regardless of who had what. We shall see why that angel presented the dispute in this way.

We are told Dawud heard from the claimant (but perhaps not from the defendant). It can be understood his focus was on the self-claimed vulnerable and innocent one with less. He ruled, **"He has definitely wronged you in demanding [to add] your ewe to his"**[642] but realised his misjudgement and understood this was a test, **"Then David realised We had tested him so he asked his Lord's forgiveness, fell down in prostration, and turned [to Him] in repentance"**.[643] The verse goes on to remove any ambiguity in the mind of the reader about the status and high regard for Dawud as a prophet following this incident, **"So We forgave him. And indeed he will have [a status of] closeness to Us and an honourable destination"**. It was fitting for him

---

[636] Qur'an, 38:22.

[637] Tafsir Ibn Kathir.

[638] Qur'an, 38:22.

[639] Qur'an, 38:23.

[640] Qur'an, 53:5-6, 81:19-21, 66:6, 2:30. Muslim (7495).

[641] Tafsir al-kashaf, tafsir al-Qasimi. Similar to how Prophet Ibrahim was adddressing as one the people in refuting their worship of idols as gods. See Qur'an, 6:76-8

[642] Qur'an, 38:24. Tafsir al-Qurtubi.

[643] Qur'an, 38:24.

to be corrected as he was to become a ruler, later showing true qualities of leadership and wisdom, "***And Allah blessed David with leadership and wisdom and taught him what He willed***".[644]

The conclusion is that these angels were sent to Dawud for him and us to see where judgement can go wrong and that inference and emotions has its limits, where evidence is required.[645] Everyone in their areas of judgment and responsibilities are being reminded. A parent with their child, teacher with their student, or a leader with their people.

One must also remember, regardless of what Dawud did or did not do, Allah ﷻ had destined this story carve out in this way and be a reason to deepen in the mind of the reader high principles of justice and fairness. Remember, the Qur'an is not a book of historical events, it is a book of guidance. A means for us to conduct ourselves in line with divine standards of integrity at times of judgement and conflict resolve. Just like Adam was destined to eat from the tree so we can learn the tactics of Satan, and as Prophet Muhammed ﷺ was destined to frown the companion so we can take wisdom and guidance from that. The reader is being reminded in last verse of chapter 12, "***in their stories there is truly a lesson for those who ponder and reason***", concluding the verse and chapter, **"*never was it [i.e., the Qur'an] a narration invented, but a confirmation of what was before it and a detailed explanation of all things and guidance and mercy for people who believe*"**.[646]

Another important point to note is how Allah ﷻ presented the story of Dawud by first saying, "***<u>have you heard</u> the story of the two disputants***".[647] Drawing attention to something important, something relevant to the reader. As mentioned earlier in this book, "*the divine miracle of the Qur'an is that it speaks to you, and you will find your own life story in it*". And mentioned also, "*It is talking to you. It relates to you and serves you. Every verse. All of it*".

It is addressing our conscious, highlighting the importance of reflecting and contemplating. Similarly, in the story of Musa, "***<u>have you heard</u> the story of Musa***"[648] just as many stories and events start with "***have you heard the story of***"[649] and even used more than once for the same story to draw the reader's attention to a new dimension(s), event(s), or lesson(s).[650]

In summary, it is about us. The prophets have departed, and mankind remain. Who through these lessons are guided to disciplined and uprightness.

"***...so Moses struck him and put an end to him***"[651]

The apparent meaning could be problematic for some. How can someone infallible attack someone leading to their death? This incident started with two men fighting. The verse describes, "***He [Moses] found in it two men fighting - one of his own sect, and one from his enemies. The one of his sect solicited his assistance against the one from his enemies***" Musa then intervened to assist and "***struck him and put an end to him***." He had no intention of harming, just attempted to stop harm inflicted upon a Jewish man from the abuse of another man. When refusing to stop and set him free he intervened.

---

644 Qur'an, 2:251.

645 Tafsir al-Qasimi.

646 Qur'an, 12:111.

647 Qur'an, 38:21.

648 Qur'an, 20:9.

649 See Qur'an, 51:24, 85:17, 88:1.

650 Prophet Musa in 20:9 and again in 79:15.

651 Qur'an, 28:15.

There are two scholarly opinions on the death:

1st opinion: although he did not attempt to harm, it still led to his death. Therefore, "**and put an end to him**" refers to Musa, unintentionally, while attempting to separate the victim and the transgressor.[652] The man could not bear the strength and power of Musa who was known to be very strong with a large body structure and figure[653] so the impact was great. The verse before describes, "**And when he [Moses] attained his full strength**".[654] An example of that strength was his ability to carry a large rock alone which ten others could not carry together.[655]

He then said, "**This is from the work of Satan**" meaning this whole incident from the start, the conflict between the two men was the plot of Satan, as one of his tactics is to cause frictions and divide.[656] As Musa was concerned about the social consequences, he felt regret and yearned, "**My Lord, indeed I have wronged myself, so forgive me**".[657] A person may apologise to another not necessarily for any wrongdoing (and sometimes with the person apologising not even involved altogether) such as "I am sorry you lost your job." Simply a heartfelt expression that they had hoped things could have worked out differently or any inflictions could have been avoided.

Another view is that man - the enemy - was a combatant where defence and attack is permitted which may lead to death. Saying, "**This is from the work of Satan**" referring to the oppressor as his actions were Satanic.[658]

2nd opinion: the death came with the punch not from it, "**put an end to him**" referring to Allahﷻ not Musa. Meaning Allahﷻ ended his life as he was destined to die at that moment not from the hit but at the time of the hit.[659] We even see this today. A person can be subjected to a car accident or assault, but a post-mortem examination shows they died from something other than or prior to the actual hit of the car or the physical assault.

"*Those who follow the Messenger, the Unlettered Prophet*"[660]

Prophet Muhammadﷺ could not read or write! Yes. Allahﷻ destined a prophet would be sent and He too destined he would not read and write. Allahﷻ knows best. Some may be surprised. Why? Because they are judging according to the circumstances we live today, that reading and writing is a necessity and an inability to is a flaw. Restricting understanding of such matters to a specific time/generation, place or expectation context can cloud understanding of Prophet Muhammadﷺ's message.

Every messenger came with their miracle. As Prophet Muhammadﷺ's miracle was the Qur'an, for this to be a challenge and extraordinary and for people to appreciate it, they needed to be focused on its content, wording, rhetoric and

---

[652] Tafsir al-Tabari, tafsir al-Razi, tafsir al-Baghawi, tafsir zad al-masir, tafsir al-Jalalin, tafsir hashiyat al-Sawi ala al-Jalalin.

[653] Qur'an, 28:26. See tafsir al-Tabari.

[654] Qur'an, 28:14.

[655] Tafsir Ibn Kathir (Qur'an, 28:26).

[656] Qur'an, 5:91. See tafsir al-Qurtubi and tafsir al-Sha'rawi.

[657] Qur'an, 28:16. See tafsir hashiyat al-Sawi ala al-Jalalin, Tafsir al-Baydawi.

[658] Tafsir al-Razi, tafsir hashiyat al-Sawi ala al-Jalalin.

[659] Tafsir al-tahrir wa al-tanwir, tafsir al-muharar al-wajiz.

[660] Qur'an, 7:157.

miraculousness and not be distracted with accusations and debate over the possibility of it been written by the Prophet﷽. It could not have. He did not read or write. The same goes for all the knowledge he had. It could not have been taught to him. He had no teachers. And if he did, surely, they would have started by teaching him the easiest and most basic thing, reading and writing![661] This shows how every plan Allah﷽ executes is measured. Being unlettered, the Prophet﷽ could not have produced the Qur'an himself which, as proof, confirms it is preserved and miraculous, and confirms the legitimacy of his prothethood.[662]

If Allah﷽ has destined the Prophet﷽ read and write, he would have been the best of writers and the most profound, owing to his perfection in everything about him and everything he does.

> *"O prophet! Why do you prohibit [yourself from] what Allah has made lawful for you, seeking to please your wives?"*[663]

Prophet Muhammad﷽ making something permissible prohibited! And for pleasing his wives over pleasing his Lord! By now, after reading this verse, the thought of even 'seemingly' should not even come to mind. Why? Because it cannot even be imagined to be true that a prophet﷽ would change a ruling of Allah﷽. Especially after knowing in the principles of *aqidah*, under what is Necessary, they have the attributes of truthfulness, trustworthiness and spreading the message as it is. Interpreting verses, hadiths, incidents, and stories of prophets in a way that goes against their infallibility is rejected. Gaining more information, commentary and depth of meaning is balance, a level of maturity, and will allow the reader to appreciate and benefit from this divine book.

Again, bringing together verses and hadiths in any subject matter gives insight and understanding. Alongside the verse mentioned above, we have a hadith that gives a detailed account and background information of what happened. Sayidah Aisha, a witness herself, reported:

> *"The Prophet, peace and blessings be upon him, would spend time with his wife Zainab bint Jahsh and he would drink a concoction of honey. Hafsa and I agreed that whomever the Prophet visited first, we would say, "I notice a strong odour of mimosa gum on you." The Prophet visited one of them and she said this to him, so the Prophet said: I have taken a honey drink at Zainab's house and I will not do it again. The verse was revealed: Why do you forbid yourself from what Allah has made lawful for you?"*[664]

Let us break this up into specific clear points:
- The Prophet﷽'s wives Aisha and Hafsa were upset he was spending time with his wife Zainab
- They knew he had a honey drink when visiting her
- They secretly agreed to pretend to be offended by the smell of that honey (*odour*)
- The Prophet﷽ did not want to cause them discomforted, so he swore an oath never to drink it again
- The verse was revealed telling him not to prohibit what is lawful

---

[661] Tafsir al-Razi (7:157).

[662] Al-Baqillani, A. *I'jaz al-qur'an*, pp.48-51. Tafsir al-Baydawi.

[663] Qur'an, 66:1.

[664] Muslim (3678).

The questions now are:

Did the Prophetﷺ overturn or adjust a divine ruling or was he just preventing <u>himself</u>?

Did he say "no one is to drink this honey drink"

Did he seek to please his wives out of desire, or did he do it out of mercy and goodwill?

Even though he only prevented himself, he was still told "**Why do you prohibit [yourself from] what Allah has made lawful for you?**" Why burden yourself? Why limit the bounties Allah﷾ has bestowed upon you? Here the Prophetﷺ was acting according to his <u>human</u> side whereas the Qur'an referred to his <u>prophetic</u> side: "**O prophet.**" This confirms that Allah﷾ not only divinely protects prophets and messengers themselves but also the message, by preventing the Prophetﷺ's personal choice/preference be interpreted as a religious command (honey drink becoming impermissible). In the verse itself it is evident the Prophetﷺ did not mean to forbid the drink as a religious command. We see the permissibility of the drink was attributed to Allah﷾ ("**what Allah has made lawful** ') and the [assumed] prohibition attributed to the prophet ("**Why do you prohibit**'). Here two opposites that cannot form a single command. So, there is no religious command prohibiting. He merely prohibited himself as a personal choice.

In one story the Prophetﷺ is told not overburden himself for the *Elites of Quraysh* and here told not to overburden by preventing himself from what is allowed. All verses are interrelated in this coherent and well-connected book. In this regard the Qur'an states a general principle, "**God wants for you ease and does not want for you hardship**",[665] a reminder for us through him. The many imbalances we fall into in different areas of life and self-created hardships.

The question still stands. Was the Prophetﷺ's judgement correct? No, it was not. But at the same time it was not a sin and it did not arise from or was driven by desire, "**Nor does he speak out of [his own] desire**".[666] The word in Arabic used to describe "**he does not speak**" (*wa ma yantiq*) does not refer to a given moment but refers to past, present and future, always. This is his nature and character.

"**Your Companion [i.e., Muhammad] has not strayed, nor has he erred**[667]"[668] i.e., he remains infallible and has not mistaken or done wrong in his actions. Strayed referring to intentionally and erred referring to [even] unintentionally.[669] Bringing together these verses draws the conclusion that he: [670]

"**Has not strayed**' i.e. he is on a path

"**Nor has he erred**' i.e., the path he is on is straight.

"**Nor does he speak out of [his own] desire**" i.e., his character is harmonious with this straight path. A person can be on a journey or path but their character and attitude be a reason for them to be disconnected, lack harmony with it or be veiled from benefiting from it.

---

[665] Qur'an, 2:185.

[666] Qur'an, 53:3.

[667] Mistaken or incorrect.

[668] Qur'an 53:2.

[669] Tafsir al-tashil le 'loum al-tanzil.

[670] Tafsir al-Razi.

Finally, no one heard this revelation as it came down to him, but still, he revealed and spread these very words of Allah☻:

"*Why do you prohibit [yourself from] what Allah has made lawful for you?*" although he knew it would be recited untill the End of Time and spread widely, correcting him. This is because truthfulness, trustworthiness and delivering the message completely are 'Necessary' qualities and attributes of prophets and messengers. And again, Necessary means it cannot not be.

Conclusion

Prophethood and infallibility is not something they trained themselves to be or develop into but is bestowed by Allah☻. It is appropriate and perfectly normal that prophet or messenger are put through such experience for several considerations and educational objectives:

- The stories of prophets are stories of human beings like us. The Creator of all humans of course knows how to address and guide them in the most suitable way that brings about success and salvation, "*your Lord knows you best*".[671] Religious discipline is being instilled through reading their practical experiences and instructive lessons. The teaching methods of the Qur'an are fitting to our human nature and structure (physically, mentally, spiritually).

- They fall into situations we can also fall into, highlighting relevance of such matters to us today and every day, and how it was resolved. This in turn helps us to be conscious and cautious, proactive and alert, adjust our ways and approaches, and avoid where necessary.

- To observe how their actions were closely monitored by Allah☻. No worthy matter was left unresolved, nor were prophets spared reminding, ensuring the message remains pure and objective, "*Allah does not shy away from of the truth*", [672] i.e., does not refrain from revealing the truth and clarify.[673]

They had no self-power. They relied on Allah☻ for support and steadfastness, guiding them through their prophethood and adjusting their ways to be in line with the highest level of representation. Allah Almighty puts things straight, "*Had We not made you steadfast, you probably would have inclined to them a little*".[674]

In conclusion, a Muslim's belief centres round the undoubtful fact that prophets and messengers are of the highest status and regard. One should not allow himself to utter the slightest remark that would even infer deranking their status, honour, or due respect. It is only Allah☻ who can apply to them any treatment He deems fit for them.

---

[671] Qur'an, 17:54.

[672] Qur'an, 33:53.

[673] Tafsir al-Qurtubi, tafsir Ibn Kathir, tafsir al-Baydawi, tafsir Al-muharrar al-wajiz, tafsir zad al-masir.

[674] Qur'an, 17:74.

The duties of prophets and messengers

There are many wisdoms in how Allah☻ perfectly plans things out for humanity in sending prophets and messengers, "*Indeed in that is a reminder for whoever has a heart or cares to listen attentively*".[675] This includes:

- Inviting and persuading humanity to the worship of Allah☻ alone.

Their main duty they were extremely devoted to. To save every soul. To guide every human being to happiness and successes in this life and the Next through the worship of the only Lord, "*And We certainly sent into every nation a messenger, [saying], "Worship God and shun false gods*".[676] *And teach them the names and attributes of their Lord*".[677]

They did this through invitation and persuasion not by forcing anyone to believe or compulsion. Islam is a belief and belief sits in the heart, so persuasion has to come from within "*there is no compulsion in religion*".[678] Every person decides for himself and faces the consequences of their choice, "*for the truth stands out clearly from falsehood*".[679] Their duty and those who come after is to preach and explain, respond to misconceptions and address ignorance, "*so that they may reflect*".[680] They were required to show patience when enduing hardship and the rude nature of some non-believers, responding with a soft and gentle heart as a means to calling them to the correct path, "*Go, both of you, to Pharaoh. Indeed, he has transgressed. And speak to him with gentle speech that perhaps he may be reminded or fear [God]*".[681] It was never about them, but the message and only the message, "*By Allah, he [Prophet Muhammad] never took revenge for himself concerning any matter*"[682] and although they were devoted to helping humanity, they were regularly reminded the liability lies on the people not on them. The conclusion to this being, "*If they have surrendered, then they are guided; but if they turn away, then your duty is [only] to convey*".[683]

- To be a good example

The benefit of this is for people to see the practical implementation of the religion's teachings. Not just in the way they presented themselves, spoke or dressed. But inwardly and outwardly. The mercy and concern they had for others, conviction to save every soul and revive the state of humanity, their sincerity and truthfulness, their charity and generosity etc. This became a powerful means for people to accept the message because:

a) Through good character and sincerity, they are approachable, kind, gentle, and accommodating

b) People see the message is practical, actionable, holistic, and harmonious

c) Learn through observation, as a powerful method, "*Those are the ones whom God has guided, so from their guidance take an example*".[684] "*Indeed, in the Messenger of God you have an excellent example [to follow]*".[685]

---

675 Qur'an, 50:37.

676 Qur'an, 16:36.

677 Qur'an, 7:180.

678 Qur'an, 2:256.

679 Qur'an, 2:256. Revealed when some Muslims tried to force Jews and Christians to convert to Islam after the Prophet☻'s migration, prohibiting forcefull or pressured conversion.

680 Qur'an, 16:44.

681 Qur'an, 20:43-4.

682 Al-Bukhari (6786).

683 Qur'an, 3:20.

684 Qur'an, 6:90.

685 Qur'an, 33:21.

- To demonstrate balance and objectivity

For several reasons people create for themselves from time-to-time imbalances. This is owed to flaws and limitations. Prophets and messengers show how a balance and measured approach should be in all our affairs; worldly gains, relationships, responsibilities, interactions, and to balance between immediate pleasures of this worldly life and the Next, "**Seek the [reward] of the Hereafter by means of what God has granted you, yet do not neglect your rightful share of this world**"[686] as there is no exception or exemption for anyone, "**On that Day [of judgement], you will be asked about the [worldly] gains and pleasures**".[687] You are taught to enjoy the bounties of God but to show gratefulness and gratitude and at the same time, "**And as for the favour of your Lord, speak of it**".[688] With everything comes responsibility and balance, which comes with teaching people purpose in life and awakening their hearts to realities, "**Did you think that We had created you without a purpose, and that you will never be returned to Us?**"[689]

They showed balance and justice through:

1) Their leadership, "**Judge between them [O Muhammad] by what God has revealed, and do not follow their desires over the truth that has come to you**".[690]

2) Staying firm on the teachings of the divine commands, "**[We said], "O David, indeed We have made you an authority over the land, so judge between the people in truth and do not follow [your own] desire**".[691]

3) Being objective, not to shying away from stating clearly there is both reward and punishment, pleasure and torture. Balance requires matters to be described as they are. They were sent to convey clearly, "**whoever follows My guidance will neither go astray [in the world] nor suffer [in the Hereafter]**"[692] and those who do not follow His guidance, "**will have a life of hardship [i.e., difficulty and misery]**".[693] As for the Hereafter, "**whoever obeys God and His Messenger will be admitted to gardens [in Paradise]**"[694] but also "**whoever disobeys God and His Messenger and transgresses His limits - He will put him into the Fire to abide eternally therein, and he will have a humiliating punishment**".[695]

---

[686] Qur'an, 28:77.

[687] Qur'an: 102:8. Al-Tirmidhi (2584).

[688] Qur'an, 93:11.

[689] Qur'an, 23:115.

[690] Qur'an, 5:48.

[691] Qur'an, 38:26.

[692] Qur'an, 20:123.

[693] Qur'an, 20:124.

[694] Qur'an, 4:13.

[695] Qur'an, 4:14.

In additional to teaching the core principles of belief, they were each sent to deal with an issue(s) and/or imbalance(s) humanity was faced with during their time (social, intellectual etc), and which recurred in later times (even today), aiming to spread necessary awareness and resolve. This could be a corrupt ideology, philosophy, mannerism, or any form of corruption.

For example:

Secularism: separating religion from day-to-day affairs. This did not merely evolve in the 'Middle Ages' in Europe, a similar ideology or way of thinking goes back to the time of Prophet Shu'aib, they asked 'sarcastically', "***O Shu'aib! Does your prayer command you that we should abandon what our forefathers worshipped or give up managing our wealth as we please? Indeed, you are such a tolerant, sensible man!***"[696] claiming there cannot be a link between prayer and managing their monetary affairs (business ethics), rejecting a relationship between God-consciousness (*taqwa*), prayer and righteousness and between financial dealings, as if to say religion has nothing to do with economy. By gathering all the verses in his story, a picture is formed on the divine way this is dealt with and how Allah﷾ taught Prophet Shu'aib how to refute.

"***We already sent messengers before you. We have told you the stories of some of them, while others We have not***".[697] This verse is a clear indicator on how practical and purposeful the Qur'an is. The 25 who were [only] mentioned were done so for a valid reason, practicality and to serve the needs and flaws of the society they were sent to and humanity thereafter. Other examples include:

- The story of Prophet Musa addressing those who asked to physically see God and how the Quran responds to ideologies that rely solely on material and physical things[698]
- The story of Prophet Lut addressing homosexuality and sexual perversion
- The story of Prophet Hud addressing military dictatorship, tyranny, greed, control and imperialism[699], and the delusion of an everlasting empire which was the ambition of several nations in history and today.

Following Prophet Muhammadﷺ

It is an obligation upon every Muslim to practice the teaching of the Prophetﷺ which should not be neglected for anyone else's word,[700] "***Whatever the Messenger has given you - accept; and what he has forbidden you - refrain from***".[701] "***O you who believe! Obey Allah and obey the Messenger***".[702]

---

[696] Qur'an, 11:87
[697] Qur'an, 4:164.
[698] Qur'an, 2:55. See tafsir al-Tabari.
[699] A strategy a country adopts to extend it's power and influence through colonisation, use of military force, or other means.
[700] Imam Malik in *al-maqasid al-hasanah* (815), imam al-Shafi'i in *al-um* (8/741).
[701] Qur'an, 59:7. Al-Bukhari (7288), Muslim (6115), Ahmad (7501).
[702] Qur'an, 4:59.

A Muslim must believe Allah Almighty sent down divine scripture to guide people to the right path, teach them good and bad, warn them, and communicate commands and prohibitions, "***Mankind was [of] one religion [before their deviation]; then God sent the prophets as bringers of good tidings and warners and sent down with them the Book [i.e., the books] in truth to judge between the people in which they differed***".[703]

Revelation was first sent in the form of pages called *Suhuf* and in the form of large volumes called *Kutub*. The later books containing universal messages are:

The Qur'an (*al-quran*), The Torah (*al-taurat*), The Gospel (*al-injeel*), The Psalms (*al-zabour*).

The Qur'an *(al-quran)*

The Qur'an is the greatest of all books, sent through the greatest of angels, Jibril, revealed to the greatest of prophets and messengers, Muhammadﷺ. As it is the word of God it is free from flaws and error. It is useful to highlight some of its key features to show how it differentiates from any other book known to mankind:

- Undoubtably sent down from God, "***And indeed, it [the Qur'ān] is the revelation of the Lord of the worlds. Brought down by the Trustworthy Spirit [i.e., Angel Jibril]***",[704] "***On the night of Glory***".[705]

- Free from deviance from the truth and crookedness, making it upright, accurate so "***unerringly straight***".[706]

- Free from contradictions, "***If it had been from [any] other than God, they would have found within it many inconsistencies***"[707] and "***free from distortion***".[708]

- Powerful and causes admiring respect mixed with fear of God, expressed remarkabley in the Qur'an "***Had We sent down this Qur'an upon a mountain, you would have seen it humbled and torn apart in awe of God***".[709]

- Powerful effect of its words, "***if there were a recitation that could cause mountains to move, or the earth to split, or the dead to speak, [it would have been this Qur'an]***".[710]

- Its miraculous nature is a challenge to both humans and jinn, "***Say, [O Prophet], "If [the whole of] mankind and Jinn were to come together to produce an equivalent to this Qur'an, they could not produce like it, no matter how supported each other***".[711] And challenges accordingly: "***Or do they say, "He [the Prophet] has fabricated this [Qur'an]!"? Say, [O Prophet] "produce ten fabricated chapters like it and seek help from whoever you can – other***

---

[703] Qur'an, 2:213.

[704] Qur'an, 26:192-3.

[705] Qur'an, 97:1. Other names: Night of Decree, Night of Power which falls in the last ten days of the month of Ramadan

[706] Qur'an, 18:1.

[707] Qur'an, 4:82.

[708] Qur'an, 39:28.

[709] Qur'an, 59:21.

[710] Qur'an, 13:31.

[711] Qur'an, 17:88.

than God – if what you say is true!"[712] and inviting them to produce not ten chapters, but even "***Produce one chapter like it, and seek help from whoever you can***".[713]

The Qur'an has been described in many ways, giving insight to its nature: guidance, the distinction [between right and wrong], The differentiator,[714] The conclusive proof and evidence,[715] The truth,[716] A mighty message, The momentous,[717] A sufficient message for humanity,[718] A spirit,[719] A teaching, warning, and admonition,[720] A healing and cure,[721] Most beautiful message, best of statement, A coherent book,[722] Wisdom,[723] decisive and unassailable scripture,[724] A noble book,[725] Glorious and honoured,[726] The great,[727] clear, detailed and perfectly explained scripture,[728] Which falsehood cannot reach.[729]

It has 30 parts, 114 chapters, 6616 verses, 77,934 words and 333,761 letters.

Preserved for over 1400 years, it shall continue to be until the End of Time, "***We [God] have sent down the Qur'ān Ourself, and We Ourself will preserve and guardian it***".[730] Preserved in several ways:

- In its book form where not even Satan is able to add, remove or adjust anything of it
- By means of protecting its carrier and conveyer, Prophet Muhammad🕊:[731] "***And Allah will protect you***"[732]
- Preserved in that it's miraculous Arabic wording, expressions and structure cannot be debated, nor room for improvement, or exceeded
- Preserved in the heart of many Muslims through memorisation.[733]

---

[712] Qur'an, 11:13.

[713] Qur'an, 10:38.

[714] Qur'an, 2:185, 3:4, 25:1.

[715] Qur'an, 4:174.

[716] Qur'an, 34:49, 69:51.

[717] Qur'an, 38:67, 78:2.

[718] Qur'an, 14:52.

[719] Qur'an, 42:52.

[720] Qur'an, 10:57.

[721] Qur'an, 17:82.

[722] Qur'an, 39:23.

[723] Qur'an, 36:2.

[724] Qur'an, 10:1, 41:41. Meaning it is unquestionable and cannot be defeated due to its adequacy and accuracy.

[725] Qur'an, 56:77.

[726] Qur'an, 50:1, 85:21.

[727] Qur'an, 15:87.

[728] Qur'an, 41:3.

[729] Qur'an, 41:42. See also 4:82, 10:37.

[730] Qur'an, 15:9.

[731] Tafsir al-Tabari, tafsir al-Razi, tafsir al-Kashaf, tafsir Ibn Kathir, tafsir al-Baghawi.

[732] Qur'an, 5:67.

[733] Tafsir al-Baydawi, tafsir al-muharar al-wajiz, tafsir al-Sha'rawi.

The relationship between the Qur'an and other books, Prophet Muhammadﷺ and other prophets

Believing in the other books is part of a Muslim's belief[734] and adherence to the Qur'an. Guidance from Allahﷻ has been provided throughout history, "**there was no nation but that there had passed within it a warner**",[735] ongoingly conveying the message intended for *jinn* and humanity. And as mentioned earlier, the message is one. Here we note some Qur'anic verses confirming this:

- With Ibrahimﷻ and Isma'il: "***Our Lord, and make us <u>Muslims</u> to You and from our descendants a <u>Muslim</u> nation***".[736]
- With Ya'qub: "***And Abraham instructed his sons [to do the same] and [so did] Jacob, [saying], "O my sons, indeed God has chosen for you this religion, so do not die except while you are <u>Muslims</u>***".[737]
- With Musa: "***And Moses said, "O my people, if you have believed in God, then rely upon Him, if you should be <u>Muslims</u>***".[738]
- With 'Isa: "***But when Jesus felt [persistence in] disbelief from them, he said, "Who are my supporters for [the cause of] God?" The disciples said, "We are supporters for God. We have believed in God and testify that we are <u>Muslims</u>***".[739]
- With Sulayman: "***Indeed, it is from Solomon, and indeed, it is [i.e., reads]: 'In the Name of God, the Most Compassionate, the Most Merciful, Be not haughty with me but come to me as <u>Muslims</u>***".[740]
- With the believers of Jinn: "***And among us are <u>Muslims</u>, and among us are the unjust***".[741]
- And Prophet Muhammadﷺ: "***Indeed, the religion in the sight of God is <u>Islam</u>***"[742] and in another verse: "***whoever takes other than <u>Islam</u> as religion – never will it be accepted from him***".[743]

Allahﷻ did not mention prophets and messengers in the Qur'an in a historical order. That is to highlight that Islam views them all as one. All devoted to one thing. Their focus being nothing but to convey the message to people regardless of where they are, when they were or how they lived.[744] Another core verse shows how Prophet Muhammadﷺ continues the message. He is commanded to follow the footstep of prophets before him, "***Those are the ones whom God has guided, so from their guidance take an example***".[745] This is also a confirmation he is the most complete human and prophet. To take

---

[734] Qur'an, 2:4, 2:136, 4:136.

[735] Qur'an, 35:24.

[736] Qur'an, 2:128.

[737] Qur'an, 2:132.

[738] Qur'an, 10:84.

[739] Qur'an, 3:52.

[740] Qur'an, 27:30-1.

[741] Qur'an, 72:14.

[742] Qur'an, 3:19.

[743] Qur'an, 3:85.

[744] Tafsir mawahib al-Rahman (Qur'an, 6:90).

[745] Qur'an, 6:90.

from them the best of their character means that what they all had collectively he had as one individual. This is one reason why he is worthy of being the seal of prophets and prophethood, and the best example of human perfection.[746]

The Torah (*al-taurat*)

The book revealed to Prophet Musa.

The original revelations share similar characteristics. The Qur'an describes the Torah as Light,[747] A distinction, A reminder, Detailed, Of clarity,[748] Guidance, Mercy, and Inclusive.[749]

The Qur'an spoke about some details of the Torah, "***In the Torah We prescribed for them a life for a life, an eye for an eye, a nose for a nose, an ear for an ear, a tooth for a tooth, and for wounds is legal retribution. But whoever gives [up his right as] charity, it is an expiation for him. And whoever does not judge by what God has revealed - then it is those who are the wrongdoers [i.e., the unjust]***".[750]

It described also what would happen to the Torah, being tampered with, "***Do you [believers] still expect them to be true to you, though a group of them would hear the word of God then knowingly twist and distort it, even when they understood it?***"[751] And likewise, distortion "***O Messenger! Do not let those who are quick to disbelief grieve you—from among those who say with their mouths, "We believe," but their hearts do not believe; and from among the Jews—listeners to lies, listeners to other people who did not come to you. They distort the meanings of [revealed] words and they say [to each other], "If you are given this ruling, accept it; but if you are not given it, beware." Whomever Allah has willed to divert; you have nothing for him from Allah. Those are they whose hearts Allah does not intend to purify. For them is disgrace in this world, and for them is a great punishment in the Hereafter***".[752]

"***Among the Jews are some who take words out of context, and say, "We hear and we disobey", and "Hear without listening", and "Observe us," twisting with their tongues and slandering the religion. Had they said, "We hear and we obey", and "Listen", and "Give us your attention," it would have been better for them, and more upright. But Allah has cursed them for their disbelief; they do not believe except a little***".[753]

And is harmonious with the Gospel, a continuation of the same message, "***And We sent, following in their footsteps, Jesus, the son of Mary, confirming that which came before him in the Torah; and We gave him the Gospel***".[754] "***And We did certainly give Moses the Book [i.e., the Torah] and followed up after him with messengers. And We gave Jesus, the son of Mary, clear proofs and supported him with the Pure Spirit [i.e., the Angel Jibril]***".[755]

---

[746] Tafsir al-Sha'rawi.
[747] Qur'an, 5:44.
[748] Qur'an, 21:48.
[749] Qur'an, 6:154.
[750] Qur'an, 5:45.
[751] Qur'an, 2:75.
[752] Qur'an, 5:41.
[753] Qur'an, 4:46.
[754] Qur'an, 5:46.
[755] Qur'an, 2:87.

The Gospel (*al-injeel*)

The book revealed to Jesus.

The Qur'an confirmed the message of Jesus and the Gospel, "*But when Jesus felt their [persistence in] disbelief, he said, "Who are my supporters for [the cause of] God?" The disciples said, "We are supporters for God. We have believed in God and testify that we are Muslims [submitting to Him]. They prayed to God "O Lord! We believe in Your revelations and follow the messenger [i.e., Jesus], so count us among those who bear witness [to the truth]*".[756]

"*And We sent, following in their footsteps,*[757] *Jesus, the son of Mary, confirming that which came before him in the Torah; and We gave him the Gospel, in which was guidance and light and confirming that which preceded it of the Torah as guidance and instruction for the righteous*".[758] "*And [I have come] confirming what was before me of the Torah and to make lawful for you some of what was forbidden to you. And I have come to you with a sign from your Lord, so fear God and obey me*".[759]

The Qur'an describes the Gospel also as Clear proof,[760] Light, Guidance[761] and a continuation of the divine message, revealing in it the sending of Prophet Muhammad☙, "*And [mention] when Jesus, the son of Mary, said, "O children of Israel, indeed I am the messenger of God to you confirming what came before me of the Torah and bringing good tidings of a messenger to come after me, whose name is Ahmad*"[762]".[763]

The Qur'an's clear statement negating the full accuracy of the Gospel, over time: "*And indeed, there are some among them who alter the Book with their tongues to make you [people] think that what they say is from the Book when it is not from the Book. And they say, "This is from God," but it is not from God [so] they attribute lies to God knowingly*".[764]

It did not go into much detail of the tampering and everything altered in the Torah and Gospel. The objective was to highlight this serious infringement and warn that they will not remain fully accurate, which took different forms:

1. The revealed text remained but explanations twisted, "*Due to wrongdoing on the part of the Jews, We forbade them good things that used to be lawful for them; and for their preventing from the way of God many [people]. And [for] their taking of usury while they had been forbidden from it, and their consuming of the people's wealth unjustly. And we have prepared for the disbelievers among them a painful punishment*".[765]

2. Fabricate stories, lies and myths about prophets and God, and attributing this to the divine book, "*Indeed, God has heard those [among the Jews] who said, "God is poor, and we are rich." We have certainly recorded their slurs and their killing of the prophets unjustly. Then, We will say, "Taste the torment of the burning*".[766]

---

[756] Qur'an, 3:52-3.

[757] I.e., following the tradition of the prophets.

[758] Qur'an, 5:46.

[759] Qur'an, 3:50.

[760] Qur'an, 2:87.

[761] Qur'an, 5:46.

[762] Ahmad is another name of Prophet Muhammad☙.

[763] Qur'an, 61:6.

[764] Qur'an, 3:78-9.

[765] Qur'an, 4:160-1.

[766] Qur'an, 3:181.

3. Claiming Jesus to be a god. In this regard, Jesus himself will respond and refute, "**And God will say, "O Jesus son of Mary, did you say to the people, `Take me and my mother as gods rather than Allah?' " He will say, "Glory be to You! It is not for me to say what I have no right to. Had I said it, You would have known it. You know what is in myself, and I do not know what is in yourself. You are the Knower of the hidden. I only told them what You commanded me: that you shall worship Allah, my Lord and your Lord. And I was a witness over them while I was among them**".[767]

4. Concealing the truth. This is two-fold.

   (a) Concealing the rulings of God (the commands): "**Those to whom We have given the Book recognize it as they recognize their own children. But some of them conceal the truth knowingly**".[768]

   (b) Concealing the sending of a final prophet and messenger, Muhammadﷺ: "**Those who follow the Messenger, the Unlettered Prophet [i.e., Prophet Muhammad], whom they find mentioned in the Torah and the Gospel in their possession. He directs them to righteousness, and deters them from evil, and allows for them all good things, and prohibits for them wickedness, and unloads the burdens and the shackles that are upon them. Those who believe in him, and respect him, and support him, and follow the light that came down with him— these are the successful**".[769]

The Psalms (*al-zabour*)[770]

The book revealed to Prophet Dawud, "**We gave David the Psalms**".[771] Among what has been revealed in it: "**We wrote in the Zabour, as We did in [earlier] Scripture: "my righteous servants will inherit the earth**".[772]

Belief in the Unseen

This is the third aspect of *aqidah*, the Unseen (what is absent, invisible) known as *ghayb* (plural: *ghaybiyyat*) or *sam'iyyat*. *Ghayb* is knowledge which we cannot acquire through our sensory organs. Allah﷾ has given knowledge of this to prophets and messengers to communicate to mankind through revelation.

Belief in the Last Day

It is an obligation upon every Muslim to believe in the Last Day, "**[true] righteousness is [in] one who believes in God, the Last Day**".[773] In this worldly-Hereafter journey there are various phases everyone shall go through and experience. Everyone alone. A day equivalent to "**fifty thousand years in length**",[774] when every person shall be brought to account and sent to their designated place in Paradise or Hellfire.

Questioning in the grave, the bliss and punishment (or torment) of the grave

---

[767] Qur'an, 5:116-7.

[768] Qur'an, 2:146.

[769] Qur'an, 7:157. See also 3:81-2 and 61:6.

[770] Can also mean 'scriptures' in general.

[771] Qur'an, 4:163. See also 17:55.

[772] Qur'an, 21:105.

[773] Qur'an, 2:177.

[774] Qur'an, 70:4.

Once a person is buried, friends and family leave, the deceased is questioned by two appointed angels called *Munkar* and *Nakir*. Their duty is to test their faith. The righteous believers will answer correctly and gain peace and prosperity, disbelievers and sinners who fail to answer correctly, their punishment will start, "**Allah will give firmness to those who believe, with the firm word**[775]**in this life, and in the Hereafter, but the evildoers He leaves to stray**".[776]

Everyone will be asked three questions: "**Who is your Lord? What is your religion? Who is that man sent to you?**"[777]

This will not be a Q&A session like the ones in this life which rely on knowledge, intellect, or memory. These are questions only the person's condition will respond to, how they lived, as believers or non-believers, righteous or sinful, pure, or corrupt.

Resurrection (*al-ba'th*)

The dead will all be raised from their graves (body and soul) and stand before Allah﷾ for judgment, "**And behind them is a barrier, until the Day they are resurrected**".[778]

The Gathering (*al-hashr*)

There will be a physical gathering where people, *jinn*, angels, and even animals come together, "**He [i.e., Allah] will gather you all together for [account on] the Day of Resurrection, about which there is no doubt.**.[779] "**And in the end they will be gathered to their Lord**".[780] And animals: "**when the wild beasts are gathered**".[781]

All creations gathered naked, barefooted, and uncircumcised as were first born. The wife of the Prophetﷺ, *Aisha* asked while astonished, "**O Prophet of Allah, men and women all looking at one another!**" He replied, "**the matter is great, the event is greater than people having the time or the mind to look at one another**".[782]

There will be those walking and those riding.[783] Disbelievers dragged on their faces while the righteous gathered as an honoured delegation.[784] The gathering will be where no one has lived before and nothing ever existed. Plain white land, "**the day when the earth will be changed into another earth**".[785]

Questioning, Judgement, Reward and Punishment

Allah﷾ shall bring us to stand before Him to be questioned - and He knows best - about every act of good and bad, obedience and disobedience. Every verbal and physical action, and intention. Nothing will be hidden or forgotten, "**Whether you reveal within yourselves or conceal, God will bring you to account for it**".[786]

---

[775] To testify: there is no god but Allah.

[776] Qur'an, 14:27.

[777] Abi Dawud (4753).

[778] Qur'an, 23:100. See also 23:16 and 36:52.

[779] Qur'an, 4:87.

[780] Qur'an, 6:38.

[781] Qur'an, 81:5.

[782] Al-Bukhari (6527), Muslim (7198), Ahmad (24265).

[783] Al-Tirmidhi (2593), Ahmad (20031).

[784] Qur'an, 17:97, 19:85.

[785] Qur'an, 14:48. Al-Bukhari (6521),

[786] Qur'an, 2:284.

"And the record [of deeds] will be placed [open], and you will see the criminals fearful of that within it, and they will say, 'Oh, woe to us! What is this book that leaves nothing small or great except that it has enumerated it?" And they will find what they did present [before them]. And your Lord does injustice to no one".[787]

Questioning will be direct, "*talked to by Allah on the Day of Resurrection, without there being an interpreter between him and Allah*".[788]

Questioning will be intense, "*asked about five things: About his life and what he did with it, about his youth and what he wore it out in, about his wealth and how he earned it, and spent it upon, and what he did with what he knew*".[789]

Then comes the outcome, the test results, "*Then as for he who is given his record in his right hand. He will be judged with an easy account. And return to his people in happiness. But as for he who is given his record behind his back. He will cry out for destruction*".[790]

The Scale (*al-mizan*)

Every deed and action is weighed so everyone can see for themselves what they have accumulated, "*We will set up the scales of justice for the Day of Resurrection, so that no soul will suffer the least injustice. And even if it be the weight of a mustard-seed, We will bring it up. Sufficient are We as Reckoners*".[791]

The Bridge (*al-sirat*)

This is a path everyone passes over, "*It is a slippery (bridge) on which there are clamps and (Hooks like) a thorny seed that is wide at one side and narrow at the other and has thorns with bent ends. Such a thorny seed is found in Najd and is called As-Sa'dan. Some of the believers will cross the bridge as quickly as the wink of an eye, some others as quick as lightning, a strong wind, fast horses or she-camels. So some will be safe without any harm; some will be safe after receiving some scratches, and some will fall down into Hell (Fire). The last person will cross by being dragged (over the bridge)*".[792]

Basin of the Prophet (*al-hawd*)

To believe there is a Basin of the Prophet, "*My Lake-Fount is (so large that it takes) a month's journey to cross it. Its water is whiter than milk, and its smell is nicer than musk (a kind of Perfume), and its drinking cups are (as numerous) as the (number of) stars of the sky; and whoever drinks from it, will never be thirsty*".[793]

[787] Qur'an, 18:49.

[788] Al-Bukhari (6539).

[789] Al-Tirmidhi (2416).

[790] Qur'an, 84:7-11. They will not be able to bear the burden of standing and be questioned for their actions, to the extent they ask to be demolished, as a way of ending their suffering for what they are experiencing and fear of what could yet follow.

[791] Qur'an, 21:47. See also 7:8-9.

[792] Al-Bukhari (7439).

[793] Al-Bukhari (6579), Muslim (5971).

Paradise and Hellfire

Both Paradise and Hellfire are created and shall remain with no end time to them.[794] Allah♦ has willed everything will end but Paradise and Hellfire shall remain everlasting with people in it. Following the scale and judgement, whoever their sins were greater than their good deeds shall enter Hellfire and whoever's good deeds exceeded shall enter Paradise.[795] All with the Will of Allah♦.

As for those whose scales are balanced between good and bad, they are the *people of heights*[796] (*al-a'raf*). Their good has prevented them from entering Hellfire and their bad preventing Paradise. They will recognise the inhabitants of both, calling out to the people of Paradise, "**Peace be upon you**." They cannot enter but are yearning to be with them, and look at the people of Hellfire pleading, "**Our Lord, do not place us with the wrongdoers**". They remain in-between until Allah♦ wills with His Mercy they enter Paradise.[797]

Paradise (*al-jannah*)

Paradise is a place created as an eternal reward for those who believed and obeyed, "**Such is Paradise which We will give as inheritance to those of Our servants who are devout**." "**Nor will they be asked to leave it**".[798] It is described as Garden of Eternity,[799] Gardens of Bliss,[800] Garden of Repose, Refuge, Restfulness,[801] Gardens of Eden, Perpetual residence,[802] Home of Peace,[803] Residence of the righteous and pious,[804] Home of the Hereafter,[805] Best reward,[806] Permanent and Everlasting Home,[807] Entrance of Honour.[808]

---

[794] Qur'an, 2:81, 4:57, 4:122, 4:169, 5:37, 15:48, 21:99, 33:64-5, 43:74-5, 45:35, 72:23, Al-Bukhari (6545), al-Tirmidhi (2557), Ibn Majah (4327), Ahmad (8535).

[795] Qur'an, 101:6-11.

[796] The *heights* is a partition [i.e., wall] that separates Paradise and Hellfire.

[797] Qur'an, 7:46-7. Tafsir al-Tabari (10/213, 10/231). Al-Bukhari (6464), Muslim (7122), Ahmad (24941).

[798] Qur'an, 15:48, 19:63.

[799] Qur'an, 25:15.

[800] Qur'an, 4:57, 4:122, 31:8.

[801] Qur'an, 53:15.

[802] Qur'an, 38:50.

[803] Qur'an, 6:127.

[804] Qur'an, 16:30.

[805] Qur'an, 12:109.

[806] Qur'an, 10:26.

[807] Qur'an, 35:35.

[808] Qur'an, 4:31.

There are several doors to entering,[809] with angels standing at them to welcome its new residents entering in honoured groups, greeting them as they arrival with "*Peace be upon you*" assuring them "*come in: you are here to stay, eternally*". Why all this? the verse continues, because "*you have become pure*".[810]

As for its description, this is beyond any imagination, beyond every beauty seen and heard of, "*no soul knows what [delight and satisfaction] has been hidden for them as a reward for what they used to do [in their lifetime]*".[811] What is prepared for the righteous believers is, "*such things as no eye has ever seen, no ear has ever heard of, and nobody has ever thought of*".[812] We have been told some of its bounties while sure the nature, quality, and beauty of anything there is beyond what has been experienced in this life in the best of times and best of places.

Its residents are in castles with layers upon layers of elevated rooms called chambers and mansions, with gardens and vineyards. Rivers running beneath, they will not be alone but secluded in their pavilions with companionship, maidens of matching age, restraining their glances as though they were rubies and corals. It is guaranteed to be "*an excellent residence and settlement*".[813] In it are date-palms, pomegranates, and fruits of every type, full of variety. While reclining on beds of silk brocade linings, green cushions and beautiful fine carpets, the fruit of the two gardens hanging low at hand reach,[814] living under thornless *lote trees*,[815] sweet-smelling plants with shades extended, and constant flowing water.[816]

They have rivers of pure water, rivers of milk forever fresh, rivers of wine delightful for the drinkers, and rivers of pure strained honey with cups of wine whose mixture is an aroma of sweet-smelling spring making it gush abundantly and another with a mixture with ginger. Paradise has not only a stock of them but a fountain of each, served by servants on trays and cups of gold and silver. Whatever their souls desire and what delights their eyes, they are given.[817]

Their clothing is from a large tree so big that under its shade a rider can travel for one hundred years without stopping. Clothed in fine silk and brocade, decorated with bracelets of gold, silver, and pearls.[818]

They are ranked as being the people of the right,[819] with the elites called the forerunners,[820] who did more in their life. These were the committed ones who devoted with serious dedication to their worship, obedience, and purification. As they were forerunners in good deeds and piety, they become forerunners of Paradise. They are the nearest to God, in Gardens of Bliss and on luxurious furnishings, reclining on them, facing one another. Serving them will be immortalised youth with luxury cups, pitchers, and sparkling drinks, causing them neither headache or intoxication. Offered fruits of their choice and meat of

---

[809] Qur'an, 13:23, 38:50, 39:73. Al-Bukhari (3257), Muslim (2710), Ahmad (22818). E.g. the door called *al-Rayan*. For those who used to fast a lot voluntarily. Al-Bukhari (1896).
[810] Qur'an, 39:73.
[811] Qur'an, 32:17.
[812] Al-Bukhari (4779), Muslim (7132), Ahmad (8143).
[813] Qur'an, 39:20, 78:32, 55:56-8, 25:76.
[814] Qur'an, 55:68, 55:54, 55:76.
[815] A believer can increase their number of trees in Paradise through Remembrance (*dhikr*). Al-Tirmidhi (3770).
[816] Qur'an, 56:28-31.
[817] Qur'an, 47:15, 76:5-6, 76:17-8, 43:71.
[818] Qur'an, 22:23, 44:53, 56:30-1. Al-Bukhari (3251), al-Tirmidhi (3577).
[819] Those given their book on the Day of Judgement in their right hand. Qur'an, 56:27.
[820] Qur'an, 65:10.

birds they may desire, with companions, and gifted with the likenesses of treasured pearls. There will be no noise or nonsense, all they will hear is "*peace, peace*", never experiencing tiredness, fatigue, hunger, thirst or be unclothed.[821]

Perseverance and effort were a main feature of their character, well-focused and undistracted from their goal, "**they are in large numbers from the older generations of believers and few from the later generations**".[822] They were not concerned with being a minority, their concern was to make purification and discipline a must.

Hellfire (*jahannam*)

Hellfire is a place prepared as a punishment for the disbelievers, transgressors, and believers who were sinful, "**O you who believe! Protect yourselves and your families from a Fire**".[823] Described as a Blazing Fire,[824] Torment of Hell,[825] Raging flame,[826] An Abyss,[827] The Crusher,[828] The Furnace,[829] and Scorching Fire.[830]

Once its residents arrive, they will be shackled with yokes around their neck, dragged in chains, and seized by the forelocks and feet.[831] It will be set ablaze and they are thrown in on their faces.[832] Its fuel will be people and stones, when it will be asked by God – and He knows best - "**Are you full?**" and it will say, "**Are there anymore?**".[833] Yes, it will speak. It is a creation that is ordered to fulfil His command and respond. From a distance you can hear its fury and roar. Its surrounding is searing wind and boiling water, and its shadow thick black smoke, neither cool or refreshing, or of any benefit to them.[834]

There are seven gates to Hellfire[835] with nineteen keepers on them or many more with nineteen being the leaders,[836] angels who are, "**harsh and severe,**" do not disobey Allah and carry out whatever they are commanded. Almost bursts with fury, every time a batch is thrown into it its keepers will remind them, "**Has no warner come to you!**"[837]

Their torture is not just one. The pain is varied, and their suffering, misery, and torment will take many forms. They are neither dead nor alive; neither finished off and die nor have punishment lightened for them or ended. Death will come to them from every direction but will not die, surely paying back for their lack of gratitude and ungratefulness.[838] They thought

---

[821] Qur'an, 56:12-26, 20:118-9.

[822] Qur'an, 56:13-4 and 56:39-40.

[823] Qur'an, 66:6.

[824] Qur'an, 25:11 and 67:5.

[825] Qur'an, 67:6 and 78:21.

[826] Qur'an, 70:15, 92:14.

[827] Qur'an, 101:9.

[828] Qur'an, 104:4.

[829] Qur'an, 37:97.

[830] Qur'an, 74:42.

[831] Qur'an, 13:5, 34:33, 41:71, 55:41, 69:30.

[832] Qur'an, 81:12, 54:48.

[833] Qur'an, 50:30.

[834] Qur'an, 2:24, 3:10, 21:98, 25:12, 50:30, 56:42-4, 66:6.

[835] Qur'an, 15:44.

[836] Qur'an, 74:30. Tafsir al-Qurtubi.

[837] Qur'an, 66:6, 67:8.

[838] Qur'an, 14:17, 20:74, 35:36.

enjoying life meant they had absolute freedom as if they created it but will realise that even freedom has its limits and comes with responsibility, especially when enjoying and living in the kingdom of the very Lord they disobeyed or rejected. Their [perceived] freedom led them to time in prison or their whole [after] life in prison.

In the heat of Hellfire their shelter will also be fire. Every time they try to get out, they are brought back into it and told "**taste the torment of Fire, which you persistently denied**839".840 The doors of Hellfire will be closed on them and they remain locked inside, screaming and pleading to the head of the keepers, *Malek*, "**O Malek, let your Lord finish us off**". He will say, "**You are here to stay**".841 And when they cry for relief, they are relieved with water like molten metal scalding their faces and ripping their intestines, given also putrid and purulent water, freezing hail, and oozing pus.842 Their food is fire into their stomach and from the tree of bitterness,843 and other food they will choke on.844

Their garments are tailored for them made from fire, and so are their beds and bedsheets. When their skin burns it will heal and replaced with new skin, so they may repeatedly taste the torture.845

They will yearn to meet those who helped them go astray, "**Our Lord, show us those who led us astray - among jinn and humans— so we shall put them under our feet, so they become of the lowest [i.e. most humiliated]**".846 They ask they share some of their punishment, but will be too late, "**[And they should consider that] when those who have been followed disassociate themselves from those who followed [them], and they [all] see the punishment, and cut off from them are the ties [of relationship], Those who followed will say, "If only we had another return [to the worldly life] so we could disassociate ourselves from them as they have [now] disassociated themselves from us." Thus will God show them their deeds as regrets to them, and they will not come out of the Hellfire**".847 They should have remembered no one can force you to sin and be disobedient, *the only barrier is you!*

While being hurled into Hellfire together with those who misled them, they will be asked, "**where are those you worshipped beside God? Can they help you now, or even help themselves?**"848 This is when the residents of Hellfire will want to disown everything that distracted them, everything they allowed to direct them away from seeking and acting upon the truth. They will deeply and shamefully regret. They will forget those pleasure they were indulged in, any achievements, and everything they gained. What remains is a burning desire to save their burning bodies. Screaming and desperate to bring a stop to their torture, at any cost. They will ask to return to life to do good. But Allah Almighty, the all-Knowing knows these are just words they say out of desperation and agony. They will go back to their old ways if they did return.849 This is when they will

---

839 Denied does not necessarily mean they rejected the fact there will be Hellfire. It also means their actions did not demonstrate they were conscious of there being judgement, punishment, and Hellfire. The effect/impact of their knowing was absent or lacking.

840 Qur'an, 32:20.

841 Qur'an, 35:36-7, 43:77.

842 Qur'an, 18:29, 47:15, 78:25, 14:16.

843 Called *zaqqum*. See Qur'an, 56:52.

844 Qur'an, 73:13.

845 Qur'an, 4:56, 7:41, 14:50, 22:19.

846 Qur'an, 41:29.

847 Qur'an, 2:166-7, 41:29.

848 Taking as a god, such as their desires, "**Have you seen he who has taken as his god his [own] desire**". Qur'an, 45:23.

849 Qur'an, 6:27-8, 14:44, 23:99, 35:36-7.

say "*If only we had obeyed Allah and obeyed the Messenger*".[850] And cry "*How sorry I am, for having neglected [my duty towards] Allah, while ridiculing [the truth]*".[851] The signs where there, the opportunities were immense, but their self-created veils they allowed to blind them.

A Day where you cannot lie, deceive, act, or pretend. Every reality is exposed and if you try to lie, there are witnesses testifying against you. These witnesses were not just with you, they were part of you, "*their ears, eyes, and skins will testify against them regarding what they used to do*".[852] Then they will turn against them and take their anger out, saying, ""*Why did you testify against us?" They will say, "Allah, Who made all things speak, made us speak. It is He who created you the first time, and to Him you are returned." You were unable to hide yourselves from your hearing, and your sight, and your skins, to prevent them from testifying against you, and you imagined that Allah was unaware of much of what you do. It is that thought of yours about your Lord that led you to ruin—so you became of the losers*".[853]

The worst of people in Hellfire and lowest are the hypocrites who shall find no help or support.[854] Only the believers who had sinned shall come out of it, eventually.[855]

Seeing Allahﷻ in Paradise

The people of Paradise will be able to see Allahﷻ "*[Some] faces, that Day, will be bright, looking at their Lord*",[856] seeing referred to as 'more' in this verse:[857] "*For them who strive for excellence will get the best [reward] - and __more__*".[858]

Intercession (*shafa'ah*)

Linguisically, it is 'to offer support to someone'.[859]
Islamically, 'to plead to God for forgiveness, support, a benefit, relief from hardship/something negative on behalf of someone'.[860]

This is not the same as intermediation which is not accepted in Islam. We have a direct connection to God himself, without needing an intermediary. It is merely out of His love towards His chosen creations He has gifted a special right that they may intercede before Him. And as with everything, it remains with His permission and His Will, "*Who there that can intercede except with His permission*".[861]

---

[850] Qur'an, 33:66.

[851] Qur'an, 39:56.

[852] Qur'an, 41:19-20.

[853] Qur'an, 41:21-4.

[854] Qur'an, 4:145.

[855] Qur'an, 11:106-7. See tafsir Ibn Kathir (2/460). Al-Bukhari (7510).

[856] Qur'an, 75:22-3. Tafsir al-Qurtubi, tafsir al-Razi, tafsir Ibn Kathir. Al-Bukhari (554), Muslim (1434).

[857] Tafsir al-Tabari, tafsir al-Qurtubi, tafsir al-Jalalin.

[858] Qur'an, 10:26.

[859] Al-Asfahani. *Al-mufradat.*

[860] Al-Jurjani. *Al-ta'rifat.* Tafsir Abu al-Saud (Qur'an, 4:85).

[861] Qur'an, 2:255.

There are two types of intercession:

(1) Concering worldly-life matters

"***Whoever intercedes for a good cause will have a share [i.e., reward] of it***".[862] Such as doing a prayer (duaa) for a fellow brother or sister. In a *hadith*, the Prophetﷺ says, "***Whoever supplicates for his brother behind his back (in his absence), the Angel commissioned (for carrying supplication to his Lord) says: Amen, and it is for you also***".[863]

(2) Will take place in the Hereafter. There are five forms of Intercession:[864]

I. The Great Intercession: the Prophetﷺ shall intercede for Judgement to start in the Hereafter, to settle the unrest, anxiety and fear of people waiting to know their fate. He is being granted an "***laudable and praised position*** (station/status)".[865] This intercession is given to him alone.[866]

II. The Prophetﷺ intercedes to enter certain people Paradise without standing for questioning. This intercession is also for him alone.[867]

III. Heﷺ shall intercede to move people in Paradise up from their level to higher levels.[868]

IV. Intercession to prevent those worthy of entering Hellfire from entering. This is not just for the Prophetﷺ.[869]

V. Prophets and righteous believers will intercede to remove people inside Hellfire out of it.[870]

Signs of the Last Day

The Qur'an and Sunnah have revealed to us there are signs that will occur before and leading up to the Last Day. These have been divided into two types:

(1) Minor signs (*al-'alamat al-sughra*)

(2) Major signs (*al-'alamat al-kubra*)

The major signs are relatively descriptive and speaks a lot about the condition and circumstances of humanity, societies, and morals as indications whereas the minor signs are usually more descriptive.

---

[862] Qur'an, 4:85.

[863] Muslim (6927).

[864] Imam al-Nawawi, rawdit al-talibeen 'omdit al-mufteen (7/13).

[865] Qur'an, 17:79.

[866] Al-Bukhari (7510), Muslim (193). See *sharh al-Nawawi 'ala sahih Muslim* (3/53).

[867] Al-Bukhari (5705), Muslim (216). See *sharh al-Nawawi 'ala sahih Muslim* (3/53).

[868] Muslim (2130).

[869] Al-Tirmidhi (2435), Abi Dawud (4739).

[870] Al-Bukhari (7474), Muslim (487, 491). See *sharh al-Nawawi 'ala sahih Muslim*.

See also The Creed of imam al-Tahawi: "The [Prophet's] Intercessions that God deferred for them is true, as narrated in the traditions" (line 51).

The Minor signs - include:

- Slave girls will give birth to their mistresses[871]
- Bare-footed, naked, destitute shepherds will compete in constructing tall building[872]
- The splitting of the moon[873]
- An increase in earthquakes, tribulations (*fitna*) and diseases/illnesses[874]
- Several individuals claiming to be prophets[875]
- Increase in deception and ignorance,[876] in fornication, alcohol drinking,[877] oppression, and unlawful killings[878]
- Excessive desire to save money and stinginess[879]
- Time passing quickly[880] such that, for example, a month feels like a week

The Major signs - include:

- The appearance of *al-Mahdi* (Muhammad ibn 'Abd Allah). A leader of the Muslims who will unite and lead justly after the world experiences great corruption and grave injustices.
- The appearance of the *Dajjal*. He will travel the earth causing havoc (prohibited from entering Makkah and Madinah). Those who are deceived will follow him and experience prosperity and wealth, and the believers who reject him will experience poverty.[881]
- The descent of Jesus. Appearing not as a new prophet to mankind but a follower of the seal of prophets Muhammad. He will rule for forty days with the Shariah Law of Islam then will die and be buried in the Prophet's holy mosque in Madinah. During his time, he will kill the *Dajjal*, smash the crucifix and kill swine (pigs) as an affirmation these were prohibitions/deceptions.[882]
- The appearance of Gog and Magog (*Ya'juj* and *Ma'juj*) which is a tribe of beasts. Muslims will be guarded from their terror by taking refuge on *Mount al-Tur*.
- The rising of the sun from the west instead of the east. At this point the door to repentance is closed.[883]
- The appearance of the beast of the earth (*dabbat al-ard*).[884]

---

[871] Muslim (97).

[872] Ibid.

[873] Qur'an, 54:1. Al-Bukhari (4825).

[874] Al-Bukhari (1036), Muslim (6792).

[875] Al-Bukhari (7121), Muslim (7342).

[876] Al-Bukhari (1036, 6037, 7061), Muslim (6792), Ibn Majah (4036), Ahmad (7912).

[877] Al-Bukhari (80).

[878] Al-Bukhari (1036, 7061), Muslim (6792).

[879] Al-Bukhari (6037, 7061), Muslim (6792).

[880] Al-Bukhari (1036, 6037, 7061), Muslim (6793).

[881] Yet the support of Allah will be with them. The food of the believers will not be food that requires money, rather it will be *dhikr*. Ibn Majah (4077).

[882] Al-Bukhari (2476), Muslim (7373)

[883] Muslim (396).

[884] Qur'an, 27:82. Tafsir Ibn Kathir. Ibn Majah (4066, 4067).

- A disastrous catastrophe (*khasf*) causing the sinking of the Arab Peninsula, returning as rivers and meadows as it used to first be.[885]

Jinn

A Muslim must believe there is a creation namely '*jinn*' who exist in a world of their own, created from fire, "***And the jinn We created before from scorching fire***".[886] They can see us, but we cannot generally see them. This does not mean a human cannot see them entirely. The Qur'an refers the reader to a specific context which should not be generalised, "***they see you from where you do not see them***".[887] It is possible, for whoever Allah﷾ wills.[888]

The *jinn* are required also to worshiping and maintain obedience, "***I did not create the jinn and the humans except to worship Me***". They are sent prophets, and like humans are accountable for their actions,[889] can be believers or disbelievers, "***And among us are Muslims [in submission to God], and among us are the unjust***" [890] who also enter Paradise or Hellfire, "***We have destined for Hell multitudes of jinn and humans***".[891]

Angels (*malaikah*)

A Muslim must believe Allah﷾ has created angels, "***The Messenger has believed in what was revealed to him from his Lord, as did the believers. They all have believed in Allah, and His angels***"[892] and warned that not believing in their existence makes the person no longer Muslim, "***Whoever rejects Allah, His angels, His Books, His messengers, and the Last Day, has certainly gone far astray***".[893]

They are real creations not imaginary, existed before humans, and do not disobey their Lord.[894]
Granted by Allah﷾ great abilities, they do not share the same characteristics as humans such as male and female gender, eat, or drink.[895] Some have two wings, others with three, others with four and others with more,[896] and can shape themselves in different ways including the image of a human being.[897] With great bodies, they are strong, beautiful, and made from light.[898] In constant worship, day and night, without getting tired or becoming slacken, and are characterised with humbleness and humility. They love believers and dislike non-believers and those sinful.[899]

---

[885] Ibn Hibban (6700)

[886] Qur'an, 15:27.

[887] Qur'an, 7:27.

[888] Tafsir al-Qurtubi, tafsir al-Baydawi. This is despite being a different kind of creation, just as the companions of the Prophetﷺ saw Angel Jibril. Al-Bukhari (50), Muslim (97).

[889] Qur'an, 51:56, 6:130. Tafsir Ibn Kathir, tafsir al-Tabari, tafsir al-Qurtubi.

[890] Qur'an, 72:14. I.e., those who deviate from the truth and act tyrannically.

[891] Qur'an, 7:179.

[892] Qur'an, 2:285. See also Qur'an, 2:177, 3:18. Muslim (93), Al-Bukhari (50).

[893] Qur'an, 4:136, 2:98.

[894] Qur'an, 53:5-6, 81:19-21, 66:6, 2:30. Muslim (7495).

[895] Qur'an, 43:19, 11:70. Tafsir Ibn Kathir. Qur'an, 3:124, 8:9, 8:12, 13:23-4, 39:68, 69:17.

[896] Qur'an, 35:1. Tafsir Ibn Kathir (3/546). Al-Bukhari (3232), Muslim (432).

[897] Qur'an, 19:17. Al-Bukhari (50), Muslim (93).

[898] Muslim (7495).

[899] Qur'an, 7:206, 21:20, 21:26, 33:43, 40:7-9, 80:14-6. Al-Bukhari (6040) Muslim (2637, 2401).

We do not know exactly how many angels there are, narrations state they are many.[900] Some have specific names and and descriptions: The Witnessers,[901] Supernal elites,[902] Soldiers,[903] Messengers,[904] Noble, Exalted,[905] *Jibril*,[906] *Mikail*,[907] *Israfil*,[908] *Malik*,[909] Angel of death,[910] *Munkar* and *Nakir*,[911] *Harout* and *Marout*.[912] They can be around people[913] and just like every creation, will die.[914] There are those who are greater than others, "**God chooses messengers from among the angels, and from among the people**"[915] and those with designated roles and tasks:

Jibril

The angel of revelation whose duty is to deliver the word of Allah❁ to prophets and messengers, "**And it is not for any human being that God should speak to him except by revelation or from behind a veil or that He sends a messenger [i.e., angel] to reveal, by His permission, what He wills**".[916]

His other names: Trustworthy Spirit (al-*ruh al-amin*), Holy Spirit (*ruh al-qudus*), and The Great Secret (*al-namus*).[917] He is also tasked to communicate with non-prophets and messengers as in the case of Mary, the wife of Emran and mother of Jesus, "**But he [i.e., Angel Jibril] called her from below her, "Do not grieve; your Lord has provided beneath you a stream. And shake toward you the trunk of the palm tree; it will drop upon you ripe, fresh dates**".[918]

Mikail

The angel dealing with the affairs of rain, seas, rivers, and provision, actioning the Will of Allah❁, "**By those [angels] lined up in rows. And those who drive [the clouds]**" and managing the affairs of the mountains.[919]

Israfil

Tasked with blowing the Trumpet/Horn on the Day of Judgement (*al-sur*) "**The sur is a trumpet which will be blown**".[920] "**On the Day when the Trumpet is blown, everyone in the heavens and the earth will be horrified, except whomever Allah wills; and**

---

900 Qur'an, 19:94, 74:31.

901 Qur'an, 40:51. Tafsir Ibn Kathir (4/84). Qur'an, 11:18. Tafsir al-Qurtubi (9/18). Muslim (2842), al-Bukhari (3207).

902 Qur'an, 37:8.

903 Qur'an, 9:26, 9:40, 33:9. Tafsir Ibn Kathir (2/346).

904 Qur'an, 22:75, 35:1.

905 Qur'an, 80:16. Tafsir al-Tabari (Qur'an, 30:54).

906 Qur'an, 2:97, 66:4.

907 Qur'an, 2:98.

908 Muslim (1811).

909 Qur'an, 43:77.

910 Qur'an, 32:11.

911 Al-Tirmidhi (1094).

912 Qur'an, 2:102.

913 Qur'an, 56:83-5. Tafsir al-Qurtubi, tafsir zad al-masir.

914 Qur'an, 28:88, 39:68, 55:26-7.

915 Qur'an, 22:75.

916 Qur'an, 33:9.

917 Qur'an, 70:4, 78:38, 97:4, 26:193, 16:102. Al-Bukhari (3), Muslim (160).

918 Qur'an, 19:24-5.

919 Qur'an, 37:1-2. Tafsir Ibn Kathir (4/2). Ahmad (2483), al-Nisa'i (9072). Al-Bukhari (3059), Muslim (1795).

920 Al-Tirmidhi (2599), al-Nisa'i in *al-kubra* (11250), Abu Dawud (4742).

everyone will come before Him in humility".[921] He will blow twice. The first time all creations will die, except whom Allah﷽ wills. The second time, resurrection commences and everyone's souls returns to their body, "**And the Trumpet will be blown, and whoever is in the heavens and whoever is on the earth will fall dead except whom God wills. Then it will be blown another time, whereupon they will rise up, looking on**".[922]

Azrael

Appointed to bring death by removing the soul from the body and has assistants, "**He sends over you guardian-angels until, when death comes to one of you, Our messengers [i.e., angels of death] take him, and they do not fail [in their duties]**".[923]

Munkar and Nakir

Given the task of questioning the dead in their grave about the Oneness of Allah﷽, the religion and the Prophetﷺ. The Muslim will be asked, "**Who is your Lord?**" and he will reply "**My Lord is Allah**". Then asked, "**What is your religion?**" He will say "**My religion is Islam**". To the last question, "**What do you say about the man who was sent on a mission to you?**" He will answer "**My prophet is Muhammad, sallallaahu 'alayhi wa sallam**". At this time, he is told he will enter Paradise. Conversely, the disbelievers will be asked the same questions but unable to answer. They are told they will enter Hellfire and will be tormented severely in their graves."[924]

Raqib and 'atid

The noble writers (*kiraman katibin*) who take account of the deeds and actions of every person, "**And indeed over you [are appointed angels], observing, Noble Writers. They know all that you do**".[925] Allah﷽ has appointed for every person two angels recording. One to a person's left and the other to their right. Everything a person does will be recorded, small or great. The one to the right records the good while the one on the left records the bad.[926]

Everyone will see the accurate record and made aware of what led to their reward and what led to their punishment. Everything is on record, "**Read your book; today there will be none but yourself to call you to account**".[927]

Malik

Angels have a role as keepers of Hellfire, including Malik, "**Those who disbelieved will be driven to Hell in throngs. Until, when they have reached it, and its gates are opened, its keepers will say to them, "Did not messengers from among you come to you, reciting to you the revelations of your Lord, and warning you of the meeting of this Day of yours?" They will say, "Yes, but the verdict of punishment is justified against the disbelievers**".[928]

---

[921] Qur'an, 27:87. 36:51.

[922] Qur'an, 39:68.

[923] Qur'an, 6:61.

[924] Abi Dawud (4753).

[925] Qur'an, 82:10-2.

[926] Qur'an, 50:16-8, 54:52-3, 82:10-2, 99:7-8. Tafsir al-Baghawi (4/222), *jaami' al-'loum wa al-hikam* (1/336).

[927] Qur'an, 17:14.

[928] Qur'an, 39:71-2, 74:26-31.

Ridwan

There are also gatekeepers for Paradise, include Ridwan. In a *hadith*, "**I will come to the gate of Paradise on the Day of Resurrection. and would seek its opening. and the keeper would say: Who are you? I would say: Muhammad. He would then say: It is for you that I have been ordered, and not to open it for anyone before you**".[929]

Al-hafadhah

Those who – with the Will of Allah ﷻ - protect people from harm that is hidden or apparent, "**For him [i.e., each person] are successive [angels] before him and behind him protecting by the command of God**".[930]

Other angels

- Give support to the believers and as a reminder of Allah ﷻ 's bounties such as the case in the Battle of Badr,[931] the Battle of Al-Khandaq[932] and the Battle of Hunnein,[933] "**O you who believe! Remember Allah's blessings upon you, when forces came against you, and We sent against them a wind, and forces you did not see**".[934]
- The travellers (*Sayyahun*), "**for Allah are (Sayyahun) angels on earth, [tasked] to convey greetings upon me from my Ummah**".[935]
- Those appointed to prevent the *Dajjal* from entering Makkah or Madinah[936] and participate in congregational prayer.[937]

Belief in the *qadar* (fate)

A fundamental principle of *aqidah* is belief in *qadar* (fate) which means pre-destining. But firstly, there are two important considerations and two terminologies we must stop at before proceeding into this subject as these are essential in understanding the concept of *qadar* in Islam.

The two considerations:

I. Attributing to Allah ﷻ perfection and flawlessness necessitates we submit wholeheartedly to the fact his knowledge is also perfect. *He has knowledge of all things. All that existed, exists, yet to exist, and will not exist,* "**And with Him are the keys of the unseen (ghayb); none knows them except Him**".[938]
II. As mentioned in the beginning of the book: *it [life] is limited, perishable, short-lived, and above all,* "**a test**".[939]

---

[929] Muslim (486).
[930] Qur'an, 13:11. Tafsir Ibn Kathir.
[931] Qur'an, 3:123-6, 8:12. Al-Bukhari (3992, 3995).
[932] Qur'an, 33:9.
[933] Qur'an, 9:25-7.
[934] Qur'an, 33:9.
[935] Al-Tirmidhi (3917).
[936] Ibn Majah (4077).
[937] Al-Nisa'i (916).
[938] Qur'an, 6:59.
[939] Qur'an, 67:2.

On the first point, with His perfect knowledge, Allah۞ knows best how to manage the affairs of everything, putting in place Universal Laws and measures.

On the second point, as life is a test, real accountability will prevail in the Hereafter, so for accountability to happen every person has choice of what path to take and choice to make. In the end, on the Day of Judgement, they are faced with the outcome and consequences of their choices and free will to do what they chose.

The conclusion to these two points is it must be worthwhile people are granted free choice to do good or bad, otherwise there is no purpose in there being a test, or having a system of accountability, reward and punishment.

Two terminologies:

Qada' is pre-knowledge and *Qadar* is the pre-known becoming reality (as it was known).[940]

I. **Qada':** Allah۞'s pre-eternal knowledge of everything that will happen and how everything will carve out, in their essence, attributes, and actions, "***and He has knowledge of all things***".[941]

Allah۞'s attribute of knowledge is eternal. His foreknowledge of everything was known to Him since pre-existence. This is in line with His pre-determined regulation of everything in accordance with a measure of rule, bringing about harmony to the universe, "***Indeed, We have created everything by measure***".[942] There is no change or substitute to these [pre-determined] Universal Laws or alteration.[943] The sun and moon is determined to be a measure of time, day and night following each other, good brings reward and bad draws punishments, are all examples:[944] He is the "***Creator of all things, and has charge of all things***".[945] The creation of human beings is part of this.

II. **Qadar:** the revealing of this knowledge. What was already known to be has come into reality.

There are two types of human related actions, both fall under the pre-knowledge of Allah۞. Actions where there is:

(a) **No free will** - e.g., when we are created, die, our height, colour, gender, race, shape of the sun etc. Calamities outside the realm of a one's own actions. As these are beyond a person's remit and abilities, he is therefore not accountable for.

b) **Free will** - human actions where there is choice and ability to action so is accountable for.

---

[940] Al-Haythami, I. Fath al-mobin bisharh al-arbain al-nawawiyah (hadith Muslim, 97).

[941] Qur'an, 57:3.

[942] Qur'an 54:49. See also 65:3, 87:2-3, 13:8, 56:60.

[943] Qur'an, 33:62, 35:43, 48:23.

[944] Qur'an, 2:189, 36:40, 6:96, 18:55.

[945] Qur'an, 39:62.

Allah﷾ having pre-knowledge of everything happening in the world, including the actions of every person, does not mean a person is compelled and without will. His knowledge is revealing and not imposing. Just like a light bulb that reveals the items in a room. It does not dictate what is in it, it just reveals. He knows what you will say, wear and do but you also chose. The knowledge of something does not necessitate intervention.

An example:

You have three children. Each of them you give an amount of money. Knowing them well enough, you predict the first child will spend it all, the second will save it all and the third will spend half and keep half. Later you ask them and find they did exactly that. Does the fact you knew what they were likely to do mean you influenced their actions or dictated it? No. They had the choice, and you were also correct in your expectations based on knowing them and experience. If this is the case with a parent towards their children (whose knowledge is still limited), how about the Creator's unlimited knowledge of those He created.

The relationship and agreement between the will of a person and the Will of Allah﷾

Although a person has free will, they will not be able to do what Allah﷾ has not permitted to happen but can do what He allows to happen, which still does not mean your actions are dictated or compelled. You have will, "**But you cannot will unless God wills**".[946] This is why Muslims are used to saying *In-shaa'-Allah* (God willing), such as "I will go to work *In-shaa'-Allah*", "I will do such and such *In-shaa'-Allah*", "I hope to marry this person *In-shaa'-Allah*" etc.

Everything needs Allah﷾ to bring into existence and to maintain its continued existence. After initiating the creation of all things,[947] they still rely on Him to continue its existence every moment. When a person is created, born and lives for 40 years, Allah﷾ did not initiate their creation and leave them. Both the creation and continued existence all along is from Him, renewing existence every moment. Everything is the same. The sun is not created and left to serve us but Allah﷾ creates its ability to function every moment. Our lungs are not pre-programmed to help us breath and left, its ability to function is created every moment. Therefore, we describe Allah﷾ not only as the Creator, but the Creator and Sustainer of all things, "***it is God who has created you and what you do***".[948]

Any action occurs when two things happen at the same time:
- Allah﷾'s Will and Him creating the action
- The person's internal readiness and intention to do this thing

The outcome and end result is from Allah﷾ according to His Will. Our choice and free will lies in the remit of His Will.

---

[946] Qur'an, 81:29.

[947] All things meaning anything other than Allah﷾ which includes the actions of people.

[948] Qur'an, 37:96.

The Will of Allah﷾ and the actions of a person

Part of Allah﷾'s way, His Universal Laws, is the Law of Causation, causality or cause and effect.[949] In relation to us humans, this means Allah﷾ has determined that everyone fulfils a duty/condition to reach certain outcomes, referred to as 'reasons' (asbab). Reasons, like everything, do not have self-power or self-ability. Allah﷾ creates the functionality in it and decides the outcome. He is in total control; we just do our part.

Examples of how a person's actions can be a cause/reason for an outcome:

- People refining and purifying themselves brings about positive change in our societies and countries, "***Indeed, Allah does not change the condition of a nation until they change the condition of themselves***".[950]
- Injustice and corruption are a reason for punishment, "***...and seized those who wronged, with a wretched punishment, because they were defiantly disobeying***".[951]

And now we see how *reasons* do not work in isolation of Allah﷾'s Will, even if He allows certain norms to exist regularly:

- We take medication when falling ill. Medicine does not have self-power of self-ability to cure. It is Allah﷾ Who creates the feature of 'cure' in it. If Allah﷾ wills, He could make a medicine not cure but a glass of water cure instead. Why? Because the attribute of cure He is the One that determines when it happens and where. He creates it. He has control over it.

- Eating food removes hunger. But the attribute of 'filling' is created by Allah﷾ in food when He chooses, not that food has it itself. He could choose that a person eats a lot but is not filled or eats little and is filled. And He can choose something other than food fills a person. At the End of Time when the *Dajjal* comes and there will be severe poverty, the food of the believers will be *dhikr* (Remembrance).[952]

- Fire burns, but with Prophet Ibrahamﷺ it did not. Why? Because even though Allah﷾ allows this norm to exist (that fire burns), the attribute of burning is created and determined by Him on every occasion. On that occasion He commanded, "***O fire, be cold and safe for Ibraham***".[953] So it is He who orders a fire to be hot and it is He who orders it to be cold. Everything is a creation of His and submits accordingly, "***To Allah [alone] submits all those in the heavens and earth – willingly or unwillingly***".[954] "***There is not a single thing that does not glorify Him with praise, but you do not understand their [way of] praising***".[955]

---

[949] A cause is a 'means' or 'way' conditioned or provided by Allah﷾ to achieve something. It is He who created causes and producing their effects, just as He created everything. If it was not for Him creating causes or effects, there would be none.

[950] Qur'an, 13:11.

[951] Qur'an, 7:165.

[952] Al-Hakim (8773).

[953] Qur'an, 21:69.

[954] Qur'an, 13:15.

[955] Qur'an, 17:44.

- Likewise, He ordered the knife not to slaughter Ismaeel although it normally does,[956] the whale not to eat Yunus although it normally does,[957] and the Sea not to drown Musa although it normally does.[958]

- *"From a sperm-drop He created him and enabled him"*.[959] This does not mean it has self-power to form a human. It is only a *reason*. And any reason is useless unless and until Allah☾ creates the attribute in it.

- *"Have you seen that [seed] you cultivate? Is it you who make it grow, or are We the Grower?"*[960] You do your part, it is Allah☾ Who allows it to nourish and grow not the seeds themselves.

- *"Have you seen the water you drink? Is it you who sent it down from the clouds, or are We the Sender?"*[961] The cloud is just a *reason*, it is He Who allows it to rain not the clouds.

- *"Have you seen the fire you ignite? Is it you who produce its tree, or are We the Producer?"*[962] The tree is just a *reason*, it is He Who allows this to happen not the trees.

If a person chooses to be content with the *Qadar* of Allah☾, they will live with great inner-peace and acceptance. And if one chooses to transgress or oppose, they are the losers. They will live in misery and anguish and become worn out, still only receiving what is destined for him.

---

[956] Qur'an, 37:102-7.
[957] Qur'an, 21:88.
[958] Qur'an: 26:63-6.
[959] Qur'an, 80:19.
[960] Qur'an, 56:63-4.
[961] Qur'an, 56:68-9.
[962] Qur'an, 56:71-2.

CHAPTER SEVEN

The Book of Ihsan
Tazkiyah
(Purification)

What is *Ihsan*?

Linguistically, *Ihsan* means 'perfection and excellence'.[963]

Islamically, is "**to observe and worship Allah as though you could see Him, for though you cannot see Him yet He sees you**".[964]

Reaching *Ihsan* is a journey; to become manifested with perfect traits and excellent character. Constantly developing, from bad to good and good to better. Whilst it works on the heart, it impacts every aspect of the human being, so is the pursuit of all-round perfection. It refines a person's dealings towards himself, towards Allah✆, people, animals, plants, and objects. Perfection in everything you do and everything about you, "**Indeed, God commands justice and excellence**".[965] "**Verily, Allah has prescribed excellence in everything**".[966] i.e., it is an obligation.[967] The *hadith* then continues by giving an example of how everything means everything, even with animals when slaughtering, "**If you are to slaughter, slaughter with excellence. Let the person sharpen his knife, so the animal is spared of suffering**".

What does the knowledge of *Ihsan* cover?

This knowledge is about how to embark on a journey to Allah✆ in removing negative inner traits (sins, egoistic desires and attachments) and replace with perfection, righteousness, positive traits, and deal with the obstacles that prevent this process to continue[968] while elevating through ranks of piety, ongoingly, "**And worship your Lord until what is certain comes to you [i.e., death]**".[969]

Before excelling in perfection there must be the removal of inner-impurities, flaws and deficiencies that prevent reaching this, done through the methods of purification of the heart. The heart is the command centre, if it is pure and sound everything about you will take a ripple effect in being pure and sound, "**Verily, in the body is a flesh which, if sound, the entire body becomes sound, and if corrupt, the entire body is corrupt. Verily, it is the heart**".[970]

If you are really looking to refine yourself and purify in the most perfect way, there is only one right way. The divine way. It does not make sense to look elsewhere. If it is Allah✆ Who created you and He Who commanded you, why then go looking for methods elsewhere other than what He has prescribed. It is all there. Everything you need. And if it is not there then it is not required of you or will not help you fulfil the objectives in reaching the aim. You can try everything else in the world to help you refine, you will simply be going round in circles, doing an incomplete job, and will never reach the true levels of *ihsan*.

---

[963] Al-Jurjani. *Al-ta'rifat.*

[964] Al-Bukhari, (50) Muslim (97).

[965] Qur'an, 16:90.

[966] Muslim (5055), Ahmad (17113).

[967] Jaami' al-'loum wa al-hikam (1/290).

[968] Qur'an, 91:8-10. Tafsir al-Tabari, tafsir al-Baydawi, tafsir Ibn Kathir, tafsir zad al-masir.

[969] Qur'an, 15:99.

[970] Al-Bukhari (52), Muslim (4094), Ahmad (18374).

There are many illnesses of the heart that must be treated. This way a person becomes spiritually healthy and progresses. *Ihsan* is never about just moments of spiritual uplifting, an occasional boost, or glimpses of good character. It is about consistently developing into levels of godliness and noble character; inwardly and outwardly.

This subject a lot of people may be unfamiliar with as it is not spoken about enough, in depth. Broadly, we hear of needing to become better people with better hearts, good intentions, and good feelings towards one another, but it is rare anyone can guide you to the 'know how' and practically assist in reaching *Ihsan*. This is because it requires a person take you on this journey who themselves have gone through, developed, purified and became qualified and permitted to take others on it. Reaching *Ihsan* is not by a list of actions. It is a journey which involves actions and responsibilities but under the supervision of a 'spiritual guide', "***ask the people of knowledge if you do not know***".[971] They will guide you on removing bad inner and outer traits, replace with good, work with you to overcome barriers, and help you understand changes and new experiences while on that journey. This is the path to true everlasting success, "***he has succeeded who purifies himself. And he has failed the one who corrupts it***".[972] 'Corrupts it' includes those who do not work on purifying themself, allowing it to remain corrupt or deteriorate.[973]

But all this requires something very important. **To take control**. Control of yourself.

Know that purification starts with reclaiming your heart. You cannot change or refine something you do not have control over. Once you take control you become the driver. Control over all forms of egoistic urges and manipulations of the inner self or externally (people, worldly pleasures, deceptions etc).

Secondly, humility is essential. It is no option. How can you refine your self if at the same time it is idolised with arrogance, preconditions or admired with itself! You are useless without the interventions and support of Allah✲ to help achieve success on this path, "***it is certainly upon Us [alone] to show [the way] to guidance***"[974] so be like those who plea, "***[O Allah] guide us along the straight path***"[975] and acknowledge, "***We would have never been guided if Allah had not guided us***".[976]

Thirdly, part of being in control is to observe maturity. Being content and disciplined to do things the way they should be done. Purification is a process not an overnight miracle and one must be patience in accepting this. If you have a glass of dirty water, you cannot in a single moment convert it into clean water. There must be a process of either pouring out the dirty water and cleaning the cup to pour in clean water or continue pouring in clean water until it outweighs the dirty. Our hearts are more complex than a glass of water. Our hearts have accumulated a lot more dirt!

---

[971] Qur'an, 16:43, 21:7.

[972] Qur'an, 91:9-10.

[973] Tafsir al-Tabari, tafsir al-Qurtubi.

[974] Qur'an, 92:12.

[975] Qur'an: 1:6.

[976] Qur'an: 7:43.

Importance of *Ihsan*

- To fully practice the religion is to implement **all** three aspects: Islam, Eman and Ihsan
- It is to do with the most important part of an individual, the heart
- When the heart is refined and pure, the whole body and mind will fall in line with purity and righteousness

Every Islamic teaching a Muslim is required to follow is divided into two categories: an **outer** and an **inner**:

The outer/body actions which are two types:

Fulfilling commands: prayer, fasting, giving everyone their rights, good dealings with people etc

Avoiding prohibitions: theft, fornication, gambling, drinking alcohol etc

The inner/heart actions which are also two types:

Fulfilling commands: faith, sincerity, truthfulness, honesty, humility etc

Avoiding prohibitions: disbelief, arrogance, envy, hatred etc

Both the inner and outer are important and must be dealt with simultaneously: "***Say, He has only made forbidden all corrupt acts, [both] those that are <u>apparent</u> and those that are <u>hidden</u>***".[977] However, actions of the heart in the sight of Allahﷻ are the most important. The inner **must** be adressed just as we are clear about addressing the outer. Salvation in the Hereafter relies on salvation of the heart - with the mercy of Allahﷻ - by cleansing it of vices and immoral traits and replace with positive and beautiful traits. By not doing so, a person is reckless, displeasing their Lord, causing negative traits to stay, accumulating more on top of them, and depriving himself from good character and a righteous condition. Purification is a religious obligation as it is a human necessity. One disease of the heart is the egoistic desires of the *nafs* (*shahawat).* That is when the desires of a person go beyond its natural state, such as when people live to satisfy urges that are unlawful or excessive and become led by them. Islam provides this body of knowledge that guides to the methods, through a journey, for hearts to become sound and safe, inclined to morality.

A person may not be aware of their inner diseases and deep-rooted issues causing them to think their heart is sound, especially if they have general kindness. This is far from the truth. Firstly, to think you are fine and need no treatment is itself arrogance, becoming the first disease you need to overcome! Allahﷻ draws attention to this due to its great importance, "***Do you see those who claim purity for themselves?***"[978] and in another verse, an order, "***So do not claim yourselves to be pure***"[979] why? The verse continues, "***He knows best who is mindful of Him***" i.e., He knows who is truly cleansed, of a pure condition, and righteousness. And in a *hadith:* "***Do not claim yourself to be pure. It is God alone who knows the people of piety among you***".[980] He knows the inner and outer.[981] Sometimes we think we do not have certain diseases only because we have not been confronted and tested with situations that expose these diseases. Therefore, one must accept – out of humility and sincerity – he has all diseases until proven otherwise. For example, someone cannot claim

[977] Qur'an, 7:33.

[978] Qur'an, 4:49.

[979] Qur'an, 53:32. Tafsir al-Razi, tafsir al-Kashaf, tafsir al-Baydawi, tafsir al-Sha'rawy.

[980] Muslim (5609).

[981] Tafsir al-tahrir wa al-tanwir, al-tafsir al-wasit lilquran al-kareem.

to not have desire for recognition or status if they live a life with no status opportunities that exposes their heart.'s condition accordingly.

Someone may be asking: is this not too harsh? To think of myself as having every possible disease?

No. It is not about being harsh on yourself or becoming negative about yourself. It is about being conscious. Imagine that person is suddenly given high recognition or some sort of status in life, their lack of attentiveness in the possibility of having this disease could make it worse. When one has a disease and it is (knowingly or unknowingly) being aplified, they are endangering their heart condition and at risk of decline and corruption. As for the one who is conscious, should this happen, they are well alert and take the experience as a 'testing ground' to see where their heart stands with status and recognition. If they are in control and not manipulated by it, they are grateful and remain steadfast but if they find they became self-admiring, have self-pride, or feel superior, they now know to work on the root cause of this disease. It is not about waking up every day and saying to yourself you have this disease and that disease listing everything you can think of. It is about not rejcting you may have a disease you are not aware of. It is also also about getting to know yourself better. Again, how can you refine what you do not know!

Saying that, not many people commit to embarking on a purification journey. This should not put you off nor should you be intimidated by being a minority. Stay focused and do not allow anything to be an obstacle or distract you. The Prophet makes this point very clear, "***Do not let yourselves be 'yes-men', saying: 'If the people are good then we will be good, and if they are wrong then we will be wrong. 'Rather, make up your own minds, if the people are good then you are good, and if they are evil, then do not behave unjustly***".[982] This is reminding that everyone has their own will. Do not be like a sheep led by a herd. Know that we all will stand before Allah on the Day of Judgement <u>alone</u>. Every person in panic and terrified about their fate with even the closest of people running away from you. All you will be hearing is "myself, myself, myself," engaged only with themselves, in fear and entirely helpless.[983] On this Day when **your** purification will be questioned, as on this Day nothing shall be of benefit except those who return to Allah with a sound and pure heart.[984]

The knowledge of purification gives understanding of the heart, how to reclaim it, taking control, cure methods, practical solutions, all while maintaining humility, strive, and perseverance which are a core part of the change process. Let us look at verse 69 of chapter 29, "**As for those who <u>struggle</u> in Our cause, We will surely <u>guide</u> them to Our way**". The more strive and effort put in, the more guidance you gain. And the first strive is to be in control of yourself.

An example:

You are travelling from one city to another. You first make a decision to go on this journey, your decision is firm and decisive, you reflect on the means that get you there, you are conscious of any hidden or apparent hindrances that could delay or pull you back, you prepare to embark on the journey through its proper means even if you are not the driver, and you remain focused with an ongoing strive to pursue and overcome any distractions. This way you are in control.

---

[982] Al-Tirmidhi (2125).

[983] "The Day when a person will flee from his brother. And his mother and his father. And his spouse and his children. Every one of them, on that Day, will have enough to preoccupy him". Qur'an, 80:34-7 and "when no friend will ask about his friend". Qur'an, 70:10. Al-Bukhari (4712), Muslim (480).

[984] "The Day when neither wealth nor children will be of help. Except the one who returns to Allah with a pure sound heart". Qur'an, 26:88-9.

The purification journey is the same:

Starts with a decision

It starts with you and is all about you!

You need to ask yourself what you really want. Do you want to continue the way you are? Consciously or unconsciously telling yourself there is nothing to change or "I am not that bad!" Do you want to remain passive with your desires, sins, and negative traits and continue running away from them? Or do you want to confront the truth, address the self-deceptions, and face your fears? Choose to stop hiding behind excuses in changing and choose to live with real inner peace and self-harmony, "**Do they not reflect within themselves?**".[985]

These questions only you can answer. What you really want only you decide. If you want, you can choose not to do anything and remain asleep. But know that sleep is like death and rising is like resurrection, so choose if you want to rise in this life with responsibility or wait to rise in the Next life with accountability!

Knowledge can guide you on what to do once the decision is made but will never make the decision for you. Many times, we get answers to our problems, but the issue is not in getting the answer, the issue is in the willingness to accept the responsibility that comes with the answer. A sense of urgency to resolve, determination to refine and the courage to take necessary steps. Even then, there is a difference between resolving a certain problem and between embarking on an all-round-purification journey. Refining you totally as a person.

Sincerity

Once you have decided, the choice cannot be half-hearted. It is either a yes or a no. It must be decisive. Not ambiguious and not controvertial. No ifs and buts. You should have thought about this carefully. No one has forced you to decide. It must be definite and settled, and most definitely non-negotiable. Once you have decided you cannot be the teacher and student at the same time. Let go and submit to the way it is done not the way you want it to be. This is not sincerity, "**those who repent, correct themselves, hold fast to Allah, and dedicate their religion to Allah alone. These are with the believers; and Allah will give the believers a great reward**".[986]

Many people when embarking on this journey want to be in control of it. This is **not** the control we mean. We mean control in terms of the commitment to proceed with determination and self-discipline. Be sincere. Be devoted to doing it the right way. If this is all about purifying for the sake of Allah, why would you choose to choose? If the Prophet was sent to show us how, why would we dare to make changes. Do not allow yourself to dictate. Do not let your *nafs,* the very thing you are here to purify be the obstruction.

Remorse and repentance

Repent from the past. Seek to clear all you have accumulated. Make it a new start and start on the terms of Allah and the Prophet and repent from the arrogance of not changing yourself before, totally. Remind yourself: the deficiencies are

---

[985] Qur'an, 30:8.
[986] Qur'an, 4:146.

143

because of you and so are the veils, "***Verily, when the slave (of Allah) commits a sin, a black spot appears on his heart. When he refrains from it, seeks forgiveness and repents, his heart is polished clean. But if he returns, it increases until it covers his entire heart. And that is the 'Ran' which Allah mentioned: 'No, their hearts are encrusted[987] with what they have done[988]*".[989]

Repentance is the first stage on the journey and the first level of truly seeking your Lord. At first, the heart needs to awaken from the slumber of heedlessness and be conscious of a corrupt condition. Only then is there something to be purified. How can you purify what you have not even acknowledged or what remains asleep!

Humility

Humility removes the veils on the eyes and hearts to be able to see the truth of oneself. Not what is said or how others perceive you, but the truth. Then comes accepting this. This is where a person's truthfulness and sincerity are tested and exposed. They can choose to end it here or go all the way in doing something about it. For the truthful, knowing their reality creates a sense of shock and urge for change. For others, they may be sincere in wanting to change, but it remains a wish and hope. And as for the ones who have not realised or accepted the need to change, they remain asleep.

Still then, you need the means for purification to help reveal your inner self in greater detail. One important method is Remembrance (*dhikr*). *Dhikr* is light and light is revealing. Then, the more you know about your inner self the more you (a) acknowledge ignorance and weakness in not having known before (b) know about your deep-rooted flaws and failings. All strengthening the sense of humility and urgency to resolve.

Humility works to ensure the flames of your passion have been extinguished and replaced with the light of glorification of Allah☼ that shines the heart. At this point, the passion fades away, the heart is given a new life and the limbs surrender themselves likewise to humility. Humility is in the heart. Downcast appearance and slumped shoulders do not define the essence of humility. The great companion Huzayfa warned of 'hypocritical humility'. When asked to clarify what this was, he said "where the body is in humility, but the heart is not". The companion 'Umar once ordered a person to raise their neck as humility is not in the neck but in the heart.[990] And as the master of humility, Prophet Muhammad☸ teaches, If the heart were [truly] humble, the limbs would naturally follow.[991]

If there is no humility, you have already multiplied your obstacles and thickened the veils before even starting your journey. If there is humility, there can be a sincere decision, wholehearted submission, remorse, repentance, and you will ignite the light that enlightens your path and the fuel for continued progress and refinement, "***Whoever humbles himself by a degree for Allah, glory be to Him, Allah will raise him by a degree. Whoever is arrogant to Allah by a degree, Allah will lower him by a degree until he is made 'the lowest of the low*".[992]

---

[987] I.e., covered with a hard surface layer. Meaning they devoted to committing sins until their heart became coated and rusted. Tafsir al-Baydawi.

[988] I.e., their sins.

[989] Al-Tirmidhi (3334).

[990] Ibn al-Qayyim. *Madarij al-salikin* (1/521).

[991] Al-Bukhari (52).

[992] Ibn Majah (4176).

And now comes: *to be in control*

Once you have decided to submit to the requirements of this journey, repented and admited your faults and delay in refining, and entered through the gates of humility, you now start to take control. Just the start!
It is not about taking control of everything that happens. It is about you. The inner you. The firmness to progress on this path with sincere servitude, goal-oriented, driven by the real priorities, and most definitely wholeheartedly.

Embarking on this journey under the supervision of a guide means you are not limiting yourself to the theoretical teachings of *Ihsan* but enjoining with its practical teachings and manifestations. You would be handheld through the stages of awakening, refinement, and spiritual progress. They themselves would have gone through the process and mastered it by refining themselves and gaining broad and deep understanding of purification. And importantly, are qualified and permitted by their guides to take others on such journey. They serve you by their condition not volumes of words and books, echoing the way the Prophet✺ mentored and developed his companions. When his wife Sayyida Aiysha described Him, it was the manifestations that stood out to her, saying "***Verily, the character of the Prophet of Allah was the Qur'an***"[993] meaning his character mirrored and embodied the Quran, which itself affirmed, "***you are truly [a man] of outstanding character***".[994]

The elements and process for purification:

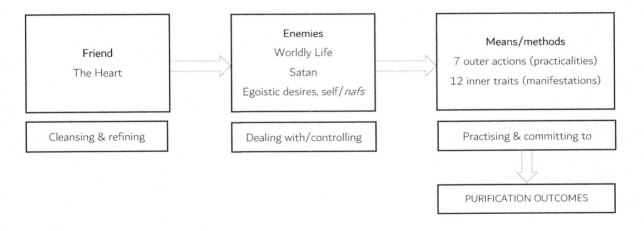

[993] Muslim (1739) Ahmad (24269).
[994] Qur'an, 68:4.

The Practicalities

There are 7 practices that contribute to purification you need to embrace. These are outward body actions. Although purification is directly concerned with the inner, it never disregards the outer which also supports developing inner traits. These should not be approach as something done one-off or occasionally. You should build a relationship with them. They will serve you if you serve them. Take them seriously and maintain with sincerely. But if you do them just for the sake of doing, you are unlikely to gain the fruits and will not aid your purification. Believing in them is believing in the way Allah﷽ has carved out this religion. You are the one in need of these means to the aim. He Almighty has given us everything and loves for us salvation but as a person is not compelled to do wrong, is not compelled to do right either. It is up to us to make the right choices, with the right inner intensions and outer actions, "**What would God do with [i.e., gain from] with your punishment if you are grateful and have attained faith? And ever is God Appreciative and All-Knowing**".[995]

One: who are your friends and companions?

From this point onwards there shall be much focus on matters of the unseen. Spirituality, the inner self, and the heart are all hidden. Many who fail or do not progress on this path is because they over rely only on what is apparent and physical. The Qur'an focuses a lot on the importance of the unseen. Those who benefit from its guidance and refine are "**those who are mindful and conscious of God**",[996] and those who are mindful and conscious are "**those who believe in the unseen**".[997] The more the impact of the unseen is on a person, the greater the success, balance, and development.[998]

Choosing your friends and companions is no different. You will be affected by those you choose to be with and amongst. The effect is inward (spiritually) and outward (taking from their behaviour and traits). Associating with people's negativity, corruptions, and darkness will slowly and unnoticeably penetrate your character and impact the heart. And likewise, being amongst the godly, noble, and righteous will have a profound and penetrating impact, so "**follow the path of those who turn to Me**".[999] Here friends and companions is not meant in the broad social context, those family, friends, neighbours, and colleagues we spend time with and admire the company of, but those who are God-fearing, who face us with our errors and flaws, remind us of the true nature of life and remind of God. When Prophet Nuh said, "**O My Lord, my son is of my family**",[1000] Allah﷽ responded by saying, "**O Nuh, he is not of your family. He is [one whose) deed is unrighteous**".

One clear example is how the companions became that great calibre of believers by surrounding and being in the presence of the best character, the Prophetﷺ who himself points out, "**a person shall be like those he friends, so be careful who you take as a friend**".[1001] Be with those who exceed you in spiritual state and can help you accordingly, "**be with the truthful**".[1002] Build with them a bond of real companionship and friendship, "**And keep yourself patient [by being] with those who call upon**

---

[995] Qur'an, 4:147.

[996] Qur'an, 2:2.

[997] Qur'an, 2:3.

[998] Tafsir Ibn Kathir, tafsir al-Tabari, tafsir al-Qurtubi, tafsir al-Baydawi.

[999] Qur'an, 31:15.

[1000] Qur'an, 11:45.

[1001] Al-Tirmidhi (2535), Ahmad (8028), Abu Dawud (4833).

[1002] Qur'an, 9:119.

their Lord in the morning and the evening, seeking His countenance. And let not your eyes pass beyond them, desiring adornments of the worldly life, and do not obey one whose heart We have made heedless of Our remembrance and who follows his desire and whose affair are scattered, and priorities confused".[1003]

The Islamic tradition of Spiritual Guidance/mentoring:

There are many Muslims who can recite and memorise the Qur'an and have much knowledge yet complain about their spiritual state and limited progress in refining their character. They yearn for solutions, especially that this can go on for several years and prolong for tens of years. An ill person cannot treat himself by reading books on medicine but must have a doctor who is qualified to diagnose and treat. Likewise, to practically purify and refine, it is essential to have a spiritual guide who is qualified and permitted, is pious and has inherited their methods and cures from the teachings of the Qur'an and Sunnah. You must have a sincere desire to be guided the prophetic way while content with whom Allah﷾ appoints to take your hand on His path.

To become righteous and pious is to shadow and relate to those who are righteous and pious. And to gain perfection is through those who have taken from the most perfect beingﷺ. It will not come from books and lectures.[1004] The companions benefited from 'being with' the Prophetﷺ not just hearing His words or about him. They observed his character and imitated. To be knowledgeable, one must study, but to be refine, one must observe. This is why they are called 'companions'.

But there is an important condition with regards to a spiritual guide. They must be an inheritor of the Prophetﷺ. You seek to join the chain, the connection leading up to the Prophetﷺ where inheritance flows down. This is known as *sanad*. Generally, *sanad* means a chain of narrators who have transmitted the text from its original source. As for the purification journey, over decades *sanad* has been the chain of interconnected guide-seeker relationship. From the Prophetﷺ right the way down to those permitted guides we have today. The Prophetﷺ mentored and took on a spiritual journey the companions. Having succeeded as noble and righteous believers and became knowledgeable in the methods of purification, they were qualified to take the people of the next generation on a journey, and the chain continues down. It is the mercy of Allah﷾ that this method has not only been consistent in the past but is a prophetic tradition that has been preserved and continues. A clear and straightforward model or 'template' we replicate, that assists in fulfilling the purification commands that goes for everyone, from the time of the Prophetﷺ to the End of Time.

In *sanad* there is great blessing as the circles of this chain are bonded with one another until reaching the Prophetﷺ. His light runs through the chain, circle to circle, generation to generation. The one with a *sanad* is stronger with this connection. He is not speaking on behalf of himself but transmits from their spiritual guide who transmitted from their guide right the way up, holding those attached to it firm on the path of the Prophetﷺ. Just like a person is connected to the *sanad* of a hadith is protected with sound knowledge and authenticity, those with the spiritual connection are protected and guided. Just like a hadith is transmitted down and helps implement the practical [outer] elements of the religion, the 'spiritual chain'

[1003] Qur'an, 18:28.

[1004] Knowledge is essential. However, the context here is on the practical means for change, refinement, and purification.

helps develop and solidify the [inner] spiritual side. This is normal and is very fitting as the religion commands that both the outer and inner go side by side, hence everything has reached us through a chain and transmission.

The great scholar of Islam Abdullah Ibn al-Mubarak explained, *"Isnad is part of religion (deen), and if it was not for Isnad, one would have said whatever one desired"*,[1005] and said: *"The one who seeks matters of his religion (deen) without Isnad is like a person who attempts to climb a roof without a ladder"*.[1006]

Sufyan al-Thawri, the great Islamic scholar and jurist warned, *"Isnad is the weapon of a believer. if he does not possess a weapon, then with what will he fight with?"*.[1007]

With your spiritual guide you are a companion of the spiritually developed and righteous, taking from them guidance and observing them as a living example and manifestation of the [inner and outer] teachings of Islam, Eman and Ihsan. The mother of Imam Malik understood this very well. She used to instruct him to be in the companionship of a righteous scholar named Rabi'ah, advising him that before taking from his knowledge, to observe and take from the manifestation of his knowledge and character, he explained, *"My mother would dress me up in the clothes of the scholars while I still was a young boy and she would tell me, 'go to the Masjid and seek knowledge from Imam Rabi'ah, study his manners before you take from his knowledge"*.[1008]

Two: what are you looking for in your Spiritual Guide?

The world we live in today has influenced people and societies to be affected by (and indulged in) its trends and tendencies which impacts and manipulate the way we do and perceive things. We mentioned in the last section that not everything is governed by what is apparent and physical but also hidden and unseen. For this reason, one must be mindful of their ways when on a journey they have no knowledge of or experience in. Intellect and desire must be controlled. Scholars teach us an important principal (of jurisprudence), *"the judgement on something is an outcome of how it is perceived"*. Therefore, limiting your understanding of this path and journey to what you think it is could lead to incorrect judgements, restricting the benefits, and causes disconnection.

If you want to get from one place to another, do you need to place pre-conditions such as the person you ask must be a highly qualified tour guide with 40 years of life experience! Surely not. You need to be focused on what they can offer that is specific to your need. In the same way, looking for a guide who has many followers and is charismatic is irrelevant and can be a distraction. You should be concerned with what they have that makes them qualified and able to support and mentor you. Look at how the Prophet☿ advises us to be focused and mature in such matter, **"The example of a good pious Companion and an evil one is that of a person carrying musk and another blowing a pair of bellows. The one who is carrying musk will either give you some perfume as a present, or you will buy some from him, or you will get a good smell from him, but the one who is blowing a pair of bellows will either burn your clothes or you will get a bad smell from him"**.[1009]

[1005] Introduction of Sahih Muslim (32).

[1006] Al-Baghdadi, A. *Sharaf ashab al-hadith*, p.42 (80).

[1007] Al-Qari, A. Sharh nokhbat al-fikr, p.617, sharaf ashab al-hadith, p.42 (81).

[1008] Al-Qadi Iyadh. *Tartib al-Madarik* (1/130).

[1009] Al-Bukhari (5534), Muslim (6692), Ahmad (19624).

This is what you should be looking for and should have the commitment to find anywhere. Do ill people not travel from one country to another to find specialist doctors, advanced treatment methods, and medicine? How about the doctor of our heart! Do not limit your commitment and strive. Ask Allah﷽ to choose a guide for you, the all-Knowing, the all-Merciful. In the darkness of the night ask him, in your prostrating ask him, and keep yearning. It is easy to find teachers/guides in many fields but if you seek a spiritual guide, you will find few, but Allah﷽ will make it happen if you remain sincere and persevere. And If you are blessed with one, hold on to them and show gratitude through the way you follow their instructions. Even if you have not yet been blessed with this one, follow through. Continue to be truthful and have strong trust in Allah﷽. Do not limit the extent of what He can do for you and increase in *salawat* on the Prophetﷺ with the intention of finding a guide.[1010]

Just like with any teacher, there are conditions that must be in a Spiritual Guide:
1. Must know the obligatory commands of Allah﷽, to implement and the impermissible, to avoid
2. Knowledgeable and experienced in heart purification and refinement methods – having gone through the process themselves, mentored by their guide
3. Has the permission of their guide, to guide others and hence given a license or *ijaza*.
4. Has a spiritual connection transmitting up to the Prophetﷺ. To be discussed in practicality three.

You may be asking a rightful question. What if you do not find a guide or it does not seem like there are any?
Be rest assured there are spiritual guides. Many are hidden as righteous pious people do not like to be known and would never claim to be pious, but Allah﷽ will bring the Seeker and the Guide together. Have trust and confidence in Him. Know that everything falls in His remit, His dominance and control. Secondly, we mentioned above that this is the way of the Prophetﷺ and this is how the companions were guided. The guide-seeker relationship (and necessity) went on throughout the history of Islam. You would not be required to purify yourself yet prevented from the guide that will lead your journey! Keep the heart asking and your limbs searching. The Quranic story of Prophet Musa and al-Khadr (chapter 18) is an example of how Allah﷽ made such a meeting happen and journey together set off. The Prophetﷺ affirms, "**A group of people from my Umma will continue to fight in defence of truth and remain triumphant until the Day of judgment**".[1011]

Before looking **you must let go** of your tendencies. If you start to draw a picture of your guide and draw up a checklist (apart from the conditions mentioned) then you will be faced with difficulties. If you are asking Allah﷽ to bring to your way a spiritual guide out of trust why then would you be pre-conditioning. Show utmost respect to your Lord and His choices. If you let go and show absolute submission then the journey has started and you will be astonished how Allah﷽ paves the way for things to unfold. This is no magic! This is the manifestation of "**Whoever relies on Allah - He will suffice him**".[1012] One of His names is 'the Opener' (Al-Fattah). Who allows things to open up and barriers removed.

[1010] Al-Tirmidhi (2625).
[1011] Muslim (1923).
[1012] Qur'an, 65:3.

Three: the pledge of faithfulness and commitment

To succeed on a spiritual journey, the Seeker must be willing to accompany and adhere to the advice of their Guide. The more you devote the more you benefit. Remember, they are the choice of your Lord for you. And while you are entrusting them and committed, you are devoting to Allah﷾. Just as following the advice and instructions of a qualified teacher of *fiqh* or *aqidah* still makes it for the sake of Allah﷾. The Qur'an is clear, there is no issue in making such pledge and does not contradict sincerity, "***Indeed, those who pledge allegiance to <u>you</u> [O Muhammad] are actually pledging allegiance to <u>Allah</u>***".[1013]

You make the pledge to your guide just like he made to his guide and his guide did with his guide and the chain continues right the way up to the Prophetﷺ. But it does not end there. The Prophetﷺ took from Angel Jibril revelation (who was permitted to transmit) and Jibril given from Allah Almighty. So you see how connection, chain and permission are a key feature of this religion. The Prophetﷺ explains, "***The scholars are the inheritors of the prophets. The prophets do not leave behind gold coins nor silver coins. They only leave behind knowledge, so whoever takes hold of it has taken an ample share***".[1014]

There are many occasions where companions made a pledge to the Prophetﷺ and in some cases he even asked them to.[1015] This included female and young companions[1016] and even companions to companions.[1017]

The Seeker is required to maintain good manners and humility with their Guide. Just as you submit to a doctor and trust them to be qualified, experienced, able to determine the condition, prescribe medication and set the doses, your Guide is also qualified, experienced and able to prescribe to you what you need, and you should be submitting to them too. They will know what to instruct you with in an experienced and measured approached. But the relationship on your part cannot be halfhearted. There must be certain manners upheld. Surely the one taking you on a *sacred journey* deserves to be highly regarded and respected. Think of how attentive and disciplined a person is with their doctor; listens, trusts, and obeys. Likewise, your 'spiritual doctor'. And think about the manners and principles the companions observed the Prophetﷺ which allowed them to develop. With your guide:

(1) Follow all instructions with humility and acceptance. Here you are not cancelling your identity or following blindly in a negative sense but are accepting to be led by an experienced specialist having known they fit the criteria of being qualified. When you are convinced a medical doctor is qualified and experienced and has the expertise, you follow their instructions with total submission. The idea is the same. Although many, if not all people, do not check their doctor's qualifications, yet walk into a medical centre or hospital and submits fully!

[1013] Qur'an, 48:10.

[1014] Al-Tirmidhi (2877), Abu Dawud (3641), Ibn Majah (223). Mentioned by al-Bukhari in his Sahih, Book of Knowledge, chapter: knowledge precedes speech and action.

[1015] Al-Bukhari (1401, 3893, 4894, 7199), Muslim (199, 4461, 4464, 4768), al-Tirmidhi (1505), al-Nisa'i (4149, 4150), Ibn Majah (2866), Malik (445) Ahmad (22679).

[1016] Al-Tirmidhi (1687), al-Nisa'i (4192), Ibn Majah (2875), Malik (982).

[1017] Ibn Saad. *Al-tabaqat al-kubra* (7/15).

(2) Do not oppose their ways and methods. You did not know the methods of purifying yourself and were unable to benefit yourself, otherwise you would not be here seeking to be guided and purified. The reality is you need help. Do not create barriers and veils out of ignorance. Now is a time to listen attentively and practice vigorously. Build with your Guide a bond of trust, faith, and confidence. Overcome your egos and the 'Me' and 'I' that tries to rebel against much needed help and discipline. Students who put their head down, focus, and do their work are the ones who flourish, excel, and get high grades.

(3) No matter how righteous and pious your guide is, they will never be infallible. It is possible they may fall into slips and errors but saying that they are pious people who do not persist in wrongdoing and are quick to repent and come back. Know that their hearts remain attached to Allah.

In summary, humble yourself with sincerity and love towards your Guide. Good feelings towards them will bring out the good in you and open door for progress. Protect their dignity and reputation as righteous friends of Allah. Observe calmness and tranquillity in their presence and be patient with their methods of developing you. Know that they went through all this and succeeded. They are not testing on you, they are simply replicating Islamic methods and reasons for purification and salvation.

Four: purification without knowledge is controversial & knowledge without purification is negligence

What good is there in knowledge if a person does not develop with it. Knowledge can lead to strengthening consciousness and mindfulness of Allah [1018] and is the means to fulfilling all aspects of the religion. This does, however, depend on the readiness of the receiver (the heart). The heart cannot react with or show emotions towards something unless it rationally makes sense of it, which is why knowledge is key. Knowledge, although does not strengthen consciousness *per se,* it provides the rational foundations for the heart to react and become more conscious. [1019] Knowledge is clarity and clarity allows you to be efficient, have sound [heart] judgement, reliability, and develop in competence and robustness. But it starts with acquiring it then practising it.

There is no benefit in knowledge without action and no good in action without knowledge. They go side-by-side and should never be separated. Your journey is about practically implementing Islam inwardly and outwardly. A seeker without knowledge is no way like a seeker with knowledge [1020] and Allah raises in ranks those who gain knowledge. [1021] As this path is based on the noble knowledge of *Ihsan*, it is therefore centred on adherence to the Qur'an and Sunnah and the rejection of unfounded or heretical innovations.

[1018] Qur'an, 35:28.

[1019] Qur'an, 35:28, 18:68. Tafsir al-Razi, tafsir al-Qurtubi, tafsir Ibn Kathir, tafsir al-Baydawi, tafsir al-muharar al-wajiz, tafsir Abu al-Saud, tafsir al-Sha'rawi. Qur'an, 29:69. Tafsir al-Razi.

[1020] Qur'an, 39:9.

[1021] Qur'an, 58:11.

It is important to know the three types of knowledge and what one's approach should be towards them:

Knowledge that is obligatory

- Start by learning the *aqidah*. The true *aqidah* that goes back to the time of the Prophet ﷺ, companions and authentic scholars, while knowing general proofs from Qur'an and Sunnah to safeguard your faith, overcome any doubts and refute misconceptions. Also matters of *fiqh* that relate to your rituals and daily affairs
- Know what is lawful to adhere to and what is prohibited to avoid
- Know about manners and morals, conduct and essential principles a Muslim is expected to maintain

Recommended knowledge

- Learn about heart purity and spiritual healthiness; sincerity, reliance on and deepening trust in Allah ﷻ, diseases of the heart such as self-pride, arrogance, envy, bad feelings towards others, hypocrisy, unlawful desires etc and learn how to overcome these through repentance, accountability, supplication, *dhikr* (Remembrance) etc.[1022]

Knowledge that is prohibited

Refrain from engaging in knowledge that is insignificant and counterproductive such as corrupt ideologies and beliefs unless you are looking to refute them and prove their falsehood. If this is already being done by others, you should avoid as should be left to those with advanced knowledge and specialism. Focus on enhancing your obligatory knowledge along with implementing.

Knowledge that is permissible

- Any knowledge that would allow you to enhance morally, develop intellectually and spiritually
- Any knowledge that will help you serve society and fellow brothers and sisters in Islam and humanity
- Broader and detailed matters of *fiqh*.[1023]

Five: are you willing to put in the effort?

The real question is: to what extent? All the way? Confronting any distractions? Dealing with the obstacles and coming out of the comfort zone?

There are no miracles on this path. There are practicalities and hard work. Relaxing, hoping, and just being motivated will not work. Allah ﷻ sets the condition for those who want to be guided. Through strive and perseverance comes guidance. There is no purification without effort. The purpose of this 'spiritual struggle' (*mujahada*) is to take control of the temptations and negative tendencies, as a start to the purification process; the readiness to receive divine light and guidance which leads to becoming characterised with obedience. This is where the very veils preventing spiritual healthiness and progress lies. This is where the barriers come down in dealing with the ego of the self.[1024]

[1022] This shall be covered in the remaining sections of this book.

[1023] The elements of *fiqh* which relate to your everyday responsibilities and practices should always take priority. Thereafter, you can study other areas of *fiqh*.

[1024] See Tafsir al-Jalalin, tafsir al-Baghawi, tafsir Abu al-Saud, tafsir al-Baydawi, tafsir hashiyat al-Sawi ala al-Jalalin, tafsir al-Sha'rawi (Qur'an, 29:69).

You cannot struggle against the self and at the same time be feeding it with sins and excessiveness of worldly pleasures. That would be sheer ignorance. The heart is a tree watered with obedience. Having no remorse and treating sins as something trivial is arrogance and a dangerous position to be in. The Qur'an warns, "**And you consider it insignificant, yet in the sight of Allah is greatly serious**".[1025] Even if a sin is considered just a spark, a spark can lead to burning acres of land.

The human self can be the biggest danger and enemy or it can be a means to success, depending on whether it enjoys sinning or enjoys obedience.[1026] Whether you decide to do what is right or leave it to do what it [unlawfully] inclines towards. Whether you battle it, or it batters you. If you are focused, you will have no time to waste or be focused on the flaws of others. You have enough to work on to keep you occupied. Do not focus on the flaws of others if you have flaws and because you have flaws, so focus on yours alone. Those who do not strive will remain on a standstill or gain very little benefit while the ones who succeed are the active ones, "**O Allah, we have wronged ourselves, and if You do not forgive us, and have mercy on us, we shall surely be of losers**".[1027] They acknowledge, admit, and strive to move on, to become better.

You are striving to overcome flaws, which are two:

(1) **The outer**: the uses of your limbs. What you say, what you hear, see and touch. Your legs, stomach, and your private parts. All these are protected by the outer commands of the religion. For example, you put effort and strive into preventing your legs take you where is forbidden, do not touch what does not belong to you, lower your gaze with your eyes, do not hear the private conversations of people or accept to hear backbiting, and do not overfill your stomach as the spiritual consequences to this is detrimental and so on.

(2) **The inner**: the strive to deal with traits such as arrogance, anger and envy replacing with humbleness, calmness, contentment, and acceptance.

The condition of the heart is unsteady and volatile and does not remain in one condition. Your role is to develop so it remains submissive and steadfast. The strive may be difficult in the beginning but over time eases once you start to gain more control and instinctively devote to what is right. The more you persevere in the beginning the quicker and more effective the change will be.

You must accept that dealing with the human self is complex. The experience, permission, and qualities your Guide has is vital. By observing attentively and listening, you pick up messages and signs on how to conduct yourself. However, your Guide can only do so much, it is up to you to move forward. It is about nurturing (and sometimes forcing[1028]) the self to oppose what it desires. Here you need to be very firm and persistent. The more you are in control the more there is space to replace with good and righteous traits. The result is that you bring the self in line with divine guidance as the practical alignment between strive and guidance, "**Those who <u>strive</u> hard for Our cause, We shall be sure to <u>guide</u> to Our ways**".[1029]

[1025] Qur'an, 24:15.
[1026] Qur'an, 79:37-41.
[1027] Qur'an, 7:23.
[1028] But still with balance. Refer to our book, Abouzaid. A., *"So they may attain taqwa"*, A Practical Approach.
[1029] Qur'an, 29:69.

Six: do you expect a journey to Allah۞ to be without remembering Allah۞?

Here we come onto a topic which is either neglected by many or not given enough focus. Remembrance (*dhikr*). This is a form of spiritual reflection in which certain prayers and supplications are repeated, to remember Allah۞ and be in His presence[1030]

Dhikr awakens the heart. You cannot be on a journey if you are dormant, living in drowsiness or have your 'Do Not Disturb' sign up! A seeker of something should be conscious and always remembering of it. A seeker of Allah۞ needs to be remembering of Him, "**So remember Me, and I will remember you**"[1031] meaning He shall guide and guard you.[1032] He advises his servants and seekers to remember Him and praises those who are in Remembrance and do it regularly, warning those who prevent themselves and others.[1033] The difference between the one in Remembrance and the one not is the difference between a dead and a living.[1034] The one who is in Remembrance their worldly and religious matters are settled and organised and those who are not, their affairs are scattered and will have a life of difficulties and discomfort.[1035] The Prophet۞ describes the places where collective *dhikr* is conducted (*dhikr* circles) as "**Gardens of Paradise**".[1036]

The heart can easily rust just like metal and as metal requires treatment the heart's cure from rusting is *dhikr*.[1037] There are *hadiths* that encourage it be done loudly and collectively, *hadiths* that encourage it be silently,[1038] and verses that encourage an in-between loud and silent.[1039] It is advisable to do silently if one fears doing it insincerely in front of people. Whether silent or loud, alone or in a gathering, the important thing is to have presence. That is to be in full concentration and [spiritually] disconnected from your surrounding so that what you are repeating is real, can be felt, penetrates the heart, and impacts. If especially in the early days you do not feel presence this should be no reason or excuse to stop doing *dhikr*, to become complacent or demotivated. Remember: purification is a process over time, so requires patience and spiritual struggle.

Doing alone has a deep effect as it involves seclusion/isolation with your Lord. One should create these moments of quality time, alone just you and Him, Almighty.[1040]

[1030] Leading also to protection and healing (Qur'an, 10:57, 13,28, 17:82, 41:44), inner peace and contentment (Qur'an, 13:28), divine light and purification of the heart (Qur'an, 33:43) moving away from hypocrisy (Qur'an, 4:142) and many other forms of reward and benefit.

[1031] Qur'an, 2:152.

[1032] Tafsir al-Tabari, tafsir al-Qurtubi, tafsir al-Razi, tafsir Ibn Kathir.

[1033] Qur'an, 2:152, 2:114, 63:9, 2:200, 3:41, 3:191, 4:103, 33:41, 62:10, 29:45, 24:37, 33:35.

[1034] Al-Bukhari (6407), Muslim (1823).

[1035] Qur'an, 18:28, 20:124. Tafsir al-Tabari, tafsir Ibn Kathir.

[1036] Al-Tirmidhi (3819).

[1037] Al-Tirmidhi (3624), Ibn Majah (4244), al-Nisa'i in *al-kubra* (10179).

[1038] Al-Bukhari (7405), Muslim (6805, 6902), al-Tirmidhi (3375), Ahmad (7422, 8187), al-Nisa'i (2753).

[1039] Qur'an, 7:205, 17:110.

[1040] This could be a daily morning and evening sitting whereas the collective *dhikr* in congregation a weekly or occasional gathering.

There are two types of *dhikr*:

Restricted *dhikr*: done at specific times (during and after prayer, before and after eating and drinking, before and after sleeping etc.) and specific places (during *hajj*, entering and exiting the toilet, upon entering the house, the mosque etc).[1041] Remembering your Lord comes in different forms. An opportunity to ask of something, be grateful for something or glorifying Allah. You are always conscious of your Beloved.

For example:

- When entering the toilet, you say the *dhikr* taught by the Prophet seeking Allah's protection from the harm of Satan who reside in such placed, "***In the name of Allah. O Allah, I seek protection in You from the male and female Shaytan***".[1042] And when leaving the toilet, you show gratitude through the *dhikr* of gratefulness for the removal of human waste from the body and your wellbeing, "***[O Allah] I seek forgiveness and pardon from You". All Praise be to Allah, who has taken away from me discomfort and granted me relief***".[1043]
- When you ride a form of transportation you are grateful for this ease to get to places, saying, "***Glory to the One Who has subjected these [transportations] to us, and in no way could we have done it ourselves***".[1044]

Slowly introduce in your day the different forms of *dhikr* and do ponder on the miraculous wording of each one and its context. Do not just utter. You cannot be asking for something or praising your Lord yet do not know what you are saying.

Unrestricted *dhikr*: this can be done at any time and in any place. We are encouraged to always be remembering Allah just as the Prophet always used to.[1045] This could be a name of Allah, glorifying and praising Him, repenting, salutations upon the Prophet, or affirming His oneness. The principle here is to remember your Lord and remember Him a lot.

<u>Daily duty:</u>

It is advisable to create some time in the morning and the evening to have a sitting in isolation with Allah. An opportunity for reflection and to develop through three essential forms of *dhikr*. Each come with their unique importance and impact on your spiritual state. But first decide, do you want to be one of the masses who deal with *dhikr* in a limited way and so what they gain back is very limited? Or do you want to be from the foremost who gain the real fruits and prosper?

The masses - those who do it just for reward and good deed yet remain in their sins, desires, and heart diseases.

The foremost - those who do with true presence and want to refine. They commit to these specific forms of *dhikr* which they know will act as spiritual cure and remedy – by the Will of Allah, removing veils of darkness and contribute to [deep-rooted] purification.

[1041] These are all listed in books of Remembrance '*The book of Remembrance*' (*al-adhkar*) by the renowned scholar imam al-Nawawi is a great book.

[1042] Al-Bukhari (142), Muslim (831).

[1043] Al-Tirmidhi (7), Abi Dawud (30), Ibn Majah (300).

[1044] Qur'an, 43:13. Al-Tirmidhi (2602), Abi Dawud (2602), al-Nisa'i in *al-kubra* (8748).

[1045] Al-Tirmidhi (3671), Ibn Majah (3793), Muslim (826).

These are:

Daily times	Type of Remembrance	Transliteration
Morning: Fagr to Sunrise (to Zuhr if time runs out)	Repentance (*istighfar*) - 100 times استغفر الله العظيم الذي لا اله الا هو الحي القيوم واتوب اليه	Astaghfir Allah ala'zeem al-ladhy la ilaha ila huwa al-Hay al-Qayoum wa atoubu ilayh
	Salutations on the Prophet✸ (*salawat*) - 100 times اللهم صل على سيدنا محمد النبي الامي وعلى آله وصحبه وسلم	Allahuma sali 'ala sayyidna Muhammad alnabi alommi 'ala aaleehi wa sahbihi wa salim
Evening: Maghreb to Isha (to midnight if time run out)	Oneness of Allah✸ (*al-tawhid*) - 100 times لا إله إلا الله	La ilaha ila Allah

What are the benefits of devoting to these three forms of *dhikr*?

(1) Repentance (*istighfar*): removes bad qualities in the self

While pondering on sins and shortcomings, with presence, the general experience inwardly is the removal of the darkness of sins, and outwardly brings the person back on track, renewing their pledge to their Lord, by:

- Feeling remorse over committing the sin – acknowledging wrongdoing with truthfulness and humility
- Have a firm desire to leaving the sin – willingness to manifest with religiously-lawful behaviour
- Determined to never return to the sin – perseverance and spiritual struggle
- Returning due rights to its owner - honouring the importance of justice and rights of others in Islam

This is your repentance from specific sins and desires. Also, pondering on your overall condition and need to be obedient and upright in your ways, steadfast and adhering to the command of your Lord. Renew this commitment and strive to do better. This is done in the morning for sins of the evening and night and repeated in the evening for sins of the morning and day. Even as one progresses and develops into greater depths of [instinctive] obedience doing what is right, they still ponder, regret and repent. But here the focus is on what they could have done better. Questioning why they did not do things with greater attentiveness and finness, knowing Allah✸ is observing them and is worthy of anything done for His sake is to be done with utmost excellence. Afterall, *ihsan,* as mentioned in earlier pages is about, "*the pursuit of all-round perfection. It refines all aspects of a person's dealings, towards himself, towards Allah✸, people, animals, plants, and objects. Perfection in everything you do and everything about you*".

(2) Salutations on the Prophet✸ (*salawat*): adorning the self with good qualities.

Sending salutations (or abundant blessings) is to ask Allah✸ to bring His mercy upon the Prophet✸.[1046] It is a way to show gratitude towards him, love, and respect. The more it is repeated the more the love, appreciation, and devotion towards him increases. This devotion over time has an outer and an inner manifestation. A spiritual bond with a strong desire to follow his footsteps, imitate his good character, and commit to his teachings.

[1046] Imam al-Tirmidhi narrated from Sufyan al-Thawri. See al-Tirmidhi (485).

This is when a person becomes adorned with good character:

Outwardly: a loving desperacy to act upon his sayings and teaching.

The body and limbs eagerly searching for anything from him and about him. For he prepresents human excellence and perfection. And works to align himself to the four (discussed in chapter three):

Believe

Honour

Support

Follow the light which is sent down with him

Inwardly: spiritual enlightenment:

We are commanded to send salutations, "***Indeed, Allah and His Angels send blessing upon the Prophet, and His angels. O you who have believed, ask [Allah to send] blessing upon him and peace***".[1047]

In this is an ongoing spiritual return.

How?

Every time you do *salawat* seeking Allah's mercy upon the Prophet, Allah responds by sending His mercy on you, ten times, "***Whoever sends blessings upon me, Allah will send blessings upon him tenfold***".[1048]

But what does this mercy do to you? What impact does it have?

This is the result: "***it is He [Allah] Who showers His mercy upon you, and His angels, so that He may bring you out of darkness and into light***".[1049] So for every salutation done, you move further away from darkness and closer to light. This is divine light i.e., purification against darkness (spiritual illnesses). A reminder that the Prophet is not just as a teacher but also a purifier, a reason for reaching purification.[1050]

There are many other benefits to sending salutations on the Prophet. When the companion *Ubai Ibn Ka'ab* asked the Prophet what if he dedicated all his *dhikr* towards sending salutations upon him, the Prophet replied, "***then your needs will be fulfilled and your sins will be forgiven***"[1051] which includes the needs of the Next life, "***the closest of people to me on the Day of Resurrection will be those who sent the most blessings [i.e. Salawat] upon me***".[1052]

[1047] Qur'an, 33:56.

[1048] Muslim (912), Ahmad (8854).

[1049] Qur'an, 33:43.

[1050] See Qur'an, 2:151 and 3:164. See also *al-mufradat fi gharib al-qur'an* (al-Raghib al-Asfahani), p. 287 (commenting on the word '*al-salah*' in Qur'an, 9:103).

[1051] Al-Tirmidhi (2625).

[1052] Al-Tirmidhi (490).

Imam [al-Hafidh] al-Sakhawi lists several benefits for sending *salawat*, including:[1053]

Relationship with Allah﷾	Protection	Your condition	In the Hereafter
Aided by Allah﷾	A spiritual healing	Removal of sins and cleanses the heart of its rust	Barrier to Hellfire
Gain the love of Allah﷾	Protects from forgetfulness of Allah﷾	Awakens the heart and induces the love of Allah﷾	Reason for entering Paradise
Chosen ally of Allah﷾	Saves the tongue from falling into sinful talk	Softens the heart and increases piety	A seedling of the plants of Paradise
Closeness to Allah﷾	A reason for salvation from punishment	Creates internal happiness, joy, and satisfaction	To be under the shade of Allah﷾'s Throne
God-fearing and increased consciousness	Gains Allah﷾'s protection	Success in all affairs	Saves from severe regret and despair
Opens the door of elightened realisation	Support in difficult times	Inner tranquillity and contentment	Increases ranks of Paradise
Glorifying of Allah﷾	Eliminates the abilities of Satan	Adorns you with good character and increase in excellence	Closer proximity with the Prophetﷺ
Develops a great awe[1054] towards Allah﷾	Causes Satan to stay away	Actions become refined and perfected	Immense reward
A deep devotion to turning to and reliance on Allah﷾	Attracts provision and blesses it	Strengthens the soul and relieves the mind from anxiety and worry	Intercession of the Prophetﷺ

(2) **The Oneness of Allah (La ilaha ila Allah, *al-tawhid*):** strengthening one's faith through affirmation.

When repeating La ilaha ila Allah there is benefit through two stages: (1) La ilaha (2) ila Allah

La ilaha – there is no god

Ila Allah – except Allah﷾

A process of constantly negating and affirming, removing and replacing.

Removing anyone and anything you have allowed to carry an attribute of God and replacing with redeclaring that only Allah﷾ is God, and the only One worthy of being in your heart. This does not mean a person is willingly or consciously worshiping other than Allah﷾. What it does mean is that you may be acting towards something in a way that is submissive and allowing yourself to be controlled by. The Prophetﷺ mentions in a hadith a few examples, "**Let the _slave_ of _Dinar_ and _Dirham_, of _Quantify_ and _Khamisa_ (i.e. money and luxurious clothes) be in loss for he is pleased if these things are given to him, and if not, he is displeased**".[1055]

A person can allow himself to be enslaved to these and other desires as if they have become a god he worships, "**Have you seen the one who takes as his _god_ his own desire?**"[1056] whereas a true believer is able to "**restrain the self from desires**".[1057]

[1053] Al-qawl al-badie' fi al-salah ala al-habib al-shafeei'.

[1054] A feeling of respect mixed with fear and glorification.

[1055] Al-Bukhari (2886).

[1056] Qur'an, 25:43.

[1057] Qur'an, 79:40-41.

There is danger in neglecting *dhikr*. The hypocrites are the ones who "**remember God only occasionally**".[1058] Now ponder on these two verses:

(1) "**And whoever turns a blind eye to the Remembrance of the Most Merciful - a devil shall be assigned to them and remains their Companion**".[1059]

(2) In chapter 114, (verses 1 and 4-6) we seek refuge from the whispers of Satan, "**Say, "I seek refuge in the Lord of mankind...From the evil of the sneaky retreating whisperer.**[1060] **Who whispers into the hearts of people. From among jinn and among people**".

Putting the two passages together, it can be concluded that that turning towards *dhikr* is a reason to be free from Satan's assignment and their evil whispers and that of humans. Turning away from *dhikr* shall be a reason whispers and assignment to exist and remain.

The first thing your spiritual guide will do is assign to you is a set of *dhikr* for the morning and the evening known as a *wird*[1061] and is very important. It consists of the three types mentioned above[1062] and certain supplications.

Seven: understanding your journey and its experiences

On your journey, as you start to progress, changes to your condition will be necessary and is natural. Your thoughts will develop as they become purer, your inner conscience and feelings will enlighten as they become purer, and your spiritual state will advance. This is about 'Spiritual Maturity'. It is important to ask questions and seek advice from your Guide. They will know what you are going through. Will know what to explain and reveal, what not to, the stages you are going through, and what will develop naturally as part of the overall remedies he prescribes.

One remedy, for example, could be seclusion. Where your Guide requests you isolate for some time and be given a certain form of *dhikr* to constantly repeat. This could be the name 'Allah' or 'Subhan Allah' intended to serve a purpose in your condition. During this, the effect slowly moves from verbal to a deep-heart-effect and purification impact. Seclusion is something the Prophetﷺ used to do[1063] and we follow his methods accordingly. As for repeating the name 'Allah' or 'Subhan Allah', this falls under the general rule of "**And remember the name of your Lord, and devote yourself to Him wholeheartedly**".[1064] The verse does not specify what to say when 'remembering the name of your Lord' nor does it specify how many times, or durations. It only says to remember. Likewise, "**O you who believe, remember Allah with much remembrance**".[1065] Again, it is open. No specifics and no limitations, just remember a lot and frequently.

[1058] Qur'an, 4:142.

[1059] Qur'an, 43:36.

[1060] I.e., a devil who makes evil suggestions to man.

[1061] *Wird* is a commonly used word which means to do something regularly. It is used when someone reads a portion of the Qur'an daily/on a regular basis. Hence called '*wird* of the Qur'an' and similarly, a '*wird* of *dhikr*' is to devote to it regularily.

[1062] The formular of each may differ. The Prophetﷺ mentioned several formulars.

[1063] Al-Bukhari (3).

[1064] Qur'an, 73:8.

[1065] Qur'an, 33:41.

Seclusion allows you to isolate from worldly distractions and ponder deeply on your condition and conduct. Other benefits include:

- **Behavioural control.** Bringing your heart and limbs to the state it should be in. Calm and free from corruption. When a person is amongst people, they may fall into backbiting for example. Seclusion is an opportunity to practice silence and be reminded how your conduct should be, so when returning back to be amongst people are able to control yourself having brought the heart and limbs to upright conduct and practiced silence,[1066] along with the strive to maintain obedience and lawful behaviours having reflected and renewed intentions.

- **Pondering on the reality of this world.** A temporary stopover every person shall move on from. This is an opportunity to question your relationship with this world. Are you becoming attached to it? Is it taking over your heart? Are you allowing it to affect, dictate, or drive your priorities? etc.

- **To move away from people for a short period.** When a person is constantly in a setting they can become accustomed and [unknowingly] manipulated and shaped by it. This requires an opportunity to renew principles and make necessary decisions away from the effects and influences.

- **To taste the beauty of worship.** As a motivation to continue, perfect, and increase.

It is essential to communicate your desires, difficulties, and developing thoughts and experiences to your Guide. Here you are not exposing your sins and negativities in a way that the religion prevents you from doing.[1067] Rather, a Seeker with their Guide is like a patient exposing his pains, sufferings, and difficulties to a doctor.

Reaching Allah﷾

The expression of 'reaching Allah﷾' or the path 'to Allah﷾' may be ones you come across. This means reaching his presence and closeness, spiritually. The more a person develops in being conscious of Allah﷾ (*taqwa*) the more they increase in receiving knowledge from Allah﷾, "**Be mindful of Allah, and He will teach you**"[1068] and the purer a person becomes, the more they receive knowledge which is beyond academic knowledge in books; deeper and far beyond what is granted to the masses. This is called *Inspirational Knowledge*.[1069] This is why the righteous and noble are also called 'the knowers of Allah' (*al-'arifoun billah*).[1070] They see and know realities of things with divine light from Allah﷾,[1071] The Prophetﷺ asserts, "**Beware of the believer's intuition, for indeed he sees with Allah's Light**". Then he recited: "**Surely in that are lessons for those who read signs**[1072]".[1073]

[1066] Refer to our book for more insight on this (Abouzaid, A., The Sacred Journey: "**so they may attain taqwa**". A Practical Approach). Yet to be published, if Allah﷾ so wills.

[1067] Al-Bukhari (6069), Muslim (7485), *sharh al-Nawawi 'ala sahih Muslim*.

[1068] Qur'an, 2:282.

[1069] Qur'an, 18:65. *Al-Khadr* was known to be a righteous man.

[1070] Tafsir al-dur al-manthur (7/20-3), Abi Dawud (362). Al-Bayhaqi, *al-madkhal ila 'ilm al-Sunnan* (529) Al-Darmi (363). Abu Na'im, *hilyit al-awliya'* (7/259).

[1071] Qur'an, 15:75. Tafsir al-Tabari, tafsir al-Qurtubi, tafsir Ibn Kathir, tafsir al-Razi, tafsir al-Baydawi, tafsir al-Baghawi, tafsir al-Nasafi, tafsir Abu al-Saud, tafsir al-Alusi, tafsir al-Sha'rawi. Al-Tirmidhi (3392).

[1072] Qur'an, 15:75.

[1073] Al-Tirmidhi (3392).

Inner (heart) traits

Like a mirror, the heart can become obscured by emotions, negative attitudes, thought, superficial levels of opinion, desires, and with pressures such as social conditioning, inherited ideas, and ideologies which causes the knowledge of the heart to becomes veiled. It can also be in a state of softness or hardness, sensitive or insensitive, awake or asleep, healthy or sick, and open or closed. Its ability to reach soundness, realisation, and purity depends on its condition.

In this section the focus shall be on the spiritual side that needs much attention by working on healing the heart and paving the way for it to be charcterised with essential inner traits. To remove what is corrupt (*takhliyah*) and replacing with what is beautiful (*tahliah*).

One: clear the heart, to pave the way – repentance (*tawba*)

Tawba linguistically is 'to retract from a sin'.[1074]
Islamically, 'committing to move from negative actions to positive ones'.[1075]

You must repent from every single sin, no matter how big or small they seem. Although - in principle - a believer is focused not on how small a sin is perceived but on how great the Lord they disobeyed is. This way your attention is on glorifying Allah﷽ in your heart and having remorse for a lack of discipline at any given moment. This is where success lies and is the essence of awakening and realisation. An awakened heart knows when it has gone wrong and knows how to retract: feeling of remorse, a firm desire to leave that sin, determined to never return to it and returning any due rights. If any of these are missing, repentance is not accepted.[1076] Renew your repentance regularly and appeal for forgiveness. Repent also from anything that disengages you from Allah﷽ and remember that choice of friends and companions has an effect.

Side-by-side with repentance there must be a positive attitude. Be optimistic about your path, certain that "**Allah loves those who always turn to Him in repentance and those who purify themselves**".[1077] Treat every repentance as a milestone to becoming better, with hope and strength. Be purposeful in everything you do and insist on becoming maturer in your ways.

(a) To move on, start with a good deed to counter the bad[1078]

(b) Learn from mistakes to assist in developing your 'Spiritual Character'

(c) Look for the root cause and internal triggers

By 'spiritual character' we mean the self (nafs) that is being moulded. Part of the purification process is to get to know your inner self better. To understand more its ways, its triggers, methods, tactics, deceptions, and know how to deal with and control. The teachings of the Qur'an and Sunnah are full of solutions and your spiritual guide will assist with suitable option, such as *dhikr* given to you as a *wird*, as mentioned earlier.

[1074] Al-Jurjani. *Al-ta'rifat.*

[1075] Ibid.

[1076] Riyadh al-salihin, p.14.

[1077] Qur'an, 2:222.

[1078] Al-Tirmidhi (2102).

The *nafs* requires a balance between firmness and encouragement. Just like a child, when moulding their character with discipline you create a fine balance between encouraging them and punishing them. Your inner self is your child that works in the same way. You cannot all along be punishing nor all along be encouraging. By replacing a bad deed with good, this is a form of encouragement that gives you assurance you are worthy of being upright and strong-willed, if you so choose. And practically reminds you: these are the kind of actions you should be engaged with, going forward, not the unlawful ones.

To learn from mistakes to make you a better person is where you create for yourself a golden opportunity. Whilst you should be consciously avoiding all sins, shortcomings, and resist temptations, when a sin is committed you should straight away be adamant to learn from this. Grasping this opportunity or neglecting is the difference between sins and desires remaining or proactively understanding how to restrain and develop out of it. This is where maturity comes in to serve you and your path. Maturity to look beyond "I committed a sin and won't do it again". This is to look deeper internally, inside your heart and your self.

Let us take anger as an example. There is no good saying "that person made me angry" or "that person intimidated me". The obvious fact is that no person had control of your inner self, your actions, or your choice of reaction. Stop looking outside and look inside where it all started. This goes back to what we discussed earlier: "*one must accept – out of humility and sincerity – he has all diseases until proven otherwise*". If there is no willingness to accept the person has root causes leading to anger, they will continue to blame anything and anyone else. And if there is the readiness to accept they may have this and other illnesses, the person has passed their first hurdle and there can be more positive to come.

If you want to get into the habit of repentance, let no moment pass without reflection. Reflect on your day's actions, words, and thoughts, and on your condition. Reflect on how you are progressing and remember there is no time; your existence is on countdown and your physical being is *wear and tear!*

Two: awaken to take accountability and be accountable to remain awakened

To be 'awaken' is when the heart is conscious and on alert. Knows what is right and knows when it is blameworthy. In wrongdoing, it is fast to acknowledge and quick to return. For this to be the case the person must be accountable. Accountability is something we apply every day at work, school, home etc and observe throughout the day. Therefore, it can be done and is done. One should be aware of where they stand with accountability and where they contradict themselves by being accountable in things and not in others, being firm and principled in things but slack and egoistic in others.

Accountability is a true treasure. Along with repentance it is fundamental for progression and refinement. It humbles you and ensures you maintain humility. You should be content to frankly say to yourself "*I was wrong, and I shall correct myself*" leaving behind any demotivation or loss of hope. The story of Prophet Adam and Satan is repeated in the Qur'an several times. This is to remind us that the satanic way is to be arrogant and not admit your fault and the way of the sincere and humble is to admit and correct.

Your inner self, like a child, if you allow it to do what it desires or belittle its faults and errors it will become spoilt, complacent and lack self-correction, and if disciplined will mature with integrity and conscious morality. Accountability keeps the hearts wideawake and softened. When Allah﷾ is disobeyed the heart becomes like the eclipsed sun overshadowing the light of faith. Accountability reminds you that you have not been created haphazardly but for a noble purpose and you shall – without a doubt – return to your Lord and be accountable, "**A wise man is the one who calls himself to account (and refrains from doing evil deeds) and does noble deeds to benefit him after death; and the foolish person is the one who subdues himself to his temptations and desires and seeks from Allah the fulfilment of his vain desire**".[1079]

Three: fear (*khouf*)

Linguistically, 'to be alarmed and distressed'.[1080]
Islamically, 'the fear of an unwanted gain or loss of what is appreciated'.[1081]

This is when the heart feels pain when committing a sin or realising one's condition is declining. Fear of future consequence. The bitter taste of knowing you disobeyed and displeased your Lord and not progressing in purification and refinement. And knowing there is consequences on The Day where there are no excuses or hiding away.
While this is not a good feeling as there lies in it regret and shame, it is necessary. The one who does not feel fear in these situations needs to think deeply and be concerned. Being content or lacking remorse when committing sins or satisfied with their [unrefined] condition has a ripple effect and can be distorting. One of the serious developments it can lead to is to start creating excuses for not having regret and remorse and excuses for not doing something about bettering your condition. Some of the excuses we hear:

- o "Our times are different to the 'Golden Age' of the Prophetﷺ and companions".
- o "It is harder because I am living in a non-Muslim country or a non-fully complying, God-conscious environment".
- o "Family life, children, responsibilities, and life constraints take up a lot of time and is stressful".

Whatever the excuse, time, place, or people, these are barefaced coverups you have created for yourself, attempting to throw the blame elsewhere, "**God does not burden a soul beyond its capacity**".[1082] There is no burden, there is strive and a sincere willingness to be open and transparent with yourself. Not doing anything to resolve your issues or not putting in the effort is no excuse and does not strip a person off their responsibility. It is a decision only you make. No one has control over you, and you cannot deceive Allah﷾. Show respect to your Lord and with Him be principled. Ask yourself: is there pain and regret? Or is there no reaction and cold emotions? Fear is not just about shedding a tear. Fear is to move away from what you are punished for and distancing far from displeasing Allah﷾.

[1079] Al-Tirmidhi (2627), Ahmad (17123), Ibn Majah (4260).

[1080] Lisan al-arab, al-qamous al-muhit.

[1081] Al-Jurjani. *Al-ta'rifat.*

[1082] Qur'an, 2:286.

Four: hope (*rajaa*)

Linguistically is 'optimism'.[1083]

Islamically, 'convince in the heart of a positive thing in the future'.[1084]

While there must be fear, it should not lead to loss of or weakened hope in the mercy of Allah. This contradicts the positive attitude of a Muslim. Imagine yourself living with two wings that allow you to be well-balanced. One is fear and the other must be hope.[1085] Hope is to have a feeling of inner calmness and assurance. It allows you to think and feel beyond the wrongdoing, especially when you accept – as mentioned before – purification is a process and the scope for improvement and development is beyond every limit. Hope allows you to continue to be focused, your vision remains crystal clear, and your perseverance increases intensity. Your wrongdoing, despite regret and disappointment, has opened a whole new avenue. But hope without repentance is deception and blindness. How can you jump on the hope waggon, wanting to change, but have not felt any guilt or acknowledged any wrongdoing in the first place!

Listen to the words of Prophet Adam and his wife Eve, "***Oh Lord, we have wronged ourselves, and if You do not forgive us and have mercy upon us, we will surely be among the losers***".[1086] Repentance and hope go together. They immediately reverted to Allah, seeking his forgiveness, affirming that He is the one that will change their situation to the better. The Prophet teaches, when we ask for something, "***No one of you should say: O Allah, forgive me if You will; O Allah have mercy on me if You will; O Allah, grant me provision if You will***".[1087] There must be hope and certainty when asking. You are asking the Lord of the worlds. Then Allah responded to them saying, "***All of you get out! You are each other's enemies***[1088]".[1089] They were then sent down to earth knowing Satan is an enemy which shows there was an opportunity for them. They and the rest of mankind got to know the subtle tactics of their distractor, Satan who will persist to keep us in falsehood and darkness. Is this not a positive advantage they gained from their repentance and optimism.

Listen to these heartfelt words, as if a whisper to fill every inch of your heart with the comfort that you can be forgiven and you can move on, "***O My servants who have exceeded the limits against their souls! Do not lose hope in Allah's mercy, for Allah certainly forgives all sins. He is indeed the all-Forgiving, the Most Merciful***".[1090] No matter how great your sins are, they cannot be greater than the Mercy of Allah. But do remember, having hope is not to just 'wish and want'. It is the one who is actively working to reach what he hopes for. A sign of sincerity is when the heart *hopes* and the limbs *work* to achieve. Again, the outer and inner side-by-side, "***So whoever <u>hopes</u> for the meeting with their Lord, let them <u>do</u> good deeds and associate none in the worship of their Lord***".[1091]

[1083] Al-Jurjani. *Al-ta'rifat*.

[1084] Ibid.

[1085] Ibn al-Qayyim. *Madarij al-salikin* (2/145).

[1086] Qur'an, 7:23.

[1087] Al-Bukhari (7477), Muslim (2679).

[1088] Satan is the enemy of mankind and vice versa.

[1089] Qur'an, 7:24.

[1090] Qur'an, 39:53.

[1091] Qur'an, 18:110.

Five: truthfulness (*sidq*)

Linguistically, is 'the opposite of dishonesty'.

Islamically, 'the matching of a person's outer with their inner, in the remit of obedience to Allah﷾'s command'.[1092]

This is about habitual truthfulness not just spoken words. About being honest with yourself arising from a goal that fills the heart, and one becomes driven by. When the goal is living with Allah﷾ in this world, being a righteous servant to Him, and a burning desire to meeting Him, everything in your life serves that purpose. You develop a habit of being goal-conscious in your speech, thoughts, intentions, and actions while seeking to develop in the stages that lead to reaching that goal. The stronger the willingness to reach that goal, the more these all become well-harmonised.

It is to implement every aspect of your religion requested of you (Islam, Eman and Ihsan). Truthfulness then becomes a weapon used to deter any distractions and drawbacks. A quality that manifests and allows the priorities to lead the way and one falls into the category of, "***Among the believers are men who have proven truthful to what they pledged to Allah***".[1093] As for the hypocrites, "***it surely would have been better for them if they were truthful to Allah***".[1094] Success on the Day of Judgement is for the loyal and truthful, "***this is the Day when [only] the truthful will benefit from their truthfulness***"[1095] and a means to ultimate success, "***Truthfulness leads to goodness, and goodness leads to Paradise***".[1096]

Truthfulness develops tranquillity in the heart and peace in the mind. When there is transparency and self-harmony, there is no reason to be unsettled and disturbed. However, the Prophetﷺ did set a condition, "***leave what causes you doubt for what does not cause you doubt, for truthfulness is contentment and untruthfulness is unease***".[1097] And in a verse, a clear instruction, "***And do not pursue***[1098] ***that of which you have no knowledge. Indeed, the hearing, the sight and the heart - about all those [one] will be questioned***.[1099]

Six: sincerity and pure intentions (*ikhlas*)

Sincerity or *ikhlas* is core and a must. It is to maintain a state of the heart that is free from motives, urges and thoughts that displease Allah﷾. Sincerity is so crucial that in its absence good deeds will not be accepted and instead will surface a corrupt, egoistic, and evil side. It is closely related to having pure intention (*niyyah*) and God-consciousness (*taqwa*) in that sincerity is the perfection of intention and the outcome of *taqwa*.[1100]

[1092] Al-Asfahani, *Al-Mufradat*.

[1093] Qur'an, 33:23.

[1094] Qur'an, 47:21.

[1095] Qur'an, 5:119.

[1096] Al-Bukhari (6094), Muslim (6637), Ahmad (3727).

[1097] Al-Tirmidhi (2687), Ahmad (1723). Al-Nisa'i (5711).

[1098] I.e., do not assume and do not say.

[1099] Qur'an, 17:36.

[1100] Qur'an, 98:5. See also Qur'an, 15:39-40 where Satan, despite his willingness to deceive all of mankind admits is unable to deceive those who are sincere (which is an outcome of their God-consciousness and rejection of what is contrary to the path of Allah﷾). So, it is either the straight path or Satan's path. Qur'an, 36:60-1.

Sincerity is that no one knows and there be no intention to impress anyone or seek recognition. Your eye is solely on satisfying your Lord, aiming to always improve and increase its purity. This is the bedrock of every action, deed, and being pious. It determines if a deed is corrupt or correct, accepted or rejected. As for piety, people look at your outer and Allahﷻ is only concerned with your inner. So why be concerned with satisfying anyone which may over time corrupt that inner! Be focused, you have not passed the test yet. Even the great Khalif 'Umar said, "**If a caller from heaven announced that all people would enter Paradise together but for one man, I would fear that I am him. And if a caller announced that all people would enter Hellfire together but for one man, I would hope that I am him**".[1101]

If you are calm, at peace, and at ease, you will have the time and inner tranquil to examine your intentions before taking an action or speaking a word. When this falls in line with your goal to be God-conscious, everything you do and everything about you becomes measured and religiously sound. The righteous friends of Allahﷻ mentioned in the Qur'an, the *awliyah*,[1102] historically have been known to speak little and when they sit and do their morning and evening *dhikr* pondering on their day's actions, they are able to count the [minimal] number of words they spoke. If there was good, they thank Allahﷻ and if was was bad, they repent. These are indeed inheritors of the Prophetﷺ. He rarely spoke and when he did, he was able to express himself with few deep, meaningful words. His speech was productive and purposeful.[1103]

Important considerations:

(a) <u>aiming to say or do something</u> - if the person is goal-conscious, speech and actions will reflect that. Whatever the heart is filled with will spill out on to everything else.[1104] It is all to do with what you choose to contain in the heart. This requires the person to be goal-focused and always conscious of their mission in life and priority.

(b) <u>having decided to say or do something</u> – which is triggered by the state of the heart. The aim is to have the heart contained with the desire to do what is right. Even when things are doubtful, you move to what is undoubtful, ensuring every move is founded with integrity, "**enlightened with [sacred] knowledge**"[1105] and when intentions are pure, the heart becomes blessed with enlightened realisation and led with divine guidance.[1106]

Here we mention some reasons that trigger insincerity and impure intentions:

<u>Feeling of self-pride when achieving something.</u>
Gratefulness is different to self-pride. When you achieve something there is nothing wrong with feeling relieved you have met a target or succeeded in fulfilling a task.[1107] However, the deeper feeling should be gratitude. Reminded that everything initiates from Allahﷻ and nothing would have been fulfilled without Him. When it becomes "*I did this*" or "*it was me*" this becomes Satanic.

[1101] Hilyit al-awliya' (1/53).
[1102] Qur'an, 10:62.
[1103] Al-Bukhari (3567, 3568), Muslim (6399, 7509), Ahmad (24865).
[1104] Al-Bukhari (54), Muslim (4927), Ahmad (168).
[1105] Qur'an, 18:65.
[1106] Qur'an, 2:282.
[1107] Ahmad (22166, 22199), al-Tabarani in *al-kabir* (7540), al-Hakim (33).

There are two types of 'me' and 'I':

The positive: when you repent and admit your shortcomings by saying only 'I' am to be blamed, 'I' sinned, 'I' committed, 'I' did wrong.[1108] This is humility and a good trait.

The negative: the pride 'me' which can be a reason for arrogance to enter the heart leading to levels of corruption and injustices.[1109]

Seeking reward from other than Allah.

Desires that have not been dealt with can stand in the way of sincerity. A desire to get something in return for good deeds is dangerous and jeopardising. This could be seeking recognition; being told you are righteous or wanting people to acknowledge certain deeds or trait. It takes many forms. The essence of gratefulness is for the heart to be aware that all provisions and all favours are from Allah alone and nothing reaches us or is accomplished solely through our ability.

In summary, your actions should not be reliant on, seeking to impress, awaiting reward or acknowledgment from anyone other than Allah *"they were only commanded to worship Allah [alone] with sincerity and uprightness"*.[1110]

Seven: patience (*sabr*)

The linguistic meaning of *sabr* is 'to endure, as in to persevere and persist'.[1111]
Islamically, to 'refrain from complainting to other than Allah, be steadfast and settled with heart acceptance'.[1112]

Patience is the state of a person when they experience difficulties, calamities, setbacks, undesired outcomes or need to assert effort, persevere, strive, or required to achieve or prevent something. It is the ability to accept and tolerate without becoming anxious, troubled or complain.[1113]

Patience is a very exalt and necessary quality for the one on a mission and has a goal. Its beauty stands out when a person endures calamities and pressures yet strives to carry on with their life. Without patience one cannot gain any valuable achievement. This is a reality you cannot disguise because you cannot change what has been destined but should be wise to work within the scope of what has been destined, *"**And never say about anything, "I will do that tomorrow. Without saying, "If Allah wills"**".*[1114] All prophets and messengers, had it not been for their patience and persistence they would not have been victorious or the message have become widespread today, *"**So be patient, [O Muhammad], as were those messengers with resolve and determination**".*[1115]

1108 Qur'an, 7:23, 11:47, 27:44, 28:16.
1109 Qur'an, 7:12, 38:76.
1110 Qur'an, 98:5.
1111 Lisan al-arab.
1112 Al-Jurjani. *Al-ta'rifat.*
1113 Ibn al-Qayyim. *Madarij al-salikin*, chapter of patience.
1114 Qur'an, 30:30.
1115 Qur'an, 46:35.

Patience is a divine shield, "***Allah is with those who are patient***".[1116] He loves and gives glad tidings, describes as being mindful of Him, worthy of Paradise, humble before their Lord, and are promised forgiveness and great reward.[1117] Those who face difficulty yet persist on the right path and respond to evil with good are given double reward.[1118]

Patience comes in different forms:

<u>Patience in time of afflictions:</u> to bear the bitterness of troubles and hardship.

Life is a test and believers shall be tried in their faith. Anyone can claim to be a believer and godly. It is the tests that practically confirms what is claimed verbally, "***Do people think once they say, "we believe," that they will be left without being put to the test?***"[1119] and the next verses goes on say, "***Yet certainly We certainly tested those before them. And [in this way] Allah clearly distinguishes between those who are truthful [in their claim] and those who are liars***".[1120] **We will certainly test you [believers] until We prove those of you who [truly] strive [in Allah's cause] and remain steadfast, and reveal how you conduct yourself**".[1121] The wise and sensible is he who accepts there will be no change to what Allah﷾ has destined.

<u>Patience in adhering to the commands of Allah﷾:</u> to bear any difficulty in performing the commands.

To remain steadfast requires patience, which holds in it dedication, "***so worship Him and have patience for His worship***".[1122] While aiming to perfect every act of worship, one must be devoted to each day being better than the one before, continuing to progress in quality and slowly in quantity.[1123] Never compromise on quality, always be conscious of the One you are worshiping not just the act of worship itself. Glorify your Lord through your rituals, intentions, contemplations, and *dhikr*. You should enjoy worship and not treat as a burden. Love what you do, to become amongst those in success.[1124]

<u>Patience to abstain from sins:</u> the strive to refrain from falling into sins.

The persistence to go against the egoistic desires of the self. To be dedicated and strong-willed despite the temptations that may come with sins and the whispers of Satan and urges of one's self, remembering that every unlawful satisfaction is limited in time but the bitter regret remains. Know that what Allah﷾ holds for you in reward for your focus and determination greater and everlasting.[1125]

Knowledge is important. Those who have knowledge are most likely to be abiding, "***Of all of Allah 's servants, only the knowledgeable [of His might] are [truly] fearful of Him***".[1126]

[1116] Qur'an, 2:249, 8:46, 8:66.

[1117] Qur'an, 3:146, 2:155, 33:35, 2:177, 3:142, 22:34-35.

[1118] Qur'an, 28:54.

[1119] Qur'an, 29:2. A rhetorical question intended to make a point.

[1120] Qur'an, 29:3.

[1121] Qur'an, 47:31.

[1122] Qur'an, 19:65.

[1123] Qur'an, 67:2. Tafsir al-Tabari, tafsir al-Razi, tafsir al-Baydawi, tafsir al-muharrar al-wajiz.

[1124] Qur'an, 103:1-3.

[1125] Qur'an, 3:14.

[1126] Qur'an, 35:28.

Purifying yourself and developing through its stages allows patience and all other traits become a natural habit, without having to act or pretend to possess them. This should be the intended result. This is what we mean by the outer being the same as the inner. However, in the meantime, there is no harm to act 'as if' you have a positive trait. You are not deceiving yourself or others, you are performing this outwardly to nurture yourself into attaining it inwardly. Patience and practice help develop a virtue over time. It is essential your intention remains pure.

Eight: scrupulousness (*wara'*)

Wara' is linguistically defined as 'being morally conscious with integrity'.[1127]
Islamically, 'avoiding doubtful and suspicious matters out of fear of falling into what is forbidden'.[1128]

A tendency to be anxious about committing sins and the quality of being adequate about religious behaviours and decency. The aim is not to be excessively overwhelmed in horror or intense fear, it is to be conscious and attentive to avoid wrongdoing and about knowing yourself. For example, you do not have a desire towards food, so eating something you like will not lead to eating or thinking about excessively, or the prohibitions of causing yourself illness, diseases, and obesity, as a result. However, you may get engaged excessively with social media causing neglegance and much time to be wasted, weakening the sense responsibilities and fiulfilling obligations, so you limit its use out of scrupulousness compared to the first example with food. This comes from two important attainments:

An outer: by gaining knowledge you know what is clear-cut in religious matters to help tackle doubt, ambiguity, and be balanced. For example, you make a certain mistake when praying so revert to repeating that prayer out of [supposed] scrupulousness. However, the knowledge of *fiqh* states there is a resolve for error and forgetfulness such as making up for it in the prayer and/or prostrating twice for forgetfulness. So, while you intend to be sincere and anxious about fulfilling the ritual correctly, you could end up practising incorrectly. Pleasing your Lord and obeying, as with everything, comes with responsibility. Being responsible is to seek knowledge to do things correctly.

An inner: a purified condition of the heart through *dhikr* and other means allows it to see clearly, be in line with sound decisions, and clear distinction. Its god-consciousness naturally moves you from dark or blurred areas to light and clarity. An example of this is in the effects of sending salutations upon the Prophet☀ "*So that He may bring you out of darkness and into light*".[1129] And distancing oneself from boarder lines, "*The lawful is clear and the unlawful is clear, and between the two of them are doubtful matters about which many people do not know. Thus, he who avoids doubtful matters has protected his religion and honour, and the one who falls into doubtful matters will fall into the prohibited as the shepherd who pastures near a sanctuary, all but grazing therein. Verily, every king has a sanctum and the sanctum of Allah is His prohibitions*".[1130] A clear *hadith* affirming that through knowledge comes clear direction and balance.

[1127] *Lisan al-arab.*

[1128] *Al-ta'rifat, fath al-Qadeer* (1/349), *nihayit al-mihtaj* (2/176).

[1129] Qur'an, 3:43.

[1130] Al-Bukhari (52), Muslim (4094).

Falling into doubts and grey areas can be avoided — by the Will of Allah☬ — through 3 things:

1. To ask and investigate. If you are unaware or unsure, revert to those who are. Ask Allah☬ to bring you clarity and knowledge and ask the people of sound understanding and knowledge.[1131]

2. Safeguard yourself from immoral dealings and unlawful practices. To lie, deceive, conceal truths, cheat etc, to gain or achieve something. Both the aim and the means should be pure.[1132]

3. Avoid excessively indulging in worldly matters. Food, clothing, property, everything. Stay far from lavishness. be moderate and purposeful in your purchases and consumptions.[1133]

Nine: asceticism (*zuhd*)

Linguistically *zuhd* is 'to avoid inclining towards something'.[1134]
In the Islamic context is 'to repulse this worldly life' or 'to replace comfort in this life with that of the Hereafter'.[1135]

This does not have to be physical worldly gains but any worldly matter which can have an attachment to the heart or distracts it, whether physical or not. This can even be something that occupies the mind.[1136] There is a common understanding that *zuhd* is associated only with forms of luxury. This is not necessarily the case. It is more to do with the 'desire' for worldly things. For some their *zuhd* is to control themselves from luxury but that is because for them luxuries or lavishness is dear to their heart and occupies their mind. However, this must be something a person can reach, possess, or own. A poor person, for example, is not practising asceticism if they have no money. How can they show a balance or self-control with something they do not have in the first place. As for the one who does own or have access to, it is about maintaining in their hand not their heart.[1137]

Although Muslims are permitted to enjoy lawful provisions and pleasure Allah☬ has gifted, those who maintain moderation accelerate in their journey. Asceticism is a spiritual state and is among the stages of the spiritual journey and encompasses restraint and self-sacrifice. To have no regard for worldly life and high regard for piety and simplicity, seeking closeness to your Lord and acceptance, "**Repulse the worldly life and Allah will love you. Renounce what people possess and people will love you**".[1138]

[1131] Qur'an, 16:43, 21:7.

[1132] Qur'an, 67:2, 18:110. Al-Bukhari (54), Muslim (4927), Ahmad (168).

[1133] Qur'an, 10:24. Tafsir al-Razi.

[1134] Al-Jurjani. *Al-ta'rifat*.

[1135] Ibid.

[1136] Ibn al-Qayyim. *Madarij al-salikin* (2/12-5).

[1137] In the hand a person is holding and controlling it, if it overtakes the heart, it controls you,

[1138] Al-Bayhaqi, *shuab al-eman* (10523).

Some may consider this too harsh or find it wrong to deprive people from what is permissible. This is not the case and can be refuted in two ways:

1) It is about having meaning and purpose for everything you acquire and consume. Not acquiring for the sake of it and not consuming wastefully or out of uncontrolled urges. To be a person of discipline, in control of one's self, not allowing it to dictate, manipulate, or blindly follow trends and social tendencies.[1139]

2) It is about removing attachments to worldly matters, replacing that space and capacity with the quest of beauties and bounties of the everlasting Hereafter. Creating a balance of not to grieve over what is lost and not to over delight with what you are given, **"Allah does not love those who are self-admiring, the boastful**".[1140] **"Say, "My Lord commands justice"** i.e., moderation.[1141] **"And be equitable. Allah loves the equitable"**[1142] i.e., those who are balanced and reasonable.[1143]

Attaining asceticism is done step-by-step. One should not make big sacrifices in the early stages of their journey as this can backlash and have a negative affect. For example, to give out a large portion of your salary to charity imitating the generosity of the companions of the Prophet but to end up realising you were not ready and overburdened yourself financially. There must be a *nurturing process*. Sacrifices must come gradually so it becomes unwavering and deep-rooted, done through stages of spiritual struggle to slowly overcome stinginess and force off Satan who tries to instil fear of poverty.[1144] There are three stages to attaining asceticism:

First initial stage:
A person may already be inclined towards worldly excessiveness but through spiritual struggle prevents himself.

Second stage:
Can give up such excessiveness voluntarily but with a motivation to gain blessings, rewards, and bounties of the Hereafter. Here there is still a desire to have something in return for what they are given up.

Third stage:
Giving up voluntarily by choice without considering it a loss or wanting anything in return.
Although the person is holding back on things, is in fact gaining greatly in return. Afterall, a real seeker on a real journey is working to empty their heart from all attachments but Allah. This world is too trivial to be occupied with and dragged by attachments. Trivial matters are the interest of trivial people, serious matters are the interest of serious and goal-conscious people.

Your spiritual guide will assist you in making the right decisions in a measured way.

[1139] Refer to our book for more insight on this (Abouzaid, A., The Sacred Journey: "*so they may attain taqwa*". A Practical Approach).

[1140] Qur'an, 57:23.

[1141] Tafsir al-Baydawi, tafsir Abu al-Saud, tafsir al-Alusi.

[1142] Qur'an, 49:9.

[1143] Tafsir al-Tabari, tafsir al-Razi.

[1144] Qur'an, 2:268.

Ten: satisfaction (*rida*)

Satisfaction in its linguistic meaning is to 'have happiness in the heart and no hatred'.[1145]
Islamically, 'to be happy and content with what Allah﷾ has destined'.[1146]

This is a heart-state of stillness, calm, peacefulness, and trust in Allah﷾.

Even after exerting effort in trying to do what is best (actions of the body) you are deeply convinced that whatever has been destined shall come and whatever has not been shall never come to you. That your Lord has every attribute of perfection, managing the affairs of this universe so perfectly and flawlessly. Confident that He is all-Knowing, the Greatest and indeed al-Salam: the source for peace and security (actions of the heart). Know that a heart that is not content with His decisions and Will is in loss, in turbulence and self-destruction.

Allah﷾ says, "***perhaps you dislike something which is good for you and like something which is bad for you***".[1147] How many times has this happened in our lives, taking sometimes years to come to terms with the reality that a perceived good turned out to be bad and a perceived bad that turned out to be good. Therefore, the verse goes on to conclude, "***And Allah knows and you do not know***". With satisfaction comes freedom of the heart, the release of worry and concern of the mind, and creates optimism and assurance, "***how wonderful is the affair of the believer, for all of his affairs is good, and that applies to no one except the believer. If something good happens to him he is grateful and thankful, and that is good for him, and if something bad befalls upon him he bears it with patience and satisfaction, and that is good for him***".[1148]

Satisfaction is a great position to be in. If a person is characterised with it, they are equipped to face burdens and calamities in life. Not only feels satisfied but is happy to accept, with submission, every decree of Allah﷾ which carries His Wisdom too. This comes by knowing more about Him and His Magnificence. Another essential method of attaining satisfaction is increased *dhikr*. The Prophetﷺ used to instil satisfaction in the heart of the companions. One method was to encouraging them to regularly say, "***I am satisfied with Allah as my Lord, with Islam my religion, and with Muhammad my prophet and messenger***".[1149] He also taught, "***Whoever is focused only on this world, Allah will confound his affairs and make him fear poverty constantly, and he will not get anything of this world except that which has been written for him. Whoever is focused on the Hereafter, Allah will grant him peace of mind and make him feel content with his lot, and his provision and worldly gains will come to him regardless (of circumstances, obstacles or people)***"[1150] and in a conclusive statement, he said: "***Wealth is not having many possessions, but rather (true) wealth the feeling of sufficiency in the soul***" i.e., satisfaction and contentment.[1151]

[1145] Lisan al-arab.

[1146] Al-Jurjani. *Al-ta'rifat.*.

[1147] Qur'an, 2:216.

[1148] Muslim (7400), Ahmad (18934).

[1149] Muslim (4879), Abi Dawud (1529). It is advised to say every morning three times and every evening three times, with presence and certainty.

[1150] Ibn Majah (4105), al-Tirmidhi (2465), *sharh al-sunnah*, al-Baghawi (4142).

[1151] Al-bukhari (6446). *Fath al-Bari sharh al-Bukhari.*

Satisfaction does not mean you refrain from asking Allahﷻ or pray for something but about mature balance. Satisfied with His destiny and at the same can time pray for something reasonable. As we are ordered to be satisfied, we are also told, "***Call on Me, and I will answer you***".[1152] Nor does satisfaction mean a hungry person does not look for food and is satisfied with his hunger! Or does not work for income and satisfied with poverty out of [supposed] asceticism! Balance and harmony between the outer and inner is when the heart is settled and satisfied and the limbs working.

Eleven: reliance on Allahﷻ (*tawakul*)

Linguistically, 'to demonstrate inability and reliance on another, with submission'.[1153]
Islamically is 'to have trust in what Allahﷻ possess with a lack of interest to what is in the hands of people'.[1154]

To adorn yourself with perfect trust and reliance on Him alone. For He alone suffices and enriches. All matters are in His hand; you have nothing, He has everything, "***So glory be to Him in whose hand is the dominion of everything***".[1155]
He alone supplies every created thing with continued existence and sustenance. He created cells in your body knowing our need for it and continues to supply it with existence to stay alive and function. Air and oxygen knowing we need it and continues to supply. Lungs and windpipe for breathing and its ongoing existence as *reasons* to keep us alive. Everything He initiated and continues to supply to serve its purpose. This should develop a natural tendency to rely on Him and remove any worries or concerns from the heart in all matters and livelihood, for He has promised, "***And in heaven is your provision and what you are promised***"[1156] and to further tranquil our hearts, the next verse goes on to say, "***by the Lord of heaven and earth! indeed, this is as certain [a fact] as you speaking***".[1157] So if provision have been promised, why be concerned about even the most basic need. Simply trust and rely on the Creator of you and your provisions.

Tawakul (along with active refining) should create several heart affects:
1. The person becomes fearing nothing
2. Upholds the truth and fears not any consequences
3. Driven by pleasing Allahﷻ alone in all actions and intentions
4. The heart is free from anxiety and with no concern about provision and sustenance
5. Calm and content when problems arise and is fearless
6. Sees no doer besides Allahﷻ
7. Develops strong hope in nothing but Allahﷻ who becomes the only source for honour

---

[1152] Qur'an, 40:60.
[1153] Lisan al-arab.
[1154] Al-Jurjani. *Al-ta'rifat.*
[1155] Qur'an, 36:83.
[1156] Qur'an, 51:22.
[1157] Qur'an, 51:23.

Reliance on Allah⁛ gains His love, "**Allah loves those who put their trust in Him**"[1158] and solidifies the heart. When the companions were threatened by the enemies of Quraysh they responded, "**God [alone] is sufficient [as an aid] for us and [He] is the best protector**",[1159] the outcome was, "**they came back with a blessing from God, and grace, no harm having afflicted them. And they pursued God's great pleasures, for God is the possessor of a great infinite bounty**".[1160] Prophet Ibrahim⁛ when thrown into the fire and said the same,[1161] the outcome was Allah⁛ commanding, "**fire, be cool and safe for Abraham**".[1162] Indeed "**Whoever relies on Allah - He will suffice him**".[1163] So, "**put all your trust [in Allah], if you truly are believers**"[1164] for He is the "**Doer of whatever He wills**".[1165]

Tawakul is that you do not see the solution and you do not know will happen tomorrow but you know one thing for sure, "**with me is my Lord; He will guide me**"[1166] and are assured, "**Allah is the Best of planners**".[1167]

Twelve: gratitude (*shukr*)

Linguistically, 'to show gratitude for something gained'.[1168]
Islamically, 'to show gratitude (through intention, verbally and physically) towards Allah⁛ out of His worthiness and to negate attributing worthiness to oneself'.[1169]

This is not just about saying 'thank you' or '*alhamdollah*'. It is a mindset, a heart condition, and sense of fulfilment. Appreciating what you have been given over the desires, wants, and self-proclaimed needs. Practically, *shukr* is expressed through the very things Allah⁛ has blessed you with:

- The heart bears witness that in every moment and in every situation the Creator and Sustainer actively provides us, "**To Him belongs dominance of the heavens and the earth, and to Allah all matters are referred**".[1170]
- The tongue's gratitude by speaks of His bounties, "**And as for the favour of your Lord, speak of it**".[1171]
- The body through good deeds, charitable giving, serving people's needs, generosity etc, "**We only feed you only for the sake of Allah. We want from you neither compensation, nor gratitude**".[1172]

[1158] Qur'an, 3:159.
[1159] Qur'an, 3:173.
[1160] Qur'an, 3:174.
[1161] Al-Bukhari (4563, 4564).
[1162] Qur'an, 21:69.
[1163] Qur'an, 65:3.
[1164] Qur'an, 5:23.
[1165] Qur'an, 85:16.
[1166] Qur'an, 26:62.
[1167] Qur'an, 8:30.
[1168] Al-Jurjani. *Al-ta'rifat*.
[1169] Ibid.
[1170] Qur'an, 57:5.
[1171] Qur'an, 93:11.
[1172] Qur'an, 76:9.

And despite all He has given, "**If you are grateful, I will surely increase you**".[1173] When He gives you, you show gratitude, so He increases you more, and you in return show more gratitude so he increases you again. The giving-gratitude relationship is ongoing and deepens. A love bond between the slave and His all-Giving, all-Generous Master.

It creates also respect and appreciation towards others, "**He who does not thank people, does not thank Allah**",[1174] removing any traces of envy, jealousy, hatred, greed, and arrogances. A heart engaged with envy towards people for what they possess is sheer ignorance, focusing on what you do not have and cannot reach, distracted with thin air. When purified, the heart becomes cleansed with beautiful patience, satisfaction, and enjoys seeing others in success and happiness.

Shukr is a key to attracting provision, prosperity, and success in worldly affairs and religious practices.[1175] He has given us so much. Such that is boundless. We remain indebted and helpless in showing even a fraction of gratitude Allah﷽ is worthy of, "**if you count the bounties of Allah, you will not be able to number them**".[1176]

The fruits and outcomes of purification

Love:
"**And Allah loves those who always turn to Him in repentance and those who purify themselves**".[1177]
First and foremost, the love of Allah﷽ is gained and your heart is engraved with that love having progressed, "**And Allah loves those who excel in doing good**".[1178] What greater good is there than a person who excels in becoming [all-roundedly] pure and pious. Excells in perfection (*Ihsan*).[1179]

True slavery:
"**Say, "Indeed, my prayer, my devotions, my living and my dying are for God, Lord of the worlds**".[1180]
"**And who is better in religion than he who submits himself wholly to Allah**".[1181]
Through your love to Allah﷽ you become truly enslaved and submitting. Appreciating the beauty of living in His Kingdom knowing that everything is in the name of Allah, through Allah, from Allah, towards Allah, upon Allah, and to Allah. Everything is Allah﷽. You have no will except what He wills for you. Your happiness is in slavery and submission and your sorrow is at times of falling into sins and loosing focus of the fact He is observing you.

[1173] Qur'an, 14:7.
[1174] Al-Tirmidhi (2069), Ahmad (7504), Abi Dawud (4811).
[1175] See Qur'an, 14:7.
[1176] Qur'an, 14:34.
[1177] Qur'an, 2:222. Tafsir al-Qurtubi. See also Qur'an, 6:151 and 7:33.
[1178] Qur'an, 2:195, 3:134, 3:148, 5:13 and 5:93.
[1179] Tafsir al-Jalalin, tafsir al-Qurtubi.
[1180] Qur'an, 6:162. Tafsir al-Qurtubi, tafsir Abu al-Saud.
[1181] Qur'an, 4:125.

Desire to be with your Lord:

"But those who believe have greater love for Allah".[1182]

You enter the paradise of this world and yearn to enter the paradise of the Next Life. The first through your heart filled with nothing but Him and the Next paradise in seeing Him. The more purification is settled and positive inner traits develop, the greater the yearn to meet the One you love, acknowledging that if it was not for Him you would not have moved a single inch on a journey or found the path, **"Those God guides are truely [and rightly] guided, and those God allows to stray**[1183] **are the losers".**[1184] Your day-to-day activities and worship are with no intention but for Him. Your [purified] instinct insists on choosing not to choose and becomes passionately devoted to love what He loves and hate what He hates.

In constant remembrance, *dhikr*:

"Those who remember Allah while standing, and sitting, and on their sides; and they reflect upon the creation of the heavens and the earth: "Our Lord, You did not create this in vain, glory to You".[1185]

You do not forget Him to need reminding of Him. Nothing distracts you from Him. The fuel that enlightens your heart is *dhikr*. Your tongue is moist with remembrance and your heart soaked with affection.

Unconditional satisfaction:

"How wonderful is the affair of the believer, for all of his affairs is good, and that applies to no one except the believer. If something good happens to him he is grateful and thankful, and that is good for him, and if something bad befalls upon him he bears it with patience and satisfaction, and that is good for him".[1186]

What comes and what goes is no concern. He, your Beloved Lord wanted it to come so you love its coming, with satisfaction, gratitude, and appreciation. Or He wanted it to go so you love it to go, with satisfaction, gratitude, and appreciation of His choice. Your focus and conviction are diverted to: the real gain in life is in His satisfaction and real loss in His dissatisfaction. All you want is Allah.

The desire to connect with His Book:

"And who wants to be spoken to by Allah should revert to the Qur'an".[1187]

Becoming attachment to Him is to love anything that comes from Him, including His Word. To satisfy the eagerness to be spoken to by your Beloved is to connect with His book. The excitement to hear what comes after **"And Allah loves...."** so you can rush to do and invite others to. Determined to know what comes after **"And Allah does not like...."** to refrain from and help those around you do the same. Afterall, you do not want anyone to displease the One you Love.

Devoted to be characterised by His words and teachings. To develop the intellect in line with the Qur'an, your actions in line, and your purification and mannerism according to it. To have His book manifested in you.

[1182] Qur'an, 2:165.

[1183] As a result of persistence in evil and rejection of truth.

[1184] Qur'an, 7:178.

[1185] Qur'an, 3:191. Tafsir al-Tabari, tafsir al-Jalalin, tafsir al-Qurtubi, tafsir Ibn Kathir.

[1186] Muslim (7400), Ahmad (18934).

[1187] Al-Hassan al-Basri.

Mercy, respect and concern for His creations and severity towards His enemies:

"Do you not see how Allah presents a parable? A good word is like a good tree—its root is firm, and its branches are in the sky, yielding constant fruit by the will of its Lord. God makes such comparisons for people so that they may reflect".[1188] *"Good and evil are not equal. Repel evil with good, and the person who was your enemy becomes like an intimate friend"*.[1189] You are prompted to love and serve His creations. Your sincere love drives your heart to love anything attributed to Him. Anything He created. You enjoy serving them, support their wellbeing, and celebrate their success. You are patient with those ill-mannered and show mercy in praying for them to be guided. You love for them what you love for yourself.[1190]

As for those who oppose Him and place themselves in the position of enemy, you deal with differently by opposing their actions and stand firm against their plots. But still, in line with justice your Lord has prescribed, you do not deprive them from any rights they are due.[1191] Your objectivity is firmly in line with the command of Allah.

Balanced between fear and hope:

"So We responded to him, and We gave to him John, and cured for him his wife. Indeed, they used to hasten to good deeds and supplicate Us in hope and fear, and they were to Us humbly submissive".[1192]

Constantly in the [balanced] remit of fear and hope. The fear of displeasing your Beloved and the hope of gaining His acceptance. You never over-fear as you do not blind yourself from His beautiful names: The All-Merciful, the Loving-Kind nor over-hopeful fearing complacency and lack in glorifying Him, the All-Glorious, the Magnificent.

The relationship a hidden treasure:

"Nor will I find in other than Him refuge".[1193]

A desire to keep your love and relationship a secret. It is about just you and Him. Not for show and not for claiming to be anything. No one needs to know. You guard it like a diamond which is left alone with its beauty. No one can touch or tamper with. Although it is known to be there, the more it is not spoken about the more it remains something unique and special sitting in the room. Likewise, the relationship with Allah is caged and wrapped beautifully in your heart.

Spiritual inspiration:

"Then they found a servant from among Our servants [i.e., al-Khidhr] to whom We had given mercy from Us and had taught him from Us a [certain] knowledge".[1194]

Inspiration is light Allah places in the heart allowing a person to comprehend beyond the average/basic knowledge of things and common understanding. This is *Inspirational knowledge*, a gift from Allah to those who purify themselves and

---

[1188] Qur'an, 14:24-5.

[1189] Qur'an, 41:34.

[1190] "None of you will attain [complete] faith until he loves for his brother what he loves for himself". Al-Bukhari (13).

[1191] Qur'an, 5:8.

[1192] Qur'an, 21:90.

[1193] Qur'an, 72:22.

[1194] Qur'an, 18:65.

whom He chooses to gift. Whilst this is known to happen to prophets and messengers,[1195] it can also happen to righteous believers, as with the mother of Musa.[1196]

This is never something a person looks for or seeks to gain on their path as it can be a distraction and reason to deviate from sincerity and purity of intention. The focus is nothing but Allah ﷻ.

Spiritual unveiling:

This is also a gift from Allah ﷻ to His righteous friends. A spiritual giving that lessens the layers of veils, resulting from spiritual struggles, *dhikr* and the other means of purification which help polish the heart and enables it to see with divine light.[1197] This is no innovation. It has happened to prophets and messengers,[1198] al-Khadir,[1199] companions such as Abu Bakr and Umar[1200] and beyond.[1201]

Especially with experiences of inspiration and unveiling, a spiritual guide is crucial as they can relate to this and guide you to deal with responsibly, maintain ongoing sincerity and verify your understanding which will progress with time. Again, purification is a *process*. It is not something static but is dynamic. In other words, it is associated with constant changes and developments. This means whoever chooses to embark on this journey and succeed needs to approach with a positive attitude and energy.

As purification passing through every part of a person: the body, mind, and heart, unless it is approached as an 'all-embracing process', you will find things contradicting one another. This leads to a state of disharmony and creates inconsistencies. On the contrary, dealing with purification holistically as an all-embracing comprehensive process will allow you to flourish, see things harmonised, and the fruits and outcomes become multi-fold.

[1195] In the case of prophets and messengers it is a means of receiving Revelation.

[1196] Qur'an, 28:7.

[1197] The Qur'an states one can see with their heart (baseira) or not: "**It is not the eyes that are blind, but their hearts within the chests, that go blind**". Qur'an, 22:46.

[1198] Qur'an, 6:75.

[1199] Qur'an, 18:79-82.

[1200] Muslim (6204), *Al-tabaqat al-kubra* (3/195).

[1201] Such as Imam al-Shafi'i. Tafsir al-Qurtubi (10/44).

Throughout the book, 'realities' and 'realisation' were mentioned. These relate to the level of Certainty (*yaqin*) a person progresses through when advancing in spiritual state. There are three levels:

First level - knowledge of certainty (or sure knowledge)[1202]
This is *yaqin*/certainty which is the result of gaining knowledge of something[1203]

Second level - the vision of certainty (or certainty of sight)[1204]
This is *yaqin*/certainty that develops from seeing and contemplating.[1205]

Third level – true (or absolute) certainty[1206]
This is *yaqin*/certainty that develops through feeling and experience[1207]

Let us take two examples. One to do with something tangible/physical and another which is intangible/non-physical:

1st level: you have <u>knowledge</u> that there is something called honey
2nd level: you actually <u>see</u> honey
3rd level: you drink from it so actually <u>taste/feel</u> the honey

1st level: you learn through <u>knowledge</u> that Allah۩ has the attribute of Mercy
2nd level: you <u>see and contemplate</u> around you different manifestations of Allah۩'s Mercy
3rd level: you actually <u>experience</u> the Mercy of Allah۩

In the first level: you gained an initial level of certainty that something exists, just through knowledge[1208]
In the second level: your certainty gets stronger, having seen it (or seen the effect of it[1209])
In the third level: your certainty reaches the highest level where it is real. Such that the experience has led to a level of certainty that cannot be doubted or questioned. [1210]

[1202] Known as *'lm al-yaqin*. Mentioned in Qur'an, 102:5.

[1203] Tafsir al-Tabari, tafsir al-Kashaf, tafsir al-tashil le 'loum al-tanzil.

[1204] Known as *'ayn al-yaqin*. Mentioned in Qur'an, 102:7.

[1205] Tafsir al-Tabari, tafsir al-tashil le 'loum al-tanzil.

[1206] Known as *haq al-yaqin*. Mentioned in Qur'an, 56:95, 69:51.

[1207] Tafsir al-Tabari, tafsir al-tashil le 'loum al-tanzil.

[1208] Either something tangible or intangible.

[1209] In the case of something non/physical.

[1210] Tafsir al-Razi, tafsir Ibn Kathir, tafsir al-Baydawi (Qur'an, 56,95 and 69:51).

Why is this important?

Certainty is power, firmness and stability of faith, deep-rooted like a mountain. Such that no doubt can rock, falsehood reach, or illutions affect. This is what we mean by quality over quantity. If you are only concerned with gaining lots of knowledge and information and doing lots of actions without purification, dealing with the religion at a surface level, the impact and thus condition will also be surface level and veils remain.

Developing through the phases of purification and refinement progresses the person through these stages of Certainty, where knowledge is merely a starting point. Certainty brings you closer to the reality of things around you and creates a self-harmonious bond with Allah🕮 and manifestations of His names and attributes. In summary, the stronger the Certainty is, the finer the state of *Ihsan*, **to observe and worship Allah as though you could see Him, for though you cannot see Him yet He sees you**".[1211]

[1211] Al-Bukhari (50) Muslim (97).

CONCLUSION

This is the *Sacred Journey*, where it all starts. Implementing the three aspects of the religion correctly sets the journey off and putting in the effort and persevering leads to the fruits, the satisfaction of your Lord and Paradise. Not only will you see light at the end of the tunnel but will be guided with light through it.

Do not embark on this journey to test it. Be honest with yourself and "***follow the path of those who turn to Me***".[1212] Be with the truthful. Just as Allah﷾ has told us to be like them, He also tells us to be with them. Being with them will gradually lead to becoming like them. Truthfulness and purification are contagious.

There is no excuse. If the right steps and process is followed, the result will be correct and fruitful. The place you are in is no excuse, nor the times. The Qur'an makes this clear. In chapter 49, some companions came to the prophet claiming to be believers although belief was merely expressed verbally and had not penetrated to their hearts, "***The Desert-Arabs say, "We have believed***". Allah﷾ responded by telling the prophetﷺ to tell them, "***You have not [yet] believed; but say [instead], 'We have submitted,' for faith has not yet entered your hearts***".[1213]
These were people with the Prophetﷺ, at the time of the Prophetﷺ, and learning from the Prophetﷺ!
Although there is immense blessing and benefit in being in his presences, it shows nothing has full influence on a person practising their religion and being righteous. It is down to them to attain the knowledge and follow the steps and process, even in the *Golden Age*. A person can be at the time of the Prophetﷺ, not take the right approach and so will not reach, and vice versa a person can be in our times taking the right approach and reaches. *The only obstacle would be you!*

Your foundation must be strong, sound, and pure. Your aim is nothing, only Allah﷾. He is your focus. To succeed you need to be clear on how to describe your Lord. You cannot attribute to Him what is corrupt[1214] and expect the relationship to be in its purist form!

Your guide is the Prophetﷺ. Devote to Him not just through imitating his character and following his sayings but through a connection and spiritual commitment too.

Build a relationship with your religion. Do not treat it as a list of dos and don'ts. And do not treat it like an ambulance service, whenever in trouble and danger you call for help then in good times turn your back. Islam is a perfect vision for life. Take it seriously and with ease. Enjoy it. It will nurture and nourish you in every way.

[1212] Qur'an, 31:15.

[1213] Qur'an, 49:14. Tafsir al-Tabari, tafsir al-Qurtubi, Tafsir Ibn Kathir.

[1214] Such as having a physical hand, or physically sits or moves just as creations do! Exalted is your Lord, Lord of Glory, far above what they attribute ti Him.

Do not waste time because there is no time. Every moment that passes eats up your lifespan. The final stage of your existence and standing for accountability is just around the corner. You started as "**a sperm-drop**" [1215] then He "**eased the way**" [1216] into this world through birth. There is only one more stop for you to stand before Him, "**then He causes him to die and be buried**", [1217] this is it. Work to develop your discipline and integrity. Be principled and stand for the ethical. On the Day of Judgement you shall be a witness for yourself. No matter what defence you prepare or excuse you may present, know that "**This is a Day when the truthful will benefit from their truthfulness**". [1218]

"*Say, the enjoyments of this worldly-life is little, while the Hereafter is better for those mindful [of Allah], and you shall not be dealt with unjustly [even] as much as a thread [inside a date seed]*". [1219]

May Allah bless you and me with patience and perseverance. May we be characterised with Ihsan and become amongst His righteous servants in our outward and inward and be true inheritors of the Prophet Muhammad.

All praise is due to Allah

[1215] Qur'an, 80:19.
[1216] Qur'an, 80:20.
[1217] Qur'an, 80:21.
[1218] Qur'an, 75:14-5, 5:119.
[1219] Qur'an, 4:77.

Printed in Great Britain
by Amazon

35939824R00106